CAPTAIN ROBERT A. FRISTER

Flight of the Golden Falcon Book 2

Newhouse Creative Group

This book is dedicated to my wife Barbara, who has been at my side throughout my career during my fifty years of flight. And to my sons, United Airlines Captain, Scott A. Frister, and Southwest Airlines Captain, Keith B. Frister. Both of whom I had the pleasure to fly with, as a family flight crew while with Kiwi International Air Lines. To the men and women who have taken to the skies and challenged Mother Nature in their quest to fly.

Contents

We had climbed to our cruising altitude of 20,000 feet and were crossing over the rugged Adirondack Mountains. Some of them reach a height of over 4,000 feet. Their view was blocked by the solid cloud cover we were flying in.

Our flight crew consisted of the captain, the flight engineer, two stewardesses, and myself as the first officer. Up to that point, the flight had been uneventful, routine, just small banter between us in our cockpit and the hum of those four beautiful engines in our ears of the DC-7 we were flying.

Suddenly, the calm atmosphere in our cockpit changed when all four engines unexpectedly quit.

WELCOME TO EASTERN AIR LINES

On January 24th, 1964, I was not the only one who was taking a pre-employment physical for Eastern Air Lines. Others received a similar telegram. We, who passed the physical were hired. Those who did not were sent home.

On January 27, 1964, our ground school instructor greeted us with, "Congratulations and welcome to Eastern Air Lines." It was a proud moment for all of us fledgling airline pilots.

Our class was composed of sixteen pilots. Half of us were civilian pilots, the others were former military pilots from the Army, Navy, and Air Force. It was a good class, and I would come to make lifelong friends with many of them.

Of the sixteen I was number thirteen in seniority. A word that I was not familiar with at the time. It was based on your date of hire and your birth date. Those born before you, in your class, would always be senior to you. The classes after ours would always be junior.

On that morning, my seniority number was 2352. Another 48 pilots would be hired in the next two weeks. Then all pilot employment ceased on March 16, 1964.

It would remain that way for another eighteen months before additional pilots were hired. Eventually, Eastern would have over 4,600 pilots on its pilot seniority list. Lucky me.

Part of our indoctrination encompassed the history of Eastern Air Lines. Eastern wasn't always called Eastern Air Lines nor used their motto, The Great Silver Fleet. As I well remember listening to their radio advertisements when I was growing up.

We learned The Great Silver Fleet consisted of 90 DC-3s and 34 DC-4s, Eastern had flown during, and shortly after, World War Two. Incidentally, both aircraft were not pressurized, which led to the occasional popping of an eardrum during a descent.

As Eastern expanded, new modern aircraft that were pressurized and could fly at higher altitudes giving passengers a more comfortable flight, with just an occasional popping of an eardrum, took the place of the older ones.

The airline's growth came from a composite of assorted air travel companies. It was much like putting a jigsaw puzzle together that began in May of 1928.

Harold Frederick Pitcairn was the son of Pittsburgh Plate Glass founder John Pitcairn, Jr. An aircraft manufacturer in his own right, he had been awarded a lucrative Contract for Airmail Service from New York to Atlanta, called CAM 19.

The first Pitcairn Aircraft to fly their foremost route was an open cockpit bi-plane, two wings, one above the other, NC 2895. It still hangs in the Smithsonian Museum in Washington DC.

The CAM 19 award meant a flight would leave New York, making stops at Newark, Philadelphia, Camden, Baltimore, Washington, Richmond, Greensboro, and Spartanburg, before reaching Atlanta, its final destination.

Later, more CAMs were awarded and Eastern extended its route structure to include Macon, Jacksonville, Daytona Beach, Orlando, St. Petersburg-Tampa, West Palm Beach, and Miami.

Future airlines, such as Florida Airways, which was once owned by Captain Eddie Rickenbacker and Reed M. Chambers, would be added to the airline's growth. Both men were in the same 94th Pursuit Squadron during World War 1. Then came Ludington Air Lines and Wedell-Williams Air Service, and Colonial Air Transport.

These acquisitions led to the airline expanding its route structure to Canada, Bermuda, Mexico, and destinations throughout the Caribbean.

In 1929, Pitcairn sold his airline to Clement Keys, who owned North

American Aviation. In 1930, Keys changed its name to Eastern Air Transport. Shortly thereafter it was changed to Eastern Air Lines when it was purchased by General Motors. Nevertheless, that was not the end of Eastern changing hands.

In 1938 the airline was acquired by World War l flying ace Captain Eddie Rickenbacker from General Motors. Captain Rickenbacker remained the president and chief operating officer of Eastern until October 1959. After relinquishing those positions, he remained with Eastern as director and chairman of the board.

Malcolm MacIntyre then became its president and CEO until December 1963. It was he who initiated the famous Eastern Air Lines Shuttle in 1961. It was the only airline at that time to have the passenger pay on board the flight instead of at the check-in counter. Eventually, MacIntyre was succeeded by Floyd D. Hall on December 16, 1963.

On December 1, 1963, before the transfer of power, Eastern carried over 59,600 passengers throughout its route structure. The airline was large enough to think of as being able to transport the entire population of a small city.

On July 22, 1955, the first of Eastern's new Douglas DC-7B's began service from the Great Lakes to Florida. It was stated that the new plane would fly 40 mph faster than the DC-6, due to its Wright turbo-compound 3,350 horse-powered engines.

On its tail was the image of a Golden Falcon, then known as the fastest creature on earth. The Golden Falcon had been recorded as having a dive speed of over 200 mph. From that day forward, the Golden Falcon would be displayed on the tail of most Eastern aircraft.

Flying in the open cockpits, such as the Pitcairn Mailwing, one has to think about those pilots who had to endure the snow, sleet, rain, and fog. Crashes, injuries, and death were a part of their efforts to get the mail through.

Eastern would eventually add passenger aircraft such as the Ford Tri-Motor, Curtis Condor, DC-2, 3s, Martin 404, Convair 440, L-1049 Super Constellation, and the Douglas DC-7B.

Ever striving to serve its passengers better, Eastern added the four-engine turbo-prop Lockheed Electra to its fleet.

Then would come the first of many jet-engine aircraft, the DC-8s, and the DC-10s. Boeing's B-720s, B-727s, B-747s, and B-757s. Lockheed's wide-body L-1011 TriStar and the Airbus A300 series would follow.

Eastern had other aircraft, including the Aero Commander 500B, which was used for instrument training, and Airline Transport Pilot Ratings (ATP) for company pilots only. Another was the Lockheed L-1329 Jetstar which was used for corporate purposes as was the North American Saberliner.

The only oddity of all its aircraft was the French-designed McDonnell Douglas MD 188. Intended as a short-field take-off and landing (STOL) aircraft it saw limited use on the Eastern Shuttle.

Eastern would eventually own 1088 different types of aircraft, a huge jump from its meager beginnings.

So began my thirty-three thrilling years of airline flying.

Those years were filled with wonderful memories, but, at times, they were not so wonderful.

THE POST-WORLD WAR II YEARS

Vince Lombardi, the Hall-Of-Fame football coach, once said. "Winning isn't everything. It's the only thing!"

I will relate that to being an airline pilot but in another way. Seniority! "Seniority isn't everything. It's the only thing!" All airline pilots, regardless of what airline they fly, know this.

Seniority determines how soon you may become a captain, the number one position all pilots aspire to. In some instances, pilots have been known to check out as a captain in less than three years, depending on the airline.

If you are at, or near the bottom rung of the seniority list, depending on the airline, it could take fifteen to twenty years before becoming a captain. Seniority dictated where you would be based, and the type of airplane you would fly.

It also meant you might be furloughed, as in out of a job. This is especially if the airline was having financial woes. It dictated your working conditions, known as a 'monthly bid sheet.'

The bid sheet determined what cities you would fly to, the number of days you would fly, and the number of days you would have off.

It also dictated who you would be flying with. Sometimes that worked out well. Sometimes not so good, especially when personalities clashed in those cramped cockpits.

At that time Eastern had crew bases for pilots and stewardesses in Atlanta, Boston, Charlotte, Chicago, Miami, New Orleans, Washington D.C., and New York's John F. Kennedy Airport.

In the years to come, I was fortunate to be able to fly with pilots whose exploits were portrayed by actors in combat-flying movies that I had seen while growing up during the war years. They were the Army Air Force pilots who flew the B-17s, B-24s, and B-29s, on bombing missions over France, Germany, Burma, and the Pacific.

They were the Navy pilots who flew fighter aircraft such as the Helldivers, The Dauntless Dive Bomber, and the F4U Corsair, off aircraft carriers to engage the enemy.

No matter what that theater was of operation they had been involved in, whether it was Europe, The Pacific, Indo-China, or elsewhere, none of them professed to be heroes.

Some had been shot down and ended up in a prisoner-of-war camp. Some escaped, and others remained a pow until the war ended. A few talked about their war experiences. Most didn't. They regarded themselves as just regular guys who had a job to do and they did it. I think that is what I admired most about these guys. They just did their jobs.

GROUND SCHOOL FOR THE DC-7

Whenever we were first hired, the rumor was that most airlines would only have you on the payroll for eleven months then the furloughs would start. The idea at the time was that the company wouldn't have to pay pilot increment pay. This was additional flight pay that was based on each hour of flight time that you flew.

While as a flight instructor for Wings, mainly in summertime, I averaged about three-hundred-twenty dollars a month. Eastern started its new hire pilots at approximately four-hundred-twenty-five dollars a month the first year.

The second year wasn't much better, approximately five-hundred-fifty a month. In the third year, we received a base salary plus incremental pay for the number of flight hours we flew per month.

As a new pilot with Eastern, you were on probation for fifteen months. Screw up, fail a check-ride, or a medical examination, and you might very well be out of a job.

Even though you went through your probation period, pilots, though it's never said, are always on probation.

Most of my class would be trained to fly the four-engine Douglas DC-7B, known as The Golden Falcon. The remainder would be trained to fly the twin-engine Convair 440.

There was much to be learned about flying the DC-7B. As well as other aircraft I would eventually be trained to fly while with Eastern. Each training cycle started with weeks of ground school.

Our subjects included. Electrical systems, hydraulics systems, flight controls, fuel systems, instruments, and backup systems.

We were also required to learn Morse Code and how to interpret performance charts as to the weight and balance of the airplane and their effects on take-offs and landings.

We had to learn the definition of V-speeds. V1 was takeoff airspeed. VR was rotation airspeed, and V2 was engine failure airspeed. Added to all that was needed to review Part 121 of the Federal Air Regulations. That governs all passenger activities in the United States.

It was study, study, study. In between came barrages of written and oral exams.

Ray Gould and Tom Schineller were two pilots in my new hire class with whom I would study, and they would become lifelong friends.

They would also be two numbers senior to me throughout our flying career with Eastern. It did not matter. We helped each other.

FLIGHT TRAINING

F ollowing our completion of ground school came the instrument flight portion of our training. It began with the Link Trainer.

The Link Trainer resembled a small, cramped cockpit of a one-pilot aircraft. It had just enough elbow room to squeeze your body into.

Its short stubby fuselage, stubby yellow wings, and squat tail section reminded me of the aircraft that flew during the 1920s and 1930s air races. I recalled those early years when daring pilots flew around pylons that stood 50 feet tall, at speeds that exceeded 300 mph. Of course, that Link Trainer wasn't about to lift off and fly. Although after one hour of practicing instrument flying in it, and having to unravel myself to climb out of that cramped space, it seemed like I was flying one of those ancient racers. I would spend thirteen one-hour sessions in it.

Once the sessions in the Link Trainer were completed, we were ready for the DC-7B flight simulator.

Like all flight simulators, it was a replica of the cockpit of the aircraft that I would be trained to fly. We started with the possibility of having an in-flight emergency.

Engine failures/fires, runaway propellers, decompressions, emergency descents, electrical failures, and simulating the ditching of an aircraft in the ocean were all part of the training.

After several days of 4–6-hour sessions in the simulator ended, we were ready for the plane. What a beautiful aircraft it was.

My DC-7 flight instructor was Captain Reed Raser. The first thing he asked me was about my flying background. When I told him I had been a civilian pilot and not a military pilot, he said it didn't matter. He assured me that he treated all new hire pilots the same. His goal was to get them through the program.

Then we were given what seemed like a never-ending quiz on the DC-7. After forty minutes of questions and answers, it was out to the flight line.

As we walked out on the ramp, we looked for the aircraft we were going to fly. It sat between two other parked DC-7s. One was going through its maintenance check. The other appeared to be getting ready for a flight. Then I recognized one of its pilots standing near it.

It was Pete Coxhead, the Eastern pilot I met many months before while flight instructing for Wings of Morristown. Pete had written a recommendation to Eastern for me and helped me get an interview with them.

I asked my instructor if I could take a few minutes to speak to him and I explained our past. When he nodded his okay, I rushed over and thanked Pete for all his help. He wished me luck. We shook hands and I hustled back to where my instructor was waiting.

Then came more questioning of my knowledge. It started from questions about the nose of the aircraft, all the way to its tail. He asked me about every probe, hole, radio antenna, and whatever else he could think of.

Once we were in the cockpit, more questions followed as we went through our normal preflight duties. I was used to flying small aircraft, so I felt very comfortable. I felt confident, not because of those sessions in the simulator, but because of the many hours I spent flying the twin-engine Piper Apache.

Our in-flight training started immediately with a simulated left-engine failure, the most critical one on take-off. It was done by pulling the number one engine throttle, the left engine, back to idle. After that, it came down to extensive in-flight training. I had to demonstrate knowledge of every aspect of take-offs and landings. instrument approaches, missed approaches, holding patterns, and more simulated engine failures.

There were other simulated in-flight emergencies, hydraulic failures, and the possibility of having to dump fuel to preclude an overweight landing.

We trained for sudden decompression, quickly grabbing your oxygen mask, and then executing a rapid descent to a safe altitude.

My training was going very well. I was enjoying my time as a fledgling airline pilot. Tragedy struck a month later.

EASTERN FLIGHT 304

O
n February 25, 1964, Eastern Air Lines flight 304, a DC-8, had taken off from New Orleans International Airport at 2:01 a.m. bound for Atlanta. It was to continue to Washington's Dulles Airport, and on to John F. Kennedy Airport in New York.

At 2:05.40 a.m., EAL flight 304 disappeared from the radar screens as it was being tracked by ATC. The following are excerpts from the two-year investigation as to the probable cause of the accident.

According to the Civil Aeronautics Boards report (CAB SA-279, File No. 1-006, dated July 1, 1966), at the time of flight 304's departure, there were reports of heavy rain-shower activity in the area. Approximately five minutes after takeoff, EAL 304 disappeared from the radar.

Flight 304 crashed into Lake Pontchartrain, some 20 miles from its departure airport. All 51 passengers and 7 crew members were killed.

Of the passengers, 14 were pass-riding Eastern Air Line employees. It was a great tragedy for all the families and our airline.

Although Lake Pontchartrain was approximately 20 feet deep, the impact was so severe that roughly only 60 percent of the aircraft was recovered.

The flight data recorder and cockpit voice recorder which investigators rely heavily upon were too badly damaged to determine the actual cause of the crash.

After many, many months, the investigating team concluded that a malfunctioning pitch trim compensator (PTC) which automatically trims the horizontal stabilizer in turbulent air, and is located on the tail of the aircraft, had extended too far in a nose-up attitude, producing a stall.

To counteract the stall, the pilots trimmed the stabilizer to a nose-down position trying to overcome the malfunction. Unfortunately, it was impossible to regain control of the aircraft no matter how hard the crew pulled back on the yoke.

Ironically, during the investigation of EAL 304, the CAB and the National Transportation Board (NTSB) were also investigating two incidents that happened just months before. Both involved DC-8s.

On November 29, 1963, a Trans-Canada DC-8 took off from Montreal Airport in Canada. It climbed to an altitude of approximately 7,000 feet when the nose pitched upward and stalled at zero airspeed. The plane pitched nose down and crashed. This was very similar to Flight 304's accident.

Weeks previous to the Trans Canada accident, in November 1963, an Eastern DC-8 departed Houston, Texas, and was climbing through 19,000 feet when it also experienced a problem.

In this incident, the nose of the aircraft pitched upward, the airspeed dropped to zero, then the plane pitched into a steep dive.

The captain and first officer struggled to gain control. As a last resort, they employed full reverse on the DC-8's four engines to slow it down. You could do that with a DC-8, but not with other jet aircraft. Then both pilots pulled back on the control columns trying to get the plane out of its nose-down dive.

At 5,000 feet, the pilots recovered from the death dive, but on the pull-out, the g-forces needed to do that caused one of the engines to be ripped from the aircraft. The plane landed safely, thanks to their courageous effort.

In the ensuing years of investigating the accidents and examining their similarities, the CAB concluded, based on evidence obtained from the DC-8 flight recorders that they recovered, that the probable cause of the accidents lay with the PTC and not with the pilots.

It also came to light during the investigation that the pilots of Flight 304, Captain William Zeng, First Officer Grant R. Newby, and Second Officer Harry Idol, made a valiant effort to save Flight 304 and its passengers. The inspection team noted that the cockpit crew must have made a desperate attempt to recover the aircraft when the evidence confirmed that all four of their DC-8 thrust reversers had been deployed.

Unfortunately, when accidents such as these do happen cabin crews also perish. When pilots and flight attendants are assigned to a flight, though they may not know one another, they become bonded together.

Let us not forget about those attendants of Flight 304: Grover W. Flowers, Barbara D. Norman, Tove E. Jensen, and Mary Ann Thomas. This accident, and the loss of our friends, created a gloomy atmosphere within the Eastern family for quite some time.

The three DC-8 incidents I discussed, bring to mind three major aircraft accidents that happened while I was a Sophomore in high school. They involved Newark International Airport, not far from where I lived, and they were all related to the weather and mechanical failures.

The first occurred on December 16, 1951. A Miami Airlines C-46 crashed in Elizabeth, New Jersey. Its right engine caught fire on take-off. Less than a month later, on January 22, 1952, an American Airlines Convair 240 crashed in Elizabeth during stormy weather. The third accident was a National Airlines DC-6 which crashed in Elizabeth on February 11, 1952. Both right engines failed on take-off.

Those accidents became the main talk in one of my high school classes when my teacher, aware of my interest in flying, asked me if I still wanted to fly. Of course, my answer was yes.

While the investigating board was still in the process of determining the cause of flight 304's accident, our training continued. As it neared its end, we had to perform two simulated emergencies. The first was the immediate evacuation of a DC-7 in less than two minutes. This was accomplished in one of the Eastern maintenance hangars that were large enough to house the aircraft. Volunteers, mostly Eastern employees, and some from local groups, were recruited to serve as passengers.

With FAA inspectors watching, 102 passengers, representing a full aircraft, and a crew of five: captain, first officer, flight engineer, and two stewardesses, were ready when the command to evacuate was given.

The evacuation was completed in less than two minutes. The FAA inspectors were impressed, and that phase of our training was over.

AIRCRAFT DITCHING AND WATER SURVIVAL TRAINING

To promote flight crew awareness of what it would be like in the event of an actual water landing, we practiced boarding life rafts out in the middle of Biscayne Bay.

At that time all Eastern flight crews were trained in real bodies of water. Later that practice was abandoned. All water ditching, and survival training, was relegated to a swimming pool at a nearby hotel across the street from our training department.

Our class, along with another new pilot class, plus two newly hired stewardess classes, climbed aboard an Eastern employee bus and left for Biscayne Bay. There we boarded a twenty-five-foot Coast Guard Cutter and motored out to the middle of the bay.

With us were several instructors from our training department who were monitoring the simulated ditching. We were wearing bathing suits under our street clothes.

Upon anchoring, off came our clothes. We were ready to take the plunge into the bay. Before we did that, though we all knew what was in the three twenty-five-man life rafts, our instructors gave us a short refresher course.

Our equipment included: canned rations, water, a signal mirror, a whistle, a tarp to provide cover against the sun and rain, lip balm to help prevent blisters, a nylon anchor to help prevent drifting, a book on survival at sea, and an emergency Gibson Girl signal transmitter.

At one time, a Gibson Girl Emergency Transmitter was used to send emergency signals using its hand crank. The transmitter was named after Evelyn Nesbit, who was famous for her hourglass figure.

Nesbit, more commonly known as, The Girl on The Red Velvet Swing, during the early 1900s, had been involved in a major scandal. Her then-husband, Harry Thaw, shot and killed architect, Standford White, in a fit of jealousy announcing that White had ruined his wife.

During our ditching exercise, the wind picked up making the water choppier. By then our life-rafts had been tethered to the boat as they would be when tied to a ditched aircraft and inflated. Once they were inflated, they began to bob up and down riding the waves.

Group by group we filled the rafts and then cast off from the Cutter as you would do in a real situation before the aircraft sinks. Each raft had an instructor to show us how to set up the raft as if in a real ditching.

Before that happened, our instructor ordered us off the raft into the water and to swim twenty yards away. The idea was, in a real ditching, you might be in the water before getting into a life raft. Then he called for us to get back into the rafts.

Twenty yards do not seem to be a large distance to swim, but we were in bathing suits, and not wearing clothes and shoes like most passengers would be in an actual ditching.

As I swam back toward my raft, gusts of wind were causing foot-and-a-half waves and were blocking the raft from my view. They were also pushing the raft further away. I swam faster to get to it. As were others in my group. I was amazed at how tiring it could be.

Then came a mad scramble. On one side of the life raft was a nylon step for boarding and easier access. For those who tried to climb aboard without using the step, it was difficult. The side of the life raft is nearly fifteen inches high and the waves were making it rock back and forth. They were also lapping over the rubber and making its sides slippery. It required a lot of body strength for some of those still in the water to climb aboard without help.

Two months later, I took my proficiency check for the DC-7 with an Eastern examiner. The examiner was an Eastern captain certified by the

FAA to do flight checks for them. There was no nonsense with them when it came to a check ride.

As with all check rides, it begins with knowledge of the aircraft, from its nose to its tail. Followed by a two-hour flight check.

Thanks to Captain Raser's instruction, the examiner congratulated me for my knowledge of the aircraft and passing my proficiency check.

After 12 hours and 40 minutes of flight training, I received my Eastern Air Line Pilot Wings. It was a proud moment for me. One I will always cherish. I was finally, a First Officer for Eastern Air Lines.

But not all the pilots that were in my class would make it through the training. One had an aircraft violation on his record he did not tell Eastern about before he was hired. They found out by checking his background while he was in ground school and dismissed him.

Another new hire was asked to repeat his physical, failed it, and was also terminated. The reason was his height. When he took his first physical, his height was measured at 5' 9" inches, the minimum allowed. His second physical measured him as being just under 5' 8" inches. Apparently, he had gone through stretching exercises the night before his first physical. Somehow, they found out about it and requested that he do another. I know it sounds cruel and trivial, but at that time your height had to be a consideration. It determined if you could apply enough rudder pressure to keep piston-driven aircraft straight in the event of the left engine failing on take-off due to its drag. Sometimes, shorter legs cannot push a rudder pedal in far enough to prevent the aircraft from turning into a dead engine. This is especially on takeoff. Jet-engine aircraft don't produce that kind of P-factor, or torque. Therefore, it requires less pressure to be applied to the right rudder if a left engine fails during take-off.

Subsequently, because of those requirements, airlines had to maintain strict policies. At that time, you were fortunate to be hired by any airline.

I passed the first test. There were more to pass.

THE DC-7 JUMP SEAT

Now that I was an Eastern Air Lines First Officer, I was given my crew base assignment. The type of aircraft you were trained on determined where you would be based. For me, it would be New York's JFK. It was one of several DC-7 crew bases that Eastern had. I was fortunate because I did not have to move to another city as some of my classmates were required.

Before any of our class were allowed to fly as First Officers, we were required to have twenty-five hours of jump-seat observation time. It would be something we had to do with each different aircraft we were trained on. This meant having to sit on the jump seat directly behind the captain and observe how he and his crew conducted the flight.

On my first attempt at observing a flight, I was afraid I was going to be fired. I made the mistake of telling Captain Don Woods that I was going to sit on his jump seat. He said, "Go out the door and try again."

I thought he meant for me to go and look for another airline to fly for. Totally dumbfounded by his remark, I picked up my suitcase and flight bag and left the cockpit wondering what I did wrong.

Luckily, the second officer came after me and said, "You don't tell the captain you're going to ride on his jump seat. You ask him if you can ride on his jump seat."

With a better understanding of how sacred the jump-seat protocol was, and still is, I went back into the cockpit and humbly asked if I could ride on his jump seat.

His answer was, "You sure can. Welcome aboard Eastern Air Lines. Would you like a cup of coffee? What's your seniority number?"

What a relief.

As I sat there and observed the crew's actions, it dawned on me how competent and coordinated they were. Up to that time, I had only experienced seeing a cockpit crew perform their pre-flight duties when I was with VP-11, while they were preparing to play war games.

This DC-7 crew was preparing for a commercial flight with passengers. Totally different.

All the movies I had seen, including The High and The Mighty, starring John Wayne, briefly showed the interaction of crew members as they prepared for a flight. This was the first time that I got to see this close-up. I was impressed.

Allow me a short explanation of how flight crews prepare for every flight, no matter the airline. The captain, first officer, and flight dispatcher, who must be licensed, and is an integral part of in-flight planning, coordinate the planning of a flight. That includes the flight's route, weather conditions, flight time, fuel burn, and airport alternate if required.

The cabin crew checks to assure that all walk-around oxygen bottles for passengers are fully charged. All catering for the passengers and crew was also accounted for.

After the passengers were boarded, the senior stewardess reported to the captain. She confirmed that they completed their cabin check and the total number of passengers boarded matched the manifest.

This brings us to the gate agent who is responsible for getting the flight out on time. His job is to also confirm the number of passengers boarded, the fuel load, and the amount of cargo being carried. Then the agent fills out a weight and balance sheet indicating the total gross weight of the aircraft. This is a form the captain must sign before taking off.

As I sat on the jump seat I observed a ramp-service man standing near the nose of the aircraft waiting for the captain to start the engines.

The captain gave him a 'thumbs up.'

The ramp-service man then held up his right hand, index finger pointing to the engine to be started first. He then rotated his finger in the air.

20

Generally, the first engine to be started on the DC-7 was the number three engine. When the captain hit the start switch, the first officer looked at the engine and called out. "Eight blades." The Wright-Cyclone R3350 has a four-bladed propeller. The captain waited until the props did two complete turns before ignition to provide oil lubrication for the cylinders.

There is nothing like hearing that familiar throaty sound of a piston engine roaring to life. The sound is followed by a belch of blue-gray smoke pouring out of its exhaust stack then quickly dissipating from the blast of the whirling propellers. The remaining three engines were started, and more checklists.

As we taxied out, the second officer was double-checking the weight and balance charts, the outside air temperature, the runway to be used, and the flap setting. Which was translated to V1, VR, and V2, airspeeds. All of these are critical airspeeds when taking off.

No take-offs were allowed if the temperature exceeded 120 degrees Fahrenheit. Higher than that has a profound effect on takeoff performance. As in, you may not get airborne.

JFK had three active runways to accommodate the arrival and departure of hundreds of aircraft from all over the globe every minute of every day. Everyone had to stay alert to avoid interaction with arriving or departing aircraft before taking off.

After we were airborne, and at our cruising altitude, the senior stewardess entered the cockpit and offered us coffee. I had to ask myself. *Is this for real? Am I here, at last?*

The next few weeks had me jump-seat riding and getting a fresh outlook on how to present myself to each captain over the use of their jump seats. Then came my last jump seat ride which gave me more than the twenty-five hours that were required.

We were descending through broken clouds on our final approach to runway 22L at Newark International Airport. The approach path took us over the top of Teterboro Airport, just west of Newark International. All was well as we broke out into the open sky when the captain yelled. "Look out!" He pulled into a sharp bank to the left. That was followed by a sharp bank to the right to get back on course and land.

I had looked out my left window in time to catch a small aircraft flash by beneath us. It was a near miss. Below us was the Secaucus Dump. Seeing the dump brought back an incident I had there.

THE SECAUCUS DUMP

In the summer of 1963, I was a flight instructor for Wings of Morristown. One of my students was on a solo cross-country flight in a two-place Cessna-150. He was supposed to fly from Caldwell-Wright Airport to Trenton Mercer Airport.

Shortly after taking off from Caldwell-Wright, he became disoriented due to a rapid change in weather. He accidentally ended up on the approach path to Newark Airport. He panicked when he saw an airliner coming toward him. Then he saw the Secaucus Dump below and decided to land in it.

The only damage was to one of the brakes. That happened because he was pressing on them hard when he landed. Fortunately, he stopped the aircraft just short of the piles of garbage.

The question was how to get the aircraft out of the dump without disassembling it. Or letting the FAA know about it. The latter would have led to a lot of questions about letting a student pilot fly under such visibility, training, and all the rest that went with it.

I informed Walt Sanders, Wing's chief pilot, that it was my student who put it there, and that I would be the one to fly it out of the dump. Alone!

The only problem was the dirt road my student landed on was narrow, and winding, and its length was probably no more than 500 to 600 hundred feet. Oh yes. The road led back to the main highway and traffic.

I knew it wasn't going to be easy.

I had Sandy and Bill stop the garbage trucks and other cars from entering the dump. We had to ask those who were already there to pull off the dirt road far enough so that my plane's wings wouldn't strike them as I took off. You could see the expression in their eyes, all wondering what an aircraft was doing in their dump.

After we cleared the area, we turned the C-150 around and faced it in the direction I was going to take off. Then we pushed it back as far as we could, the tail and wings almost touching the mounds of trash.

I climbed into the cockpit and started the engine, keeping both feet on the brakes, making sure that if I had to suddenly stop, the brakes were going to work.

Almost immediately, there was a dust storm of dirt and cinders that swirled around the airplane from the propeller blast.

I dropped my flaps for a short-field takeoff. I performed my usual pre-takeoff check. I pushed the throttle to full power, just like an aircraft on an aircraft carrier readying for launch. I released the brakes and started down the dirt road.

With the engine at full power, clouds of dirt and dust from the prop wash became thicker and obstructed my forward view. I had to look out the left side window and kicked the left and right rudders to stay on the winding road.

In what seemed an eternity, I gained enough airspeed and lifted off, glancing down as I did. The truck drivers were waving and jumping up and down as I passed over them. For a moment I felt like Charles Lindbergh on his arrival in Paris after he crossed the Atlantic Ocean alone.

Once airborne, my forward visibility was limited because of the thick haze, but I breathed a sigh of relief that all was well. Until I saw the high-voltage powerlines directly in front of me. We could not see them from our position in the dump.

Here I was at low altitude, hanging on the prop, flying just a few knots above stall airspeed. I couldn't make a bank for fear of stalling out. I was in big trouble, but it's amazing how quickly your mind reacts.

If I elected to go under the wires, would the tail of the C-150 catch one of them? If I went over the wires, would the landing gear get caught on one of them?

I pushed the nose down and skimmed over the ground to gain more airspeed. Just before hitting the wires, I pulled back on the control column. I skimmed over the top of the wires, and pushed the nose down again, my landing nearly touching the weeds of the Meadowland Swamp. I regained my airspeed and flew back to Caldwell Wright Airport.

Wings charged my student for the flying time and the damage repair to the airplane. The FAA never became involved, nor was there any report of an aircraft being in the dump. Thank you, truck drivers. After that, my student quit flying.

As to the near collision, once we were inside flight operations, the captain contacted Newark's control tower and filed a near-miss report.

During my career, I would encounter numerous near-misses. Most of these incidents occurred arriving or departing an airport. I know of other pilots who also encountered them. Each one reminded me of the danger of not staying alert. Whenever I made my approach to land at Newark, I looked down at the dump and shook my head.

The good news was I finished my twenty-five hours of jump-seat time and was looking forward to my initial flight as a First Officer.

FIRST FLIGHT AS A FIRST OFFICER

O n April 12, 1964, 22 years after I first saw that yellow J3-Cub, and 10 years after my first solo, I was assigned to a flight as a First Officer.

The Captain was Les Bott whom I never met before. For those first few months, I would fly with different flight crews. Each captain that I flew with had their idiosyncrasies as to how they wanted things done, even though there were set procedures. Talk about learning the ways of an airline.

That first flight was a four-leg segment: Newark to Providence, Rhode Island was the first leg. From there to JFK, then to Boston, and finally back to JFK.

I found Captain Bott to be the type of person who made you feel comfortable in the cockpit and that you belonged there. He was very professional when it came to being responsible for the safety of his aircraft, his crew, and his passengers.

During that segment of flights, Captain Bott flew the first leg, and I flew the second to JFK. All went well, including my first landing flying the line, which was as smooth as silk. Lucky me.

Bott's comment: "Nice approach and landing. But let's be more on the numbers."

Each major airport has threshold runway markings. These include runway numbers, touchdown zones, and aiming points.

Runway numbers indicate magnetic headings in the direction you're landing. Touchdown zone markings are 500 feet from the end of the runway. The aiming point is 1000 feet from the end of the runway.

I was 100 feet beyond the touchdown zone when I landed. It doesn't sound like a lot, but on short runways, it could result in running out of a landing surface and ending up in the boonies. It was worse if the runways were covered with rain, ice, or snow. I took Bott's comment seriously. The next two segments went well.

It was Eastern policy to let the Captain decide which leg, or legs the First Officer would fly. Usually, the Captain would fly the first leg. Thereafter we would rotate additional takeoffs and landings.

At the end of our flight sequence that day, I had to give Captain Bott a survey to complete rating my performance. This was something all new pilots had to do as part of their fifteen months of probation.

Bott filled it out as 'satisfactory,' signed it, then handed it to me to sign. I had to file his report and the many others that would follow, and submit them to the Chief Pilot's office as evidence of my progress.

Some captains would not fill them out, claiming that they had not flown enough with a newly hired pilot to warrant a fair judgment. In a way, I could understand their reasoning. Approving a pilot is a huge responsibility.

NIGHTTIME AND FLASHING
LIGHTS AHEAD

Six weeks passed since my first flight as a fledgling First Officer. The night skies were clear of clouds as we made our way southwest bound from Newark to Atlanta. Above us, the sky was filled with the beauty of millions of stars that shone like luminous diamonds against a background of black. Below us, Mother Earth was bathed in nighttime darkness, no towns or the glow of city lights could be seen as we flew over the emptiness of Western North Carolina.

Suddenly, I caught a flash of light coming from one of the mountaintops ahead of us. Then another. I pointed them out to my Captain. My first thought was that it was a signal from a downed aircraft.

He looked at me and smiled. "That's an airway beacon," he said. Then, as though reminiscing of days gone by, he added, "It was used by pilots who were flying nighttime airmail flights way back when." He then proceeded to enlighten me on how the pilots of the 1920s, 1930s, and 1940s relied on those beacons.

As he spoke, I gathered that he was probably one of the few remaining pilots who needed to use those beacons to navigate the cold and dark nighttime routes. I thought about what I had learned about Pitcairn Aviation, CAM 19, and Eastern Air Line's beginnings. Despite what I thought I knew, I listened and learned more.

The Captain related to me that there had been about 1,500 airway beacons throughout the United States. They had been used to guide the pilot's visual navigation mostly at nighttime along a corridor from city to city covering some 18,000 miles. The beacons were constructed by the post office and the Department of Commerce. They had two distinct kinds of light. One was a revolving white light that flashed every 10 seconds. It could be seen up to 40 miles away in clear weather. Below the white lamp, a set of red or green course lights pointed along each airway route. The red lights identified an airway beacon between landing fields while the green light denoted an adjacent landing field. This was to ensure pilots didn't land at the wrong airport.

The course lights also flashed a Morse Code letter identifying where the pilot was. Each beacon was also identified with a sequence number along the airway to keep the pilot on course.

Eventually, the beacons were decommissioned as newer and improved navigation aids came into being. Nonetheless, they played an important part in early aviation.

That night, as I sat there sipping a hot cup of coffee, flying high above those mountain ranges, in a pressurized DC-7B. I couldn't help but think about the pioneers who flew those open-cockpit bi-planes. They were alone, flying in freezing temperatures a few hundred feet above rugged mountain terrain. Eyes straining, they searched for that next beacon, hoping to find a small grass strip of land lighted only by the glow of burning flare pots and automobile lights.

I could only imagine what early pioneers of aviation experienced. I had to admire them. They were the beacons for generations of new pilots. Would I be a beacon to others as well?

THE TWO-PERCENTER

During my first year with Eastern, all was going well. The crews that I flew with were enjoyable. Then came an experience with a captain that I would call, a 'two-percenter.' He was one pilot that if I had the opportunity to never fly with again would have been a blessing. To me, a two-percenter is a non-conformist. One, who doesn't take responsibility for their actions despite the existence of rules.

June 28, 1964. It was shortly after midnight when the crew scheduler called and assigned me to a sequence of flights that departed from JFK at 9 a.m.

I had flown with the Captain before. He was not one of my favorites. His gruff manner and handling of the DC-7 had always rubbed me the wrong way. He was always max braking, and max reversing of the engines, which is fine if you're about to run out of runway, but not when you have more than 4,000 feet left in front of you. It is jarring and adds to the wear and tear on the brakes and engines.

The flight plan for that day was to ferry the aircraft from JFK to Philadelphia. From Philadelphia, it would be a passenger flight to Boston, and then ferry the aircraft back to JFK.

We were filling in for a crew that became illegal to fly the night before because of duty time limitations.

Onboard with us were three members of the cockpit and two stewardesses. One of the latter was a new hire. Right from the beginning, I knew it was going to be a long, long, day.

There is nothing worse than tension in the cockpit, which rears its ugly head from time to time. Sitting beside someone in a cramped cockpit whom you may despise for one, two, or three days, can negatively impact the performance of the flight.

This happened to be one of those days. Before we even started the engines, the Captain said in a brusque manner, "Get our clearance!"

As I contacted clearance delivery, he then said, "Read the before start check-list!"

As I started to read the checklist, he grabbed it out of my hand, and shouted, "I said to get our clearance. I'll read the checklist." Frustration was already setting in.

Before we started our engines, I had my side window open, then closed it. Although it appeared to be fully closed. It wasn't. We found that out just after taking off.

The sound of air rushing through the cockpit from a not fully latched window is loud. The faster the airspeed, the more deafening the sound. It got to the point where we had to yell at one another to be heard. He was yelling at me to re-open the window and then close it. I tried, but because we were partially pressurized, I couldn't. He stopped yelling, but I could see he was angry.

Luckily, the weather was clear with unlimited visibility. He then told ATC that he was canceling our instrument clearance and we would fly to PHL by using Visual Flight Rules.

Fortunately, JFK to PHL was just a short hop, less than forty minutes. Since we were going VFR, he was able to fly over the area where he lived in New Jersey.

He made an announcement over the PA system asking our new stewardess to come to the cockpit. He wanted to show her what it was like in the cockpit and where he lived.

Our stewardesses and stewards were well trained in caring for our passengers, and more importantly, handling emergency procedures, including the evacuation of the aircraft, if necessary. They had to go through a rigorous training program before they could become what they now call, flight attendants. Most got through the program. Many did not. When they did, they were the best.

At the time I was still on probation. So was the newly-hired stewardess. As she entered the cockpit, the second officer left his seat so she could stand next to the Captain. The Captain told her to stand next to him and to 'widen her stance' so she could balance herself when he banked the aircraft.

As he banked left, he pointed down to the ground. She leaned forward over him to look down to where he pointed. He reached up between her legs and groped her. She let out a scream, banged her head against the overhead panel, burst into tears, and fled the cockpit. He was laughing.

I was incensed. When we landed at Philadelphia it was with max braking and max reversing again.

When the Captain went to flight operations to file our flight plan to Boston, I took the stewardess aside. I told her to file a complaint against him and I would sign it. She said if she did that, she would lose her job, and then she walked away.

I was in a bind. If I filed a report, and she didn't, it would be my word against a twenty-plus-year Captain. I was still on probation. I reluctantly let it go.

The flight to Boston was not that pleasant either. The Captain decided to cancel our instrument flight plan and fly to Boston using visual flight rules because he wanted to fly directly over New York City on our way to Bean Town.

I was doing the flying. He was directing me. He wanted the passengers to be able to see the Statue of Liberty on the right and the George Washington Bridge on the left. From my position, I could see both, but he could not. He unexpectedly grabbed the controls away from me and made a sharp bank to the left. He followed with a sharp bank back to the right. By that time, we had already passed New York City. He was not happy.

As we neared Boston, we had to contact approach control for sequencing to land. We were cruising at 310 mph. Off to our left, the Captain caught a glimpse of a Northeast Airlines DC-6.

At the same time, ATC directed us to reduce our airspeed to two-hundred-fifty knots. We were to follow the Northeast plane. He ignored their instructions and told me to slow down to 280 knots.

Approach control called us, "Eastern 50. What's your speed?"

Captain: "Eastern 50. 250 knots."

Approach control: "Eastern 50. Slow to 230 knots and switch to the tower."

As we entered the downwind leg to follow the Northeast DC-6, he carried his downwind leg further than normal. The Captain then told me to cut in front of the Northeast flight by making a short base leg. This is a turn you make before turning on your final approach. When I did that, the control tower instructed us to go around and fall in behind two more Northeast DC-6s before landing.

While in Boston, we changed stewardesses for the flight back to JFK. Before boarding our passengers, our new senior stewardess asked me who the Captain was. When I told her, she said. "There will be no service for the cockpit crew with him as Captain."

My thought at that time was that there must have been some conversation about the incident that took place en route from JFK to PHL.

Just then, the Captain walked into the cockpit. The Head Stewardess told him the same thing: "No service!"

The Captain did not respond.

She then told him not to make any P.A. announcements because "we have passengers on board who are to claim the bodies of family members who died in a car crash in New York."

During the boarding, I caught the sound of someone crying. I had assumed it was a relative of those who had perished in the accident. It was loud enough to be heard with the cockpit door partially open. It promised to be a rather grim day, for all.

In the years that followed, whenever I had to fly with this particular Captain, I never found it enjoyable. I was not the only one who had problems with him.

One of the newly hired pilots, in the class after ours, had been training with me on the DC-7 and had flown with this Captain several times. Not long after the JFK-PHL incident, I bumped into him after he had one of his flights with this Captain. He told me that if he ever had to fly with him again, he would put in applications to fly for another airline. Two months later, he resigned from Eastern and ended up flying for Pan American Airways.

Someone once told me about this Captain's background. I could never prove if it was true. This Captain had been an Army Air Force pilot during the Second World War. He flew the Consolidated B-24 Liberator, engaging in some of the heaviest air-combat raids on Germany and other targets. One of those missions was a raid on the oil fields in Ploesti, Romania, that took place on August 1, 1943. The raid was called Operation Tidal Wave. 53 aircraft were shot down and some 660 airmen lost their lives. It was noted by the United States Army Air Force (USAAF) at the time, as the "bloodiest and most heroic mission of all time."

I was told by another WWII Eastern pilot that during that raid, an artillery shell penetrated this Captain's aircraft. It went through his copilot and exited through the top of the cockpit without exploding.

After hearing this story, I thought perhaps this Captain had taken a "live for today and the hell with tomorrow," attitude. Several months later I had to fly with him again. Unfortunately, I saw him fondle another stewardess.

Just as he and I were leaving the cockpit after a flight, a replacement cabin crew came aboard. As a stewardess boarded, the Captain stepped in front of her. He reached down the front of her blouse and pulled out a gold cross attached to the gold chain she wore. She jumped back and asked him what the hell did he think he was doing. He answered, "I wanted to see what was on the chain." He then left the aircraft.

I asked her to file a complaint and said I would sign it. She, like the other stewardess, refused to do so. I couldn't file a complaint without her support.

I would often fly with him over the coming years until he finally retired. He might have been a war hero, but there was no excuse for his behavior toward women. Good riddance!

ENGINE FAILURE

I was seven months into my airline career. Up to that point, all had gone well, other than the usual weather delays or an occasional aircraft mechanical problem. That changed on July 25, 1964.

The captain was Ted Connolly, and the second officer was P. K. Murphy. We were flying westward from Newark to St. Louis. The weather was CAVU. That means ceiling and visibility are unlimited. I was doing the flying.

It was also my first time flying with Ted. Although I had heard a lot about him while in our initial DC-7B ground school. I also heard about his having to do a belly landing in a DC-7.

His landing had been filmed and it was later shown during ground schools or required re-current training programs.

The film showed the DC-7 touching down, props being bent as the aircraft slid to a safe stop and all passengers safely evacuated.

As generally was the case, when an aircraft accident or incident happens, discussions on the probable cause followed. That helped us learn how best to avoid such accidents.

While we were en route to St. Louis, I asked him about the incident. I discovered there was more to the story than what was shown in the film.

According to Ted, the incident happened when they couldn't get the landing gear to extend. He said he told his second officer to leave the cockpit and sit in the passenger cabin. He did not want the Second Officer to block his, and the first officer's exit, in case something went wrong. The flight engineer refused to do that. At that point, he ordered the flight engineer out of the cockpit. The flight engineer reluctantly complied. More on this incident later, including the real reason why he ordered him out of the cockpit.

After the successful belly landing, there was an investigation by the National Transportation Board, NTSB.

Connolly was asked why he did not dump fuel before his landing to lighten the aircraft's weight, so as not to have an 'overweight landing.' Landing an aircraft over its weight can tax the structural limitations of the aircraft. After such a landing, the plane must be thoroughly inspected. His answer to their question: "Self-preservation!"

The investigation was over.

Many environmentalists are concerned about aircraft dumping thousands of gallons of jet fuel, kerosene, or aviation fuel in such situations. They should know the fuel will, in most cases, vaporize before coming in contact with the ground. Because of its smoky-white appearance, there have been reports of aircraft being on fire, which is not the case.

All was well as we flew over Evansville, Kentucky. A half-hour later, Connolly asked me if I felt any vibration. I said no.

The engineer said he felt it.

Ted looked out his left-side window at our two engines. After a few moments, he declared he was going to shut down the number two engine.

At that time, all of number two's instruments appeared to be normal. Of course, from my position, I couldn't see the engine, so I asked him what was wrong. His answer was, "It's drooping."

He made an announcement to our passengers telling them he was doing a precautionary shutdown of the engine due to abnormal indications. He carefully avoided the word, 'drooping.'

We informed ATC of our problem and they gave us an off-airway radar vector directly to Lambert Field in St. Louis.

I eased myself out of my seat and looked at number two. It was drooping.

Usually, the Captain makes the landing when an emergency arises. Instead, he said, "It's your leg. You make the landing." It perked me up to know that even though we had never flown together, he trusted me

36

enough to let me do it.

Our straight-in approach into Lambert Field brought us over the Mississippi River, it's famed Arch off to our left. Ahead of us, we could see red flashing lights from the emergency equipment waiting for our arrival, in case something went wrong.

It was a normal touchdown and rollout with the crash trucks racing down the runway behind us. They followed us to our gate where we shut down the good engines. The flight was safely over.

From the passenger cabin came a burst of cheering. Ted patted me on the back. It was the end of my first in-flight emergency with Eastern. It would not be my last.

Outside, Ted, P.K., and I, with the maintenance team, looked up at the number two engine. We all agreed that the engine had a downward tilt of 8 to 10 degrees. Later, after maintenance thoroughly inspected the engine, they told us the bolts that held the engine to its mounts somehow had loosened causing the engine to droop and vibrate.

Had Ted relied on his engine instruments alone, and not looked out his window, it might have led to more extreme vibration and the engine may have separated in flight. It might have taken the left wing off and us with it. There is no substitute for a pilot's years of experience. Period.

HURRICANE CLEO

A month later, on August 26, 1964, a charter flight from JFK to (FPO) Freeport, Bahamas was on the menu. The captain was Karl Kloppel. The second officer was Chuck Mitchell.

Our 100 passengers were from a garment company that was located in New York City. Since it was a charter, we were operating under Part 135. This meant it was a non-scheduled flight and there was a little more leeway with in-flight rules.

Once we leveled off at our cruising altitude, Karl announced to our passengers that our flight time would be approximately four and a half hours. He then said if any passengers would like to visit the cockpit, they were welcome.

For the next four hours, the cockpit visitors came and went, but did not interfere with our duties. It was soon apparent some of the women were not from the garment industry, nor were they wives, or girlfriends. They appeared to belong to another profession, one, well, let's say, that has been around since the beginning of time. Nonetheless, that was not our concern. What lay ahead, was.

Before departing JFK, our meteorologist, who coordinates with the captain on any flight, gave us a heads-up on the formation of Hurricane Cleo. It appeared to be aiming at the Bahamas and Florida.

Our approach and landing at Freeport came with strong gusty winds. Our stay was just long enough to deplane our passengers and their baggage, re-fuel, and leave for Miami.

The short hop over to Miami was no different. We had our hands full of heavy gusty winds generated by Cleo. After parking the aircraft, we grabbed our flight bags and overnight suitcases and headed for the hotel. I was at the hotel just long enough to grab a shower, shave, and prepare to go to dinner when the telephone rang.

Eastern wanted all their aircraft flown out of Miami and taken to Atlanta because Cleo was aiming in our direction.

The three of us boarded the same aircraft we flew into Miami. Our windshields were still plastered with the tell-tale signs of what was left of insects and the guts of a bird strike when we made our approach.

Karl and I grabbed a can of club soda and paper towels. We scrubbed the windshields to get rid of the unwanted remains. Club soda works wonders for cleaning aircraft windows. Meanwhile, Chuck did a quick walk-around inspection of the aircraft.

A ground handler, whose job was to clean the windshield when we arrived, came into the cockpit. He told Karl he was going to file a grievance against both of us for doing his job. Karl threw him out of the cockpit and off the aircraft. We started our engines and made for Atlanta.

My thought during this incident was don't screw with a guy who flew 93 combat missions in a P-47 during World War Two. Karl held the Distinguished Flying Cross; the Air Medal with 4 battle stars; and the Presidential Unit Citation Medal.

The aftermath of Cleo was staggering. It was the longest-lived storm of the 1964 season. It formed on August 20th and finally dissipated on September 5, 1964. The estimated damage was well over $187 million, with a loss of 156 lives. We were lucky.

The following day, August 27, we flew back to MIA. While in flight operations, whom do I bump into, but my initial DC-7 flight instructor, Captain Raser. He asked me how I was doing. Of course, I told him all was well.

Standing next to him was a face I had seen in newspapers and read about growing up. He was surrounded by other pilots who wanted to talk to him. My ex-instructor intervened and introduced me to this legendary pioneer aviator, Captain Henry Tyndall "Dick" Merrill.

THE PING PONG FLIGHT

I know what you're thinking. How do you suddenly meet these famous aviators you read about and admired growing up? My answer has been and always will be, "Being in the right place at the right time." When you make a career of flying, and constantly find yourself crisscrossing our nation, there are going to be times when you do meet famous people.

The legend of Captain Dick Merrill speaks for itself. He was once Eastern Air Line's chief pilot, the number one pilot on its seniority list. He was Eastern's most experienced pilot at that time. Before his retirement, in 1961, he logged well over 45,000 flying hours. An aviation legend, he was regarded as one of America's finest aviation pioneers. He was also known as the highest-paid airmail pilot in the country. Think back to open cockpits.

Merrill was married to Toby Wing, a beautiful blonde movie star. She appeared in such movies as *42nd Street* with Dick Powell. She also appeared in many other movies of the 1930s.

Captain Merrill's aviation glory is well documented. He was Dwight D. Eisenhower's personnel pilot during the 1952 presidential elections. He flew the first round-trip transatlantic flight in 1936. That flight alone made him famous. The media dubbed that flight the "Ping Pong" flight.

The aircraft he flew was a beautiful-looking, all-metal, Vultee V-1A. It boasted having a 1,000 Wright Cyclone engine, and it could cruise at 235 miles per hour.

For that transatlantic flight, Merrill stowed over 41,000 ping pong balls in the hollows of the plane's wings and fuselage. He thought that if he ever had to ditch in the Atlantic Ocean, the ping pong balls would keep the aircraft afloat until he was rescued. Thankfully, he never had to test his theory.

During his career, Captain Merrill set several airspeed records. This would be the only time I would be in that famous aviator's presence. Unfortunately, he passed away in October 1982.

THESE ENGINES DON'T QUIT

F riday, October 16, 1964. It was 3 a.m. when the telephone rang. It was a crew scheduler. Who else? I would rather have it be a crew scheduler than something else. As a reserve pilot, we were always on call.

"We need you to cover a ferry flight out of JFK. How soon can you get to the airport?" He asked me.

"In a little over two hours. Where am I going and for how many days?" I asked as I rubbed the sleep out of my eyes.

"JFK to Nashville, next to Washington DC. Then you'll ferry the aircraft back to JFK."

It was what we called a 'turnaround.' I would be back home that night. I took a quick shower, shaved, packed my travel suitcase, just in case, grabbed my flight bag, and headed out the door.

From northern New Jersey, where I lived, it would have normally taken me one hour and forty minutes to drive to JFK. I always allowed myself more time, knowing what the traffic could be like at any time of day crossing the George Washington Bridge.

By the time I arrived, the captain and second officer already concluded the required pre-flight checks as did the two stewardesses assigned to the flight. He also received our flight clearance and briefed the Second Officer and me on the route and altitude he planned to fly. He warned us of the possibility of encountering icing conditions along our flight route.

The first leg of our sequence was a ferry flight to Nashville to pick up Vanderbilt University's football team, "The Commodores." Then we were to fly them to Washington D.C. to play against George Washington University's "Colonials."

We took off and promptly climbed into a cold, wet, heavy overcast sky. There was a hint of some icing, but several thousand feet higher, we broke out into the open and greeted the morning sun as it made its appearance.

Three hours and nine minutes ahead lay Nashville. We leveled off at our cruising altitude of 20,000 feet. Our aircraft was performing beautifully. Its four powerful R-3350 Wright Cyclone engines were humming in our ears.

Usually, the Captain normally did the first leg of a sequence of flights, but on this day he had asked me to do it.

Flying the DC-7 with its fly-by-wire control cables, or flight controls, always seemed to me, as though it had the power steering you have in an automobile. That was especially when cruising at more than 300 miles per hour.

Ahead of us, we could see the beginning of the weather front coming up from the southwest. It wasn't long before we were back in the clouds and flying on instruments.

As we crossed over the Adirondack Mountains, some reaching a height of over 4,000 feet, the view ahead was blocked by solid cloud cover. Too bad because the beauty of the Adirondacks is a sight to behold.

Up to that point, the flight was uneventful, routine, just banter between the three of us in the cockpit. A short time later, the Captain said he was going back into the cabin to have one of the box lunches placed on board for us.

As he exited, the second officer slid into the Captain's seat. This was not unusual when a pilot leaves the cockpit for a trip to the lavatory or some other destination. The DC-7 Second Officer's seat was small and uncomfortable. It sat between the Captain and the First Officer's seat, slightly behind the center console which housed the radios, navigation systems, and throttles. It was also wedged between the two shelves of radio racks. Behind the racks, was a narrow space for crew baggage and coat racks. Each time the pilot left his seat, the second officer had to get out of his way to allow him to pass.

The Captain was gone for about ten minutes when I noticed that the outside air temperature had dropped several degrees. A check of the engine cylinder head temperature gauges revealed they were also dropping. This was a good indication of possible icing conditions. Although I could not see any ice adhering to the windshield wiper bolts, another ice buildup indicator.

I told Dan that we better put carburetor heat on the engines to prevent carburetor icing.

Dan's answer was, "Bob, I've been flying these birds for a long time. These engines don't quit."

Just then, the Captain returned to the cockpit and told me to go back into the cabin and grab lunch. I hesitated, but he insisted that I relax and enjoy the box lunch of cold chicken, potato salad, an apple, and a cup of warm coffee.

Reluctantly, I went to the back of the cabin where there was a small horseshoe-shaped lounge. On the DC-7 model we were flying, passengers could use this lounge whenever the seat belt sign was turned off.

As I sat down, one of the stewardesses handed me a box lunch. No sooner did I place it on my lap when all four engines began to quit.

It's amazing how silent it gets when those fans stop turning. I felt a slight descent. My first thought was of those jagged Adirondack peaks below us, and that mine could be a very short career.

I told the stewardess that all four engines had just quit. It was as if the blood drained out of her body. She just stood there and turned completely white, petrified.

I rushed back to the cockpit, but I couldn't get back into my seat because the flight engineer was now back in his seat and blocking my way. All I could do was watch.

There were four pairs of hands, the captain's and the engineer's moving as fast as they could to get those props spinning again before the engines completely quit. The first thing they did was get the carb heat to all four engines.

After several minutes of being afraid they might not succeed, we heard that beautiful humming sound.

We had lost very little altitude. We climbed back to our cruising elevation and made an uneventful flight until landing in Nashville. There we boarded the football team for the two-hour and forty-eight-minute flight to DCA.

Before we restarted the engines, the Captain made only one comment, "Let's keep all four engines running this time."

What happened was the result of a combination of two things: suddenly entering an area of heavy icing without having carburetor heat on the engines. At the same time, the second officer had trouble cross-feeding from the four alternate fuel tanks when the main tanks were getting low on fuel. That caused the starvation of the engines for fuel for a short period.

The flight to DCA was uneventful except for the light to moderate turbulence we experienced throughout. Midway through the flight, the stewardess who had become an 'instant ghost' came into the cockpit and asked if we could slow the aircraft down.

When she opened the cockpit door, the stench of vomit permeated the air. It was evident some of the football players weren't used to flying in bumpy weather. The Captain advised her we were doing the best we could under the circumstances.

After we landed and were in the process of deplaning the Vanderbilt footballers, I couldn't help but notice the many pale and unhappy faces going out the door.

There was an upside. Vanderbilt's win/loss record at the time was one win and three losses. They beat the Colonials fourteen to nothing.

I like to think our bumpy flight put the fear of God into them and had a lot to do with their thumping George Washington's football team.

After that fiasco, each time I would see Dan, I would remind him by saying, "These engines never quit." We'd just shake our heads and laugh about this close call.

CAPTAIN EDDIE V. RICKENBACKER

O
n October 24, 1964, I had my first of many flights with Captain Howie James Jr. We spent four days flying together, logging over 15 hours of flight time, many of which were under instrument flying conditions.

The reason I bring up his name is, not once in those four days, or for that matter, each time I flew with him. He would never engage the auto-pilot. As most pilots would do. All of his flying was done by hand.

Still, he had no qualms if his first officer engaged the auto-pilot, which was the general routine.

I would hand fly the aircraft to altitude, level off, trim, then engage it. Then disengage it when starting a descent to a landing and hand fly it to touchdown.

He also had given me the best advice I had ever received about flying.

He said. "Bob, you're going to fly with a lot of different captains who have their ideas on how to fly an aircraft, some of which you may not agree with. One day you'll be the captain, and as a captain, you are also a flight instructor to your co-pilots. So be flexible."

I always remembered that throughout my flying career.

As far as I know, all of the captains I had flown with always engaged the auto-pilot.

There was one other Eastern captain who never engaged the auto-pilot. Though I never flew with him because he flew the DC-8. That was his father. Howie James Sr.

One of the Eastern plums was the Eastern Air Lines Shuttle.

Inaugurated on April 30, 1961, it boasted hourly airline service to four of Eastern's major airports. Newark, LaGuardia, Boston, and Washington D.C.

The cost at that time was a mere $10.95 to $12.75, and you paid on board the flight. In addition, it had a backup service.

If the aircraft was full, a backup aircraft was put into service, even though it may have only carried one passenger. I know. I flew the shuttle off and on throughout my career with Eastern and there had been many a back-up flight with only one passenger on board.

October 28, 1964. It was the end of a long day of three round trips of shuttle flying from Newark to Boston and back. The captain that day was Jim Keyser. A day that still stands out in my mind.

To begin with, Jim was a super guy to fly with, easy-going, and very helpful when asked questions concerning any aspects of flight.

He lived in a small town in Bucks County, Pennsylvania, not far from where George Washington's Continental Army attacked the British Army at Trenton, New Jersey, on December 25, 1776.

The picture that always runs through my mind when I think about him is that he's riding on an old John Deere tractor plowing up cornfields for spring planting and smoking that corn cob pipe he was always puffing on. Although I'm not sure he ever owned an old John Deere tractor or lived on a farm. Nevertheless that corn cob pipe was always present in the cockpit when we flew together. Filling the cockpit with the sweet smoky aroma from whatever pipe tobacco he was using that day.

We flew many times together over the years, not only on the DC-7 but on the B-727. I never minded his smoking, but there was always one habit he had that I didn't enjoy. Though I had never mentioned it to him. It had to do with eating crew meals.

Usually, the captain would eat first, the food tray set on a pillow that was placed on his lap. The meal was usually steak or chicken. Of course, the captain usually picked the steak. Then it would be the first officer's turn.

It was company policy that the captain and first officer would never eat the same kind of meal when flying. The thought of the possibility of food positioning from one of them. Where a crew member might become incapacitated.

When it was my turn to eat, I would place the food tray on the pillow that was now laying on my lap. Just before my first bite, Jim would pop out his false teeth, take a toothbrush and calmly begin cleaning his dentures. This procedure seemed to last all through the meal. Oh well. "C'est La Vie." Now you see why I did not enjoy this habit.

At that time, we were housed at the old Newark terminal and had to offload our passengers down portable stairs that were attached to the back of a pick-up truck. There were no jet-ways at that time.

After our passengers deplaned, it was our turn to hustle down the stairs and make our way through the small corridor that led to the main terminal and the employee bus.

I followed Jim, and he was not one to be deterred by any of the passengers ahead of us moving too slowly for his liking. His flight bag would occasionally bang into a passenger as he passed by, or if any departing passengers coming toward us did not give way, they too would get accidentally bumped.

Suddenly, Jim stopped dead in his tracks and I banged into the back of him. He put down his flight bag and stepped in front of a man coming in our direction and stopped him. He grabbed the man's hand and shook it.

The man looked very familiar. Then I realized who he was. Captain Eddie V. Rickenbacker.

Jim introduced me. I was awe-struck and mumbled a few words about how fortunate I was to be an Eastern Air Lines pilot. He shook my hand, wished me luck, and told us he had to catch his flight to Miami.

I watched as he proceeded to the gate for his departure, then disappeared into the swarm of passengers who were with him.

It would be the only time I would ever be in his presence. The joy I felt that day meeting my boyhood hero, has never gone away.

This great aviation pioneer who had shot down 26 enemy aircraft during World War One and was the founder of Eastern Air Lines, would have many, many, accomplishments attributed to him. Sadly, he passed away on

July 23, 1973.

A PLANE CRASH

O n November 10, 1964, I stopped by Caldwell-Wright Airport to visit some of the flight instructors I had worked with while I instructed for Wings of Morristown.

Unfortunately, some had the day off while others were on a cross-country flight with a student. Although I did get a chance to talk with Vic Varcardipone.

Vic was an assistant mechanic who worked with Bill Hasselbeck when I was flight instructing and with whom I had become friendly.

Vic had just obtained his commercial pilot's certificate and had been hired as a co-pilot for a new in-state airline that was to operate out of Caldwell-Wright Airport.

The corporation had purchased a Twin-Beech C-18S N39Q from Bendix Aviation which was once based at Teterboro Airport.

The inaugural flight was to be held on Monday, November 16, 1964, just six days away. As we talked, he told me he did not think the captain the corporation had hired had a lot of experience. Even though he said he did.

I advised Vic to give the job more thought. If he was not comfortable flying with this captain, to bypass the job and wait until another one came along.

He stated, that it was an opportunity for him to build his flying hours and hopefully fly for a major airline. Something I could understand. I wished him luck and said I would drop by again to see how it was going.

On November 14, 1964, I began what was to be a four-day sequence of flights with layovers in Atlanta, Mobile, and Washington D.C. On the fourth day fly to Charlestown, South Carolina then fly back to Newark.

On Sunday, November 15, 1964, we departed Mobile, made a stop in Atlanta, then it was on to Washington. The Captain was Al Powers, who happened to have relatives that Barbara and I knew and who lived a block away.

By the time we arrived in Washington, the day had been filled with pleasant discussions about family, friends, and neighbors. So, I was in a cheerful frame of mind when I entered my hotel room and turned on the television to see what the morning's weather would bring.

The television was tuned to a news channel. As I watched, waiting for the weather update, the newscaster began reporting on an aircraft accident that happened that day at Caldwell-Wright Airport.

The crash killed three people and critically injured two others. Before he said anything else, I knew he was talking about the twin-engine Beech. My heart sank as I thought about Vic and hoped he survived the crash.

The following morning, I made a hasty telephone call to Wings headquarters and inquired about the accident.

Vic and another person in the aircraft had been thrown clear when it split open from the crash. Both survived but were in critical condition with seventy percent burns when the aircraft burst into flames. The outlook for both was grim.

The question was. What had caused the accident?

After I had arrived back home, I made a hasty trip to Caldwell Airport to inquire about Vic's condition.

I was told that what was to be a joyous occasion started with a familiarization flight. Onboard were the two pilots, and three officers of the newly formed company.

They had wanted to see what it was like riding in the twin Beech and to make last-minute adjustments to flight schedules that were to begin the following day.

According to one of the flight instructors whom I knew, and who had witnessed the whole event told me. The flight had returned to land but it appeared to be too high and too fast on its approach.

He said the aircraft landed halfway down runway 22. Stating that it appeared to him the crew must have realized they couldn't stop the aircraft without running off the end of the runway and into the trees just beyond.

He said he could tell that full power had been applied to both engines and a go-around had been initiated. At the same time, he could see that the landing gear began to retract while the aircraft was still on the ground.

When that happened, the aircraft began to settle, and both propellers struck the runway, snapping off large pieces. The aircraft bounced back into the air, climbed to less than 100 feet, made a sharp right turn, struck high-tension power lines that were close by, and crashed.

He said that the next thing he saw was a great ball of fire.

When my wife and I went to visit Vic at the hospital we were told only relatives were allowed to see him. Conscious and in pain, Vic related to them what had happened. They in turn related it to us.

He told them, that once they realized they needed to make a go-around, full power was applied. Part of their go-around required them to go from a full flap landing setting to a go-around flap setting before retracting the landing gear.

Somehow in their haste, they accidentally grabbed the gear handle first instead of the flaps and put it in the up position. When the landing gear started to retract, the aircraft settled, the props struck the runway, and a portion of the blades sheared off. Out of balance, the engines vibrated so severely they thought they were coming off their mounts.

In front of them was a golf course they could have easily belly-landed the aircraft on, and, most likely, would have walked away unscathed. Then said. That there were too many golfers on it and they were afraid they might strike some of them.

They then made a desperate 270 degrees right turn trying to land on runway 13, lost control of the aircraft, and hit the power lines.

Unfortunately, both men would succumb to their burns.

The aftermath led to inquiries concerning the validity of the captain's commercial pilot's license and his experience in flying multi-engine aircraft. I was told they were not valid.

I couldn't help but think of Vic's concerns when I talked to him on the tenth.

In retrospect, although the crew lost their lives because of a mistake, in a sense, their actions were heroic. A split-second decision had to be made. It cost them their lives but probably saved several golfers from being killed.

As pilots, we know that we may have to sacrifice our lives to save others.

Shortly after Vic's accident, I had awakened in the middle of the night from a horrific nightmare. The dream had been of another aircraft accident.

Whether the nightmare was triggered by Vic's accident, I don't know but the dream still stands clearly in my mind.

I was sitting in the passenger cabin of a DC-7 waiting to take my first officer proficiency flight check.

At the controls was a new first officer who was receiving his first flight check. Suddenly the aircraft began rolling to the right and went inverted. As it continued its roll, I reacted by jumping out of my seat and racing to the back of the aircraft, knowing it was going to crash. The back as being the best place to survive.

Just before the aircraft hit the water I awoke. The dream was so vivid it took me a while before I could fall back to sleep.

On December 27, 1964, my days of flying the DC-7 came to an end. What was next?

THE SUPER CONSTELLATION

eniority rules! Something I did not have. It was goodbye to being a first officer and becoming a second officer on the Lockheed Super Constellation, which was affectionally referred to as, the Connie.

Ironically, it is interesting to note, that a Connie, named Columbine II, led to the presidential aircraft being called, Air Force One.

In 1953 a mix-up by air traffic controllers let two flights using the same flight number into the same air space. One was Eastern Air Lines flight 8610, and the other was Air Force flight 8610 which used their aircraft's tail number.

President Dwight D. Eisenhower was Inside Columbine II. The near mid-air collision over New York City spurred the creation of the unique call sign for Columbine II as Air Force One. From then on, all subsequent presidential aircraft are called Air Force One.

When our pilot class was first hired, we all knew it would be only a matter of time before we would be trained as flight engineers. Followed by weeks of ground school and days of simulator and flight training on the constellation.

The question was. Why would Eastern hire a pilot and then train him to become a flight engineer?

When we were hired as first officers, we were flying a position that was out of our seniority. Namely to fill slots of newly acquired aircraft, and the replacement of flight engineers who were no longer with the company.

To understand some of this, you would have to go back to February 1961 when many members of the Flight Engineers International Association

(FEIA) union went on strike.

Before that strike, a cockpit crew member was either a pilot and a member of the Air Line Pilots Association (ALPA) or a FEIA flight engineer. The strike also involved as to who had the final say as to the safety of the flight.

Before the flight, the captain and dispatcher would sign the necessary papers before take-off. When the flight ended, both the captain and flight engineer were required to sign the maintenance logbook. In some instances, it had become a problem.

The issue was who had more authority over the flight, and what was going to be entered into the maintenance logbook. Is it the captain or the flight engineer?

Remember the incident with Ted Connolly and his flight engineer when they belly-landed? That was what Ted had pointed out to me. The captain was in charge. Not everyone agreed.

After the strike and the many years of court hearings between the company and the FEIA. It was determined that all cockpit crew members would have to be pilot-qualified.

In turn, Eastern would pay for all the pilot training for those who wished to become pilots. If you chose to become a pilot and could not pass the flight tests, you would be grandfathered. That meant you could remain a flight engineer until retirement.

The catch was that you had to join ALPA and leave the FEIA. Many members of the FEIA union had chosen to retire. Others flat-out quit Eastern. The remaining group took advantage of the company's offer and became pilots and joined ALPA.

While instructing at Wings, one of those FEIA flight engineers became one of my students and went on to obtain his pilot's license, and returned to Eastern. Eventually, he became a captain.

Another irony. Remember me nearly being chopped up by a whirling propeller? That aircraft belonged to one of our part-time flight instructors who leased it to Wings. He too was an Eastern Air Lines FEIA flight engineer and had all the necessary pilot ratings required to fly for any airline before the court decisions.

At the time I had told him that if he did not go back to work for Eastern that he might not have a job. He insisted his union would eventually win the lawsuit.

Unfortunately, he did not go back and he lost his job with Eastern. He, like many other FEIA members who had refused Eastern's offer, ended up flying for airline freight outfits or foreign air carriers such as Saudi Arabian Airlines.

In a sense, those FEIA members who did not return to Eastern had opened opportunities for people like me to fly for them.

A FUEL TRUCK, A FIRE, A BAD MEMORY

My first flight as a Connie Flight Engineer began on January 15, 1965. It was an Eastern Air Lines backup shuttle flight from EWR-BOS-EWR. Carrying only one passenger per flight. At the time the Constellation was the only aircraft that was used for shuttle flying.

The Eastern Shuttle was an entity in itself. Each flight crew consisted of the captain, the first officer, the flight engineer, and two stewardesses.

Many of the senior pilots who flew the shuttle would choose either the prime shuttle lines of flying or the shuttle stand-by slots. Either way, it allowed them to be home each night. Rather than having a two, three, or four-day layover. Much like a nine-to-five job.

If you had little seniority as I did, you flew standby. That meant you spent most of your time sitting in the crew lounge waiting to be called to fly the backup flight. There were many eight-hour days when I didn't fly. How could anyone enjoy sitting around all day and not fly, was beyond my comprehension

Those who flew the line had a name for us stand-by crews. They called us, Pelicans. They thought we squawked every time we had to go fly. That was not my case. I itched to fly as much as I could.

The Connie was often referred to as, a bunch of spare parts flying in close formation. It was a hydraulic nightmare. But very reliable. I would spend eighteen months on that aircraft, mostly flying the Eastern Shuttle.

Part of a flight engineer's job was to make sure the aircraft was air-worthy by conducting walk-around inspections, inside and outside the aircraft.

One of the pre-flight routines was to make sure the proper amount of fuel the captain ordered was on board. To double-check the amount, you would have to drip-stick the fuel tanks and then compare the results with the fuel gauges in the cockpit.

Access to the fuel tanks was on top of the wings. When the fuel truck arrived, I would take the truck's ladder, lean it against the leading edge of the wing, then climb on top, and stick the tanks.

The first time I did that with Eastern, I had to force myself to do it. For it brought back an incident that took place on a very windy day on May 7, 1963.

While I was a flight instructor for Wings of Morristown, which at that time was based at the Caldwell-Wright Airport in Caldwell, New Jersey. I volunteered to help transfer aviation fuel from one fuel truck to another.

This was because the person who would normally have done it had the day off. At the time I was the assistant chief pilot for Wings and the only employee available.

The truck driver, whose tanker contained 5,000 gallons of 80/87 of volatile aviation fuel, told me he would direct me during the transfer.

The idea being he would park both trucks side-by-side and then transfer 1,000 gallons of the 5,000 gallons to our 1,000-gallon fuel truck.

The only problem. He did not have the correct length of hose for the transfer. Normally, it required a 20-foot hose to be attached from the bottom of his truck to the bottom of our truck. Then the fuel would be pressure fed to the receiving truck.

He then asked me to stand on top of my truck. That way we could fuel thru the hatch that was on top. Which I had thought odd, but agreed to do it. He then handed me a hose he had attached to the bottom of his truck. It was long enough to where I could stick four inches of it down the hatch.

When I saw that there was no shut-off nozzle, like at gas stations, I asked him how he was going to control the amount of fuel going into my truck.

No problem. He would control it from inside his cab by the use of a hand throttle. Just let him know when my truck was full and he would stop fueling.

By then, the Northwest winds picked up, their gusts becoming stronger.

At first, there was only a trickle of fuel flowing into my truck, and I told him. His answer. "Don't worry. I'll adjust the pressure."

Then came the sudden roar of the truck's engine followed by a blast of hot exhaust striking the left side of my body.

I had turned away from looking down inside the belly of my truck and spotted his truck's exhaust stack. It ran up the right side of his cab pointing toward the open hatch.

I shouted. "Turn off the truck!" It was too late.

From deep inside the belly of my truck came an enormous whooshing sound as though thousands of cans of vacuum-packed coffee cans burst open as the air was sucked out. Followed by a great ball of fire ignited by the gas fumes coming from inside my truck.

The limp four-inch hose that I had hold of went rigid and popped out of the hatch from the sudden high pressure.

What had been a trickle of gasoline became a roaring flame-thrower as hundreds of gallons of burning fuel were being pumped out of the transfer truck.

I yelled at the people who were standing nearby to run for their lives as the flaming fuel spread over the ramp toward them.

The swirling winds that had been comforting, me were now spraying deadly flames over me. Black oily smoke surrounded me. My clothes caught fire, and my arms, face, and hair.

At that moment, I truly believed the gas truck was going to detonate and thought. "This is one hell of a way to die!"

Then, as though being guided. I let go of the flame thrower and leaped from the top of my truck to the top of the tanker and dove off. Jamming both wrists when I hit the pavement.

As I rolled on the ground to smother the flames, I glanced underneath my burning truck. All I could see were the legs of people running. It was as though they were hanging from the bottom of the chassis of the truck. As if a puppeteer was controlling them.

It was comical. No bodies, just legs. They were churning as fast as they could and seemingly not going anywhere and I burst out laughing.

By that time the cab of the driver's truck was on fire. The engine was still racing pumping out that flaming inferno.

Then came the explosions.

Burning fuel had caught the truck's tires on fire and they began to explode. Each time one did, I covered my head expecting the next explosion to be the truck. Fortunately, that did not happen.

Then I remembered the airport crash truck we flight instructors had been trained to operate.

It was parked in a garage that was under the control tower. At first, I couldn't get the garage door to open. Then thought, If I can't, I'll crash through it. It opened on the second pull.

I pulled up twenty-feet short of the inferno. Jumped out, and opened the valves that would allow me to spray foam on it. Then climbed on top and began spraying down the fire. I almost had it under control, when I ran out of foam. By that time the local fire department had arrived and taken over.

For me, it was a trip to the hospital diagnosed with first, second, and third-degree burns and smoke inhalation. Miraculously, the burns healed without any scarring and my lungs cleared. Each time I think about that day. I thank my guardian angels.

I had to climb those Eastern fuel trucks for eighteen months as a Connie flight engineer. I never got used to doing it.

EASTERN AIR LINES FLIGHT 663

The morning of February 8, 1965, had me flying two round-trip flights from Newark, to Boston and back. The captain was Ted Anthony and the first officer was Bob Beal. We lifted off from EWR at 07:30 and finished our day at 14:33. All was well. It was a great day to fly. Or so I had thought at the time.

At 6:20 p.m. EDT that evening, Eastern Air Lines flight 663 had taken off from JFK on its way to Charlotte, North Carolina. As it was climbing to its cruising altitude, it was forced to take severe evasive action to avoid a collision with Pan American's inbound flight 212.

In doing so, the Eastern crew lost control of the aircraft and it rolled over and crashed into the Atlantic Ocean approximately 6.5 miles south-southwest of Jones Beach. 79 passengers and a crew of 5 perished in the crash. The aircraft destroyed was N849, the last DC-7 I had flown.

Most investigations of an aircraft accident take time, and the inspectors who do it are well-trained to determine the probable cause. This accident would take approximately two years before their final report was released.

On November 14, 1966, the Civil Aeronautics Board File # 1-0001 read in part, "The probable cause of the accident was the evasive maneuvers that EAL flight 663 took to avoid the oncoming Pan American Boeing 707 flight 212, which caused flight 663 to suffer spatial disorientation and the lost control of the aircraft."

The investigation also pointed out that the DC-7, at the time, was not required to have a flight recorder. Most of the information about the accident came from the crew of Pan American flight 212 and the recording of the conversation between JFK'S tower and both aircraft.

The report further pointed out that on the night of the accident, it was dark, with no visible moon or stars, and no visible horizon.

In other words, there were no points of reference for the pilots of both aircraft to determine the actual distance from each other. Each pilot thought they were about to collide and each took evasive action.

Flight 663 was piloted by Captain Fred Carson, First Officer Edward Dunn, and Second Officer Doug Mitchell, the son of our New York base Chief Pilot, Joe Mitchell. The two stewardesses were Linda Lord and Judith Durkin, both of whom I had flown with a week before.

The CAB report also speculated that had flight 663 been at a higher altitude, they were climbing through 3,500 feet, it might have avoided the crash given that there would have possibly been enough altitude to recover control of the aircraft.

As in my dream, and according to the CAB report, the DC-7 rolled to the right, inverted, continued to roll, and flattened out just as it hit the water. Why I had dreamt that nightmare before the accident. I can't say, for I have no answer.

JACQULINE KENNEDY

As an airline pilot, your career may take you around the world and to places you have never been. On very rare occasions, meet a celebrity you thought you would never meet.

While flying the shuttle there were times when a senator or a congressman would be aboard one of my flights. Especially if the flight was to Washington D. C. Most notably Senators Robert and Ted Kennedy. Usually with photographers and reporters tagging along.

Or they would take a shuttle flight to Boston from La Guardia en route to the Kennedy Compound in Hyannis, Massachusetts.

Then there was that day when I had been on an early morning shuttle stand-by. Somewhat bored, I decided to fetch a newspaper from the newsstand located in the Shuttle terminal.

As I reached down a woman wearing a dark kerchief that covered a portion of her face had also reached for a magazine.

My hand accidentally bumped her hand and I apologized. As I did, I noticed several men dressed in suits suddenly come forward and stand next to us. At first, I thought that was odd. Until I took a closer look at the woman. It was Jacquelyn Kennedy.

It suddenly dawned on me that those men were probably secret service and my hand bumping hers made them come forward.

After a couple of more apologies and a very short conversation, I found out she was taking a shuttle flight to BOS, from there to the Kennedy Compound.

For those few moments when I stood next to her, I thought her to be a most pleasant and very beautiful woman.

The Eastern Shuttle had a unique system for boarding its passengers. The process began by filling out a boarding pass, then standing in line, awaiting your turn to be seated, and paying onboard.

Sometimes those passengers would get a little too anxious to board, especially if the flight looked to be full. They would then try to edge their way toward the front of the line. Only to be turned back by the gate agent.

Our gate agents were just one of the many groups within the airline support team that kept it flying. I had always thought they were the most underrated group of all. The pressure on them at times was enormous.

They took the brunt of the passenger's wrath whose number could range anywhere from 1 to 200 or more. Particularly if a flight may have been canceled, delayed, or moved to a different concourse.

Passenger rage wasn't confined to boarding. It could occur during a flight. In one instance, although I was not involved, an incident happened to one of my classmates who had related it to me. I chuckle when I think about it.

The Connie carried potable water for our passengers. To verify the amount remaining in its holding tank, it required the use of a sight gauge similar to those that were once used on older models of automobiles. Where the gauge showed how much fuel was left in the gas tank. F, ¾, ½, ¼, and E for empty.

The water gauge was positioned on the bulkhead next to one of the lavatories that were located in the mid-section of the passenger cabin. To view the gauge, which was recessed, you had to press your eye against the bulkhead.

On this particular flight, a stewardess complained to the flight engineer about not having any water. Of course, the captain sent him back to check.

The engineer didn't know a woman passenger had entered the lavatory where the water gauge was. When he pressed his eye to the gauge, the husband of the woman saw him and assumed he was looking into the lavatory to look at his wife.

The husband got out of his seat, approached the engineer, spun him around and grabbed the engineer's necktie, and yanked down on it. He then hit him with a right-hand uppercut, nearly knocking the engineer out.

Other passengers jumped out of their seats and restrained the husband. In the meantime, the captain radioed ahead to have the police meet the flight. The husband was arrested for interfering with a crew member.

Luckily the flight engineer's jaw wasn't broken. If anything, it had taught me a lesson. Having a tie around your neck acts like a lasso, and once someone grabs hold of it, you will go where it is being pulled.

After I was told about that incident, I switched to clip-on ties. No more having nooses hanging around my neck.

ANOTHER MULTIPLE-ENGINE FAILURE

When flying, winter weather in the northeast is always a reason to be on guard. Snow, sleet, rain, fog, and low ceilings are always on the menu.

On March 5, 1965, we had taken off from LGA in clear skies on our way to DCA. As we flew southbound the weather forecast for the Philadelphia and Washington D. C. area had called for overcast skies, snow flurries, and possible icing conditions along our intended route of flight.

To give you an idea of what the layout of a Connie's cockpit looks like, from where the flight engineer sat, and, what instruments he had in front of him.

Instead of facing forward as the pilots did, he sat behind them facing ninety degrees to the right. In front of him, was an instrument panel with its tachometers, oil pressure, and fuel gauges.

He also had his own set of four throttles, mixture controls, and an engine analyzer that he used to view the firing of the spark plugs in each cylinder of each engine.

Then there were carburetor heat controls and fuel cross-feed levers. He also sat about six inches lower than the pilots because of their raised flooring.

To see out the front windshield he had to come to a standing position, which I usually had to do when helping to look for other air traffic.

Our flight was proceeding normally until we passed southwest of

Philadelphia. As I stood, to see what lay ahead of us, I noticed we were about to enter a heavy cloud layer. I had asked the captain if he wanted me to put carb-heat on the engines to prevent the possibility of carburetor icing. His answer was. "Not yet."

When we entered that cloud deck it was as if someone threw buckets of heavy slush over the aircraft. Instant icing.

At the same moment, there was a huge electrostatic discharge. This happens when molecules contact and bunch up on the nose of the aircraft, then separate. Think of walking on a carpet and getting a shock from something you touch.

When flying, when you get that kind of discharge, it has the sound as though a giant cannon was being fired. Along with a blinding flash of white light.

When that happened, both engines 3 and 4 quit. For a moment, I had thought one of the engines had exploded. Until I saw they were still there when I looked out the small round window that allows the flight engineer to view them. Then both props began to wind-mill as they lost power.

The booming discharge had brought our two stewardesses rushing to the cockpit screaming in fear as they opened the door. Both tried to enter at the same time, only to jam themselves in its narrow entrance.

With two engines dead, and their props wind-milling, the one thing I did not want was to have two panic-stricken stewardesses screaming in right my ear.

With my left hand, I tried to restart the number three engine. With my right, I pushed on the stewardess's chests to get them unstuck. After a few hard shoves, they were free. I shut the door and bolted it with them on the outside. Then spent the next seven minutes trying to get both engines back online.

I would get number three fired up, then concentrate on firing up number four. Just as I got number four going, number three would quit.

It was back and forth like that until I finally was able to get both engines back online, and humming that deep wonderful drone. Only this time with engine heat.

While I was doing all of this, I had glanced up at the captain. He was sitting there calmly, arms folded, looking at me, with a, when the hell are you going to get those engines running again, look.

When he was sure they weren't going to quit again, grabbed the PA and gave a short explanation of what caused the static discharge. Leaving out that we had no carb-heat on the engines.

We continued the flight as though nothing had happened and made a normal approach and landing. Nobody on board said a word about our incident.

On the flight back to LGA, we passed through the same icing conditions. This time, there was no sound of a cannon going off. All four engines had carb-heat on and were purring like a litter of kittens.

Normally, an air carrier will file an instrument flight plan and you will fly pre-set airways. There are times when a captain will decide to fly by VFR rules as long as the weather is in his favor.

I flew with one captain, and whenever the weather was in our favor, would fly VFR from DCA to EWR. This meant winging our way up along the New Jersey coastline.

Once we were out over the Atlantic Ocean, he would descend to 500 feet above the ocean. Then follow the coastline about a mile or so off the shore so passengers could see Atlantic City, and what the New Jersey seashore looked like.

As I think back about those low-flying aircraft that towed banners offshore, other sight-seeing aircraft, and the beach-goers. They must have gotten the shock of their life as we flew by that low.

As 1965 wore on, I would, on occasion, go back to Caldwell-Wright Airport and visit the guys with whom I worked as a flight instructor.

On April 14, everyone was out flying, so I decided to go out to the flight line tie-down area, a grass strip of land, and only a dozen yards from the active runway. I stood there leaning against a Luscombe, watching a Cessna 150 from Teterboro Airport doing take-offs and landings.

After a few landings, the instructor got out and motioned for his student to fly solo. I watched him take off and turn downwind and had planned to watch his landing but decided to leave.

The following day I had read that the student, a forty-two-year-old man, crashed, and was killed on his first solo landing. Several days later, I went back to the airport and visited the site where he crashed. It was on the spot where I had been standing.

From what the guys who had witnessed the accident said.

"The student had come in too high and was attempting a go-around. He had full flaps on and went to full power to abort the landing.

The aircraft's nose pitched upward and stalled, flipped over to the left, and crashed nose down. It bounced once and slammed into the Luscombe and burst into flames, killing the pilot."

It was the same aircraft that I had been standing next to. Fortunately for me, I had left the area moments before the crash.

WITH A SHOTGUN BLAST

I flew the Connie for eighteen months and on occasion would have a layover in BOS or DCA. Though most of the shuttle flights were two-round trips with no layover. What little seniority I had, allowed me to fly the LGA-DCA shuttle and LGA-BOS shuttle at various times for several months in a row.

While walking down a corridor on one of those trips to Boston, I noticed a young man coming toward me pushing a large wheeled trash barrel.

He looked at me and I glanced at him as we passed each other. Both of us stopped, turned around, and pointed at one another saying. "Don't I know you?"

The man was someone we called J. J. who I would hang around with while in the Navy in Brunswick, Georgia, in 1957.

He had told me he was working for Eastern as a maintenance man during the day and going to night school a couple of times a week to get his degree.

He was married and had a couple of kids. As we talked, he asked me if we could get together that evening and have a beer at a bar near the airport, and talk about old times. I had told him I wasn't on a layover, but the next time I was in town, I would look him up and we'd get together.

However, I spent the next several months flying the LGA-DCA shuttle. When I did start flying the LGA-BOS shuttle again, I decided to look for him and had asked one of the maintenance men where I could find J. J.

He stared at me rather strangely and then told me I had better talk to the supervisor. I thought that was rather odd. Did he quit? Get fired? I was baffled by this guy's manner.

The supervisor had also looked at me rather strangely, as though he was hiding something. Then the truth came out. J. J. was shot and killed at a bar several months earlier. When he told me the month and day it happened, I looked in my flight logbook. It was the same day that I had seen him.

The supervisor then related to me, that after J. J. left work that night he went to the bar he occasionally frequented. While there, two gunmen had come in with shotguns and killed the bartender. J. J., the only other person in the bar, and a witness to the killing, started running for the door, only to be hit in the back of the head from another shotgun blast.

According to the supervisor, the bartender was involved with a numbers racket and had been holding out on the local crime syndicate.

He also said that J. J. was the twenty-seventh person killed by the mob, but probably the only one not involved with the syndicate.

An innocent guy who happened to be in the wrong place at the wrong time. It still mystifies me, not having seen him for eight years, then meeting, and him being killed the same day. What would have happened if I had a layover that night?

As the saying goes. "Time and tide wait for no man."

Pilot attrition is a large factor that affects pilot seniority. Those being retirements, medical issues, and sometimes, the firing of a pilot.

All of which was moving me up in seniority. My time as a Connie engineer was finally coming to a close.

Eastern was phasing out its piston aircraft and purchasing more jet aircraft and during that time several events took place. One was somewhat comical, not really. The other. Another tragedy.

EASTERN AIR LINES SHUTTLE FLIGHT 853

Since I was becoming more senior, I was able to fly freight on several occasions. Eastern had several 1049G's which were used strictly for hauling freight, mostly out of JFK.

On this day, we were to fly from JFK to MSY (New Orleans). Part of our pre-takeoff check was to ensure that all cylinders on the engines were firing properly. The procedure was to run up engines 2 and 3 at the same time, check the engine analyzer for any fouled spark plugs, pull the power back if normal, then run up engines 1 and 4, and do the same check.

There is a point during the check when all four engines are near the same run-up power. This creates a prop wash of near-tornado proportions. Unknown to us, during the run-up when all four engines were at the same power setting, a C-172 happened to be taxiing behind us.

In a matter of seconds, the blast from our prop wash swirled under the high-wing Cessna, lifted it as though it was in a take-off mode, and flipped it over on its back.

Out came the emergency vehicles to ensure the pilot and his passengers were okay. They were, but the C-172 had a lot of damage to it. Most likely, so did the pilot's ego for not being aware of the potential consequences when getting too close to a much larger aircraft.

After this incident, I thought about putting a small image of a C-172 below the captain's cockpit window, much like the pilots did during the war when they brought down an enemy aircraft.

I had gotten that idea as a kid during the war years of WW II. We would put airplane glue on balsa wood aircraft, set fire to them, and throw them into the air. When we did that to five of them, we became air aces.

Late in the afternoon on December 4, 1965, the weather over Carmel, New York was broken clouds with tops at approximately 10,000 feet. Above that, unlimited visibility.

At approximately 16:18 (EST), Eastern Air Lines Shuttle Flight 853, a Connie, had passed over the Carmel VORTAC, a navigational aid, near Hartford, Connecticut. Captain, Charles J. White was in command.

Several months previously, Captain White, a Boston-based captain, had been temporarily assigned to our New York Base, and I had flown with him several times before he returned to Boston.

Assisting Captain White was First Officer Roger Holt, and Second Officer Emile Greenway, who was one of my new-hire classmates. The two stewardesses on board the flight were Kathy DePue and Patrice Sarada.

Up to that point, the EA853 flight had gone smoothly. At 10,000 feet the Connie had been skimming through the tops of the clouds.

At the same time TWA's Flight 42, a Boeing 707, had been en route from San Francisco to JFK. Captain Thomas A. Carroll in command. Flight 42 had descended to 11,000 feet and was also crossing over the Carmel VORTAC.

Both flights were banking. When an aircraft is in a turn–bank, it can give the optical illusion that another aircraft appears to be at the same altitude as you are. Very similar to EA Flight 663 accident.

As they were passing over the Carmel VORTAC to remain on course, both flight crews saw the other.

In situations such as these, an automatic reaction takes over to avoid a collision. Your first instinct is to pull up and not push the nose down. In this case, unfortunately, it led to a mid-air impact of both aircraft.

When EA 853 pulled its nose up, it put the plane at a higher altitude. Seeing this, TW 42's flight crew made a right turn pull up, followed by an immediate left turn, and passed under the tail of the Connie.

When that happened, the number 1 cowling and a portion of the B-707's

73

left wing struck the underside of the fuselage of the 1049G. The collision tore out the hydraulic boost package and control cables rendering the elevator and rudder flight controls inoperative and putting the aircraft out of control.

After the impact, thanks to the extraordinary efforts of the TW 42 flight crew, they were able to land their crippled jet safely at JFK.

Not so for EA 853.

To begin with, let's examine the loss of flight controls. The aileron controls are used for banking the aircraft. The rudder is used for directional control and the elevator is for the nose up and down pitch control. The hydraulic boost package is used to aid the flight controls, much like power steering on an automobile.

Without them, the aircraft was either climbing or descending and out of control.

It was then Captain White drew on his experience and manipulated the throttles. He either added or reduced power on the left wing or the right wing for directional control and to maintain some altitude. But regardless of their efforts, they were still descending.

In the meantime, Second Officer Greenway had sent out Mayday distress calls, informing ATC, and other aircraft of their collision and their intentions.

Knowing they were going to have to crash land, Captain White made announcements to his passengers to keep them informed of what his intentions were.

In the meantime, First Officer Holt had spotted a lake but voiced concerns about landing on water and the possibility of not getting all of the people out of the aircraft.

That's when Captain White spotted a small pasture on the side of a hill called, Hunts Mountain near Danbury, Connecticut.

The decision was made.

Just before crash-landing, Captain White made one final announcement for the passengers to brace themselves.

The small pasture sloped upward which created another problem.

Just before impact, Captain White applied full power to all four engines, which brought the nose up, so they would not hit the ground in a nose-down position and bury it into the side of the hill.

Then he quickly chopped the power off. The aircraft skimmed the grass and settled down, the left wing struck a tree and was sheared off. The aircraft bounced off a gully and came to rest, in pieces.

The impact caused all four engines to break free and hurl forward. Then came that awful feeling you get when you know what's going to happen next. Fire!

Inside the cabin, both stewardesses began evacuating the passengers. Due to her injuries, Stewardess Kathy DePue had to ask the aid of several male passengers to help others as she staggered out of the aircraft.

Once free, she was helped away from the aircraft by one of the several soldiers who were on board. She would later learn that she had suffered five broken bones in her back.

Stewardess Patricia Skarada had leaped out of the broken fuselage but heard the moaning of a young mother still in the cabin.

Disregarding her own safety, Pat rushed back in, grabbed the baby, and led them both safely away. She then rushed back into the burning cabin and lead others to safety.

As to the cockpit crew, there were still lingering questions as to how they escaped. First Officer Holt was badly injured. He was not sure if he crawled or fell out of the captain's small cockpit window before he collapsed in a heap.

Second Officer Greenway was also badly injured with gashes across his head and ear. His escape was through the crew door located on the right side of the cockpit.

Neither could say for certain whether they got out on their own or were rescued by Captain White. Neither had a memory as to the final approach and what took place afterward.

Captain White remained with his aircraft.

A captain's first concern is for his passengers and his crew. It is believed he went back inside the cabin to ensure all passengers were evacuated. They were not.

One Soldier, Pvt. Dennis Flucker was trapped in his seat. Several of his fellow soldiers attempted to free him but could not. Driven back by heat and flames, they had to save themselves.

Those passengers, standing outside the aircraft, said they saw Captain White in the cabin trying to free the soldier, but the flames prevented them from actually seeing him release Pvt. Flucker.

Some believed he was successful and was leading the private toward the forward galley and safety when oxygen bottles blew up killing them instantly.

Three people died in that crash. It was a miracle that more hadn't due to the courage of Captain White and his crew.

One thing about the galley on the Connie. It was located directly behind the cockpit. There was also a galley door used for catering to the rest of the plane.

One of the responsibilities of the second officer was to install the galley door bar after take-off. The bar prevented anyone from accidentally opening the door in flight.

I'm not sure, but that bar may have impeded Captain White from leaving the aircraft. I recollect that the victims were found near the galley door.

There were two types of oxygen bottles on board the doomed plane. Portable, walk-around bottles, were used for passengers who may have had medical issues. The others were oxygen cylinders that were over three feet long.

One cylinder was designated to be used by the crew in case of an emergency decompression. Another was for passenger use under the same circumstances. Both cylinders were located in the forward galley. Each was approximately under 1850 psi of pressure. They were the ones that exploded.

According to the CAB accident report File: 1-0033, dated December 20, 1966, testimony taken from both TWA 42 and EA 853 flight crews, the probable cause of the accident was.

"The board determines the probable cause of the collision accident was a misjudgment of altitude separation by the crew of EA 853 because of optical illusion created by the up-slope effect of cloud tops in an evasive maneuver by the EA 853 and a reaction evasive maneuver by the TW 42 crew."

Fast forward to today's in-flight safety. All air carriers are required to have a Traffic Collision Avoidance System, called, TCAS. It is used to avoid mid-air collisions, something they did not have before this accident. I know for a fact, they work!

Two more points about EA 853. It was shortly after that incident that I happened to watch CBS News with Harry Reasoner. He was considered their top evening news reporter.

His eulogy for Captain White and his crew, and their heroic airmanship, was far and above any eulogy I had ever heard then, or since.

Not long after flight 853's accident, I was assigned to a ferry flight from LGA-BOS. The captain I was flying with decided to go VFR and fly over the accident site. Something that you are not supposed to do.

He did it as if paying homage to those who died in the crash, more or less, a fly-over.

As we approached the crash site, he descended to an altitude fifteen hundred feet above the terrain. For me to view the site, I had to rise out of my seat and looked down. The 1049G lay charred and broken.

Suddenly, a roar of aircraft engines penetrated the cockpit as a dark shadow passed directly above us.

It was another EAL Connie, a shuttle flight most likely on its way from BOS to LGA with probably the same thought.

Then it was then full power, climb, and get the hell out of there. We estimated we must have missed one another by less than 300 feet of separation. Neither one of us had seen the other and we nearly collided head-on.

Shortly after that episode, I was assigned to fly another aircraft. The Boeing 727.

FROM THE GOLDEN FALCON TO
THE WHISPERJET

Eastern, like other airlines, were retiring their piston-driven aircraft and replacing them with newer jet aircraft.

On January 24, 1960, Eastern began jet service with a 179-passenger Douglas DC-8. Its flight from New York to Miami earmarked the real beginning of jet travel to many Eastern cities. Its next jet aircraft was the Boeing 720. Then came the Boeing 727-100.

Eastern would become the first airline to put it into service on a Philadelphia, Washington D.C., Miami flight on February 1, 1964.

It would become the most popular short-haul tri-jet to ever come off the assembly line.

Eastern employees would get to know it as the Whisperjet. It was the best of the best, a real workhorse.

Eastern also ordered Boeings 727-QCs. The QC's, Quick-Change, aircraft could be converted from passenger service into a cargo-hauling aircraft in a very short time.

The left front side of the fuselage, the first-class section, had a cargo door, when opened, was wide enough to allow the removal of all passenger seats and replace them with cargo pallets specifically designed for the QC.

In February 1966 I was back in Miami to begin training on the B-727, both as a first officer and then as a second officer. It would be known as seat-swapping.

On one flight, you would be the first officer, on the next flight, a second officer. Most senior pilots hated it.

Those of us who were junior pilots relished the chance to have the opportunity to fly again as first officers.

Unfortunately, seat-swapping had caused several ugly incidents. One happened when a senior pilot refused to swap seats with a junior flight engineer.

It had led to a fistfight in the cockpit as passengers were boarding and it nearly led to their dismissal. Lucky for them they only received a reprimand. They could have been fired.

Several years would pass before seat-swapping was phased out under a new pilot contract. All the senior pilots were very happy. Junior pilots would have to wait their turn to become first officers.

As usual, training on any new aircraft begins with ground school. It became quite noticeable that there were major differences between flying a piston, or a turbo-jet aircraft vs an all-jet aircraft.

At altitude, jet aircraft go from indicated airspeed to Mach Airspeed, which is used concerning the speed of sound. We flew the B-727 at .84 Mach, its designed cruising speed.

Cable-operated flight controls gave way to electrically trimmed horizontal stabilizers, hydraulic-controlled flight controls, flight spoilers, and yaw dampers.

Hot hydraulic fluid was cooled by running their return lines through fuel tanks. Instead of how many gallons of fuel onboard, it was how many pounds of fuel were onboard.

One vast difference between a piston engine and a turbo-jet engine is acceleration. When you throttle up on prop or turbine engines, you have immediate power. Jet engines, if at flight idle, have an 8 to 10-second delay before they spool up, or, go from flight idle to high thrust. You always had to consider that, especially in a go-around situation.

Once more, it was back to hours of study, study, study, and those four to six-hour sessions in the simulator.

At that time Eastern had a great deal of flight training ongoing. Whenever that happened, the company would send some of its pilots to a different training site to complete the flying portion of the training.

The group I was being trained with was sent to Euless, Texas. Located a short distance southwest of Dallas-Fort Worth Airport.

Before boarding my flight to Dallas from Miami, arose more excitement.

I had been looking toward runway 9L/27R, watching airplanes doing their normal landings. Then Eastern's first B-727, aircraft number 101 had come into view.

It appeared to be lower on the runway than I expected. Then I realized it had just made a belly landing. As it slid to a stop, the over-the-wing exits popped open. People were climbing out and sliding down the backside of the wing flaps. The rear air-stairs were dropped, and more passengers were scrambling out.

Since the aircraft was now on its belly, the aft air-stairs hadn't fully deployed. As the passengers exited, their heads were banging off the bottom edge of the aft air-stairs door. Thankfully, those would be the only injuries suffered.

Emergency vehicles arrived and immediately positioned themselves around the aircraft. Their water cannons and foam spray equipment were aimed at the engines in case of a fire. None happened.

Meanwhile, the flight attendants had led their passengers a safe distance away. They were then taken to the terminal.

During the investigation of the accident, it was claimed, that a hydraulic valve failure prevented the landing gear from extending.

Instead of manually hand-cranking the landing gear down, the captain thought it better to land with the wheels up.

His concern was, if only one main or the nose wheel came down, and not the other main wheel, he might have lost lose control on the landing and veered off the runway creating more damage.

It was also determined that another company had installed the hydraulic valve improperly. It was also the first landing after the repairs.

It showed me how every part of a plane plays a vital role in preventing accidents.

TRAINING DELAYS

While I was at Euless, the first order of business was to be qualified as a first officer. Normally, the flight check can be completed in a matter of days. Instead, the training was delayed due to the aircraft being needed for training, maintenance, or for passenger service. Or, our instructor had to have his days off. So, it went.

All during that time, my nose was buried in the flight manual. Two weeks later I took my first officer flight check and I felt well prepared.

Instead of an FAA flight inspector, it was with an Eastern captain who was qualified as a flight examiner.

Even though they were Eastern employees, there was no nonsense when it came to having to know all about the aircraft you were going to fly. As usual, it started with my knowledge of the aircraft.

After the oral, it was out to the flight line and the required walk-around inspection of the aircraft. Him asking me questions about the B-727 from nose to tail.

As to the in-flight proficiency check?

Instrument approaches, aborted landings, holding patterns, engine failures, take-offs, and landings. Two hours later I am qualified as a first officer on the B-727. Next up, becoming a second officer on the B-727.

This too could have been completed in a matter of five or six days. Instead, the same problems began to arise as when becoming a first officer. More delays seemed to be the norm.

Woody Mead was another one of my new-hire classmates who was being trained to fly both seats. Although we were being trained separately, we would get together, either in his room or mine, and study.

He would ask me questions about the aircraft, and I would then drill him. By the time we were ready for our second officer proficiency check-rides, we knew the B-727 inside and out.

Woody was one of those individuals who seldom talked about themselves. During one of those Q and A sessions, he had asked me, "Did I ever tell you about the time I got hijacked?" My first thought was, yeah right. Then his story began to unfold.

Years before being hired by Eastern Air Lines, Woody was a flight instructor at the Tamiami Airport. That lies thirteen miles southwest of Miami. He told me he had been instructing there for several years, and shortly after the Bay of Pigs invasion of Cuba.

On April 17, 1961, the CIA launched what they thought would be a major strike. A full-scale invasion of Cuba by 1,400 American-trained Cubans who had fled their homes when Fidel Castro took over.

The group attacked the island and it lasted for only two days. Many were killed or captured, and a few escaped.

A year and a half after the invasion, one of his students had asked him if it would be okay to take a friend along on one of his training sessions. Then afterward, fly up and down the coast of Miami Beach sightseeing.

He said they had taken off in a four-seat Cessna 172 aircraft and after the session began flying up and down the coastline.

Forty-five minutes later, when they banked south, back toward Tamiami Airport, the man sitting in the back seat pulled out a gun and held it to the back of Woody's head. Then ordered him to fly them to Cuba.

When the plane was a long distance from Miami Beach, he was instructed to fly low, and just above the waves. The hijackers hoped to be able to go under any air traffic radar surveillance.

As soon as they were out of sight of land, the two hijackers decided to kill him and throw his body into the Atlantic Ocean.

As Woody told it, he said. "If you do that, my body will hit the horizontal stabilizer on the aircraft's tail, knock it off, and the aircraft will crash."

After a heated discussion between the two hijackers, they decided it was safer to let him live.

When they landed in Cuba, the hijackers thought they would be welcomed as heroes until the authorities threw them all in the same prison where the Bay of Pigs prisoners were being held.

He also told me. While in prison there were numerous occasions when the guards would come into one of the cells and remove a Bay of Pigs invader. Put them against a wall and shoot them.

He was held there for many weeks before the American Embassy found out that he was a prisoner. In the meantime, there had been many search-and-rescue missions after he was reported missing. Those had stopped, believing he had crashed into the ocean and was killed.

After the American Embassy secured his release, Cuba sent him and the two hijackers, along with another American prisoner, back to the United States. Both hijackers were tried and convicted of air piracy and sent to a United States prison.

When he finished his story, I still had doubts about it until he reached into his suitcase and took out newspaper clippings from the Miami Herald. They read exactly as he told me. How fortunate he was in such a dangerous situation. Then it was back to more studying.

I started training to become a second officer on the B-727 near the end of February, it was now the middle of April.

Finally, some good news had come my way when I learned I was scheduled to take my flight check. The downside, most of the flight checks were done in the middle of the night and would last about four hours.

With me, would be two others who would be getting their first officer's proficiency flight checks.

The aircraft would be 102. The sister ship of 101 that belly-landed in Miami. Then came another schedule change. Instead of doing the flight checks at night, they would be done that afternoon. Great news for me. I can get out of Euless and be on my way home before nightfall.

Hold everything! Aircraft 102 made a belly landing at Carswell Air Force Base in Fort Worth, Texas. Check-rides are canceled. It was another hydraulic failure and the crew wasn't able to fully extend the landing gear ala Miami. Another wheels-up landing.

I walked out of the flight operations office very disappointed. Coming toward me was one of Eastern's flight engineer examiners. He was not one of my favorite people.

As we passed one another, he reached over and grabbed my shoulder stopping me. I told him to get his hands off me, telling him I was not in a good mood because my check ride was just canceled. As I walked away, he called out I had better study more. As if I'm being forewarned.

One hour later I was called back to flight operations. My check ride had been rescheduled for 11 p.m. that night. The flight engineer examiner who was to give me the flight check was the same one that I had words with. My first thought. This won't go well at all.

Eleven o'clock came. It seemed luck was with me. The person I had words with was called back to Miami because of a family emergency. Boyce Brown, another Eastern flight engineer examiner had taken his place. The two who were to be upgraded to first officers would be with me. One is a new-hire classmate of mine.

Their check captain had been at Carswell Air Force Base inspecting the damage to Aircraft 102. He appeared to be dog-tired and in a foul mood. As we were about to start engines, their flight checks began to unravel.

Normally, the first officer reads the before-start checklist. It's a case of a challenge and response by the cockpit crew.

As the first pilot began to read the list the captain reached over and grabbed it out of his hand. Then began to read the checklist expecting the first officer to respond to what the captain should have been responding to. He told the captain that he did not remember the responses.

From that point, things began going downhill. The captain ordered the pilot out of his seat and told the other pilot to take his place. The other pilot told the captain that he too didn't remember the captain's responses.

What was supposed to be a first officer check ride, became a four-hour training session. Two hours per pilot. Except, we never left the traffic pattern. Each landing was to a full stop and just long enough for me to fill out the take-off/landing data card.

At first, the circuits were high and wide enough for me to be able to complete my portion of the flight check.

Then the circuits became even shorter. It was. Fill out the take-off data card, take-off, gear up, flaps up, make a circuit, fill out the landing data card, flaps out, gear down, land to a full stop, and repeat the same sequence over and over again. This went on for several hours as both pilots were put through the wringer.

When it finally ended, I was a qualified B-727 flight engineer. Both pilot flight checks were written off as a training flight. That wasn't the end of it.

By the time the fiasco was over, it was 5 a.m. and we had to take a limo from the Fort Worth Airport back to our hotel fifteen miles away.

I jumped into the front seat next to the driver and Boyce joined me. I think we both knew what was coming.

For the two other pilots, it was another thirty minutes of Qs and A's on the B-727. At the hotel, I packed immediately, longing to get away from the training and get back home.

Then came a knock on my door. When I opened it the two pilots were standing there. They had wanted me to initial a complaint letter they were about to write against the captain. I told them, "Good luck. He's the check captain." I wished them well and headed out the door to catch the next flight back home.

In fairness to those two pilots. I believe the captain should have never been assigned to do any flight checks that night. Anyone could see he was fatigued and irritated from being at the accident site all day.

Instead of him bowing out, and having another check captain take his place, he chose to do it anyway. I'm sure he thought he was doing the right thing to help the company.

Had things gone well, I'm certain both candidates would have completed their portion of the program and would have been qualified as first officers on the B-727.

Incidentally, both were given their proficiency checks by another Eastern flight examiner several days later. They passed and were highly praised for their flying ability.

SUPERSONIC VS SUBSONIC

I n April of 1966, Eastern had placed a deposit of $200,000 with the FAA for two United States-manufactured supersonic (SST) transports. My first thought was that I would eventually be flying a supersonic aircraft that would soon revolutionize the speed of travel across our nation and the oceans.

Controversy soon ensued. Supersonic booms, as in breaking the sound barrier over highly-populated areas. At the same time, talks were ongoing to expand the airline by getting new routes to the Pacific, mainly to Hawaii from the west coast. Over water, the SST issue would not be a problem. It still was over land.

Later that year in November, Eastern placed an additional order for two more SSTs. In June 1967, the airline ordered two more SSTs. Then the wait began as to who would get those routes. It was not going to be Eastern.

The plans for those aircraft fell apart for a couple of reasons. The Pacific routes went to American Airlines and if Eastern did acquire the SST, they could only be flown at subsonic speeds when over the United States. That meant they would be no different than any other jet aircraft.

The corporation realized it would be more cost-wise to purchase traditional jet aircraft instead. Eventually, the project and the Eastern contract for the SST were canceled and the monies returned. So I never did get to fly one of those supersonic jets.

After my initial flight training was complete, I still had to do the mandatory twenty-five hours of cockpit jump seat time observing crews flying the jet.

On one of those flights, I had a layover in Dallas, Texas. It allowed me to visit the Texas Depository and perceive where the shots from a rifle were fired that killed President John F. Kennedy.

My first impression was that the distance from the depository to where JFK was shot wasn't that far. Especially for a so-called marksman such as Lee Harvey Oswald.

Of course, the controversy of whether there was more than one shooter will continue to go on.

A BARGAIN SALE

O n June 1, 1966, I flew with Captain Len Finley for the first time as his first officer. He, like ninety-eight percent of the captains I would fly with, were very good pilots, gentlemen, and helpful to pilots like me who had never flown jet aircraft.

Len stood a little over six feet tall, rather lean, wore a crew-cut hairstyle, and always appeared to be physically fit. I would fly with him numerous times over the next decade. I would also find out, he, like most captains, had their quirks, and Captain Finley had his.

After he entered the cockpit, out would come a spray can of Lysol. Then decontamination of the cockpit began. The oxygen mask, headset, microphone, throttles, control column, and anything he thought he was going to touch, got sprayed.

I once quipped. "Len. You know, I think a brain surgeon could perform a major operation in this cockpit and not have to worry about any germs that might be in it now that it's sterile." After I said that, I thought he would be annoyed with me. Instead, he just laughed and handed me the can of Lysol. He also had a heart of gold.

One of the sequences we flew would take us from Baltimore to Montego Bay, Kingston, Jamaica, Port-Au-Prince, Haiti, and San Juan, Puerto Rico. Where we would lay over. Then do the reverse the following day.

Each time we landed on the southbound leg into Port-Au-Prince, he would bring with him a pair of slightly-worn tennis shoes.

We would begin the 150-yard trek from where our aircraft was parked, cut across a grassy field that led to a chain-link fence and the boundary line for the airport.

Several native vendors had set up a miniature flea market on the other side. Where they sold handmade baskets made of woven palm or banana leaves, river stone carvings, hand-painted wooden bowls and spoons, and hand-carved wooden figurines. In return, they would accept articles of clothing for their crafts.

Len would give this one boy, who looked about fifteen and a little ragged around the edges, the sneakers. He had thought the shoes would help the family that he believed lived in poverty. Which they probably did. He would not accept any trinkets offered in return.

We flew that sequence for several months, and it was the same routine each time. When the station manager found out what Len had been doing told him.

The kid wasn't bringing them back to his family. Instead, he was selling the tennis shoes on the black market for an incredible amount of money. There were no more trips to the fence after that.

While with VP-11, I had the opportunity to go on a fam-flight, familiarization flight, to Port-of-Prince and had spent the night there. That was in 1956.

As I walked through the city, it opened my eyes to how poor a nation it was and the squalor its people had to contend with. That was ten years past, and nothing seemed to change.

AN ODD SIGHT BEGINS TO HAPPEN

J et flying was bringing me to more and more cities that Eastern served. It was during those many years that I began to notice an odd sight. No matter the city. Whether it was Atlanta, Boston, Chicago, Dallas, Denver, Los Angeles, JFK, or dozens of other cities, this strange sight was growing rapidly.

I would see them as we taxied down the ramps that led to our gates when arriving or departing. They were either on the baggage carts waiting to be put in or being taken out of an aircraft's cargo compartment. Every airline must have carried them.

What had started as a handful became hundreds, then thousands until finally, after nine years, it stopped. What were they?

Military caskets. The dead were brought back from the Vietnam War.

Their bodies were being sent home to the thousands of towns and cities throughout America from which they had come. An honor guard was stationed by the baggage carts protecting them.

Officially, United States advisers had been sent to Vietnam years before the Gulf of Tonkin Incident that happened on August 2, 1964.

That was when it was alleged that Communist gunboats fired upon United States Naval Vessels. President Lyndon B. Johnson, with the authority given to him by Congress, decided to escalate the Vietnam conflict. If that sounds familiar, think Korean Conflict.

Officially, the conflict began on March 8, 1965, when 3,580 United States Marines landed at Da Nang, South Vietnam. It would officially end on January 27, 1974, under a peace accord that was signed in Paris.

It was also the same day that I celebrated my tenth year with Eastern Air Lines.

There were approximately 58,200 causalities, of which 40,934 were killed in action.

For those of us who flew during those tumultuous years, each time we saw those caskets, it was a steady reminder of the men and women who were losing their lives in the hope of giving freedom to not only that country but others as well. They were indirectly preserving our freedom.

Eastern, along with other airlines, had served our country by flying for our government under what was called the Military Air Command.

Eastern DC-8's flight crews flew into South Vietnam bringing in or taking out American ground forces. The crews who flew those MAC flights saw first-hand what the war was doing to our young men and women who had to spend months and even years there. It was a lot more than what we were seeing or reading through the media.

I had talked to several flight attendants who flew some of those missions. They said that seeing or talking to those soldiers who fought there was heartbreaking.

On the other hand, for those who were done with their deployments and were boarding flights, there were a lot of boisterous cheers, huge grins, and tears knowing they were on their way back to the States and not having to go back to Vietnam.

NOT ANOTHER AIRLINE STRIKE?

The first thirty-seven days of my jet-flying went quickly. Then it all came to a screeching halt. Eastern aircraft mechanics and ground workers represented by the International Association of Machinists (IAM) went on strike on July 8, 1966.

Over 35,000 airline workers employed by five airlines, United, Northwest, National, Trans World, and Eastern, that belonged to the IAM walked off their jobs after their union failed to reach what would be the industry's first multi-carrier contract. This was after a Presidential Emergency Board, (PEB) offered a compromise package.

It would become the largest strike in airline history and would last 43 days. Some 60 percent of the U.S. airline industry was inoperative, a stunning blow to those airlines that depended largely on their summer travel season. It would not be the last of the IAM strikes to hurt Eastern Air Lines.

At the time, many of us pilots thought the strike would not last more than a week, given the idea that we were all family. How wrong can you be?

It was also the time the roller-coaster ride began. As in, is the strike over? No, it's not. Yes, it is. No, it's not.

Unfounded rumors, erroneous news-media reports, and bargaining sessions that never took place were daily occurrence.

The New York Pilots Union Council 51 which was part of the Air Line Pilots Association, (ALPA) union, kept us informed as best they could.

After the first two weeks of no income, thoughts of the Lewis-Matthis Strike had come to mind. It was a company I had once worked for to help pay for flying lessons while attending Parks Air College in East St. Louis,

Illinois.

One I won't forget. Especially when I had to go to the unemployment office to look for another job, and to receive unemployment benefits. Been there, done that. Not fun.

On August 19, 1966, the strike came to an end.

Taking a lyric from Gene Autry's famous song, "Back in the Saddle Again", I'll give you my lyric as it pertains to flying.

"I'm back in the air again. Flying the shuttle, once more, where I can look out at night and see the stars shining bright. I'm back in the air once again." I'm a better pilot than a poet.

Ah, seniority. I was slowly climbing up the ladder. New routes that were awarded to Eastern allowed me to fly to cities that I had never been to.

When I enlisted in the Navy, their motto was. "Join the Navy and see the World." That's great if you don't mind sailing on the ocean and not seeing land for months at a time. Okay, so I never had shipboard duty while serving. Though I did get to see many parts of the world while I was with VP-11.

For those of you who have thoughts of really wanting to see the world, become an aircrew member for an airline, any airline.

Whether it would be as a pilot or flight attendant flying domestically or internationally. You will see more of the world than you can imagine. Not only that, the airline will be paying you for doing it.

Plus providing hotel rooms and meal allowances. What might cost vacationers thousands of dollars, you get to do it free. But there is a catch.

BEING AN AIRLINE PILOT ISN'T ALL THAT GLAMOROUS

Tere is a downside. Flying sometimes times isn't all as glamorous as people make it out to be. Ask any crew member.

You may think the flight crew is done after you disembark from your flight, but in reality, they are probably preparing to fly to other cities. That means more take-offs and landings and venturing into Mother Nature's habit of getting uppity when you least expect it.

Some flight crews may fly for only one hour on selected domestic flights. Which equates to doing one take-off and one landing and having the rest of the day off. Other crews may have as many as four or five take-offs and landings in one day. Which can be very fatiguing.

International flights require many flight hours in the air but may do only one take-off and one landing. Then have the remainder of the day off.

What is most common are eight to twelve hours a day, and having to deal with Mother Nature in between.

Add mechanical problems, weather delays, and those, unwanted hours of circling in a holding pattern. Only to have to divert to an alternate airport when the weather at your original destination goes below landing minimums.

There are several reasons for having to divert a flight. Weather at your destination, remaining fuel on board, or a passenger's medical condition.

Then it's land, refuel, wait for the weather to improve, and then proceed to your original destination. All of this adds to a flight crew's on-duty limitation. This brings me to flight crew layovers.

Even though the FAR requires at least 8 hours of rest, in 24 hours, pilot and flight attendant contracts, can be somewhat different, depending on the airline. Still, the FARs require 8 hours of rest. Sounds okay.

Not so. Say you're the pilot and just landed in Atlanta, parked the aircraft and shut down the engines, and called in your block time. That is when your eight-hour layover begins.

First, you have to go from plane to train which brings you to the main terminal. That's fifteen minutes. Then wait for the hotel shuttle van for another twenty to thirty minutes. Check-in at the hotel is another ten minutes. Unpack, shower, change clothes, find a restaurant, and eat. Another hour passes.

Then it's back to the hotel to watch TV and wind down from a hard day of flying. Then set your alarm for that early morning departure and close your eyes. You're now down to a six-hour layover.

Wait! Your flight is scheduled to leave at 6 a.m. Your company requires you to be there one hour before departure for flight planning. Which means 5 a.m.

You had your alarm set for 4 a.m. to grab breakfast, if, their restaurant is open, which most aren't. Then catch the shuttle van, if it's not already at the airport, and wait for it to return. Followed by another ten to fifteen minutes trip to the airport. Usually at top speed.

Grab the train to plane transportation to be able to file your flight plan one hour before your departure.

A flight crew with that kind of schedule may only have five hours of rest and it happens more frequently than can be imagined. That's the reality of being an airline crew member.

When a crew member feels that they may not have ample rest, there is a word that pilots and stewardesses mention, but only to one another. That would prevent them from flying.

Although I never knew of any crew member invoking it. That word is Fatigue.

In all my thirty-three years flying for the airlines, there were times when

I was truly fatigued. One was one of those memorable flights as a captain when I should have but didn't. Another one was as a captain when I did.

With well over three decades of flying for the airlines, I've stayed at hundreds of different hotels and motels. From the top of the line to some of the dregs. No matter what city Eastern flew to, I most likely had a layover there.

Nonetheless, there is one hotel I will always remember that was used for short Chicago layovers. It was called the Colonial Inn. Our flight crews called it. "Ed's Beds."

The owners and their employees treated us, crew members, wonderfully. Although I believe the real reason Eastern used this hotel was they gave the airline an exceptional overnight rate. Unfortunately, it had some drawbacks. Starting with, it was a long way from Chicago's O' Hare Airport.

At the time, flight crews were required to be X number of minutes from the airport on short layovers. Ed's Bed's, main limo driver, Billy, was able to keep us within the allotted number of minutes required by driving at speeds that sometimes exceeded 80 miles an hour.

It was always a thrill a minute going to and from the airport with his pedal-to-the-metal driving. Although I don't remember any crew member complaining.

For that matter, it seemed no matter what hotel we would stay at, the limo driver always seemed to have a heavy foot on the gas pedal. I always believed they were trying to make as many round trips to and from the airport as possible for the tips that they would receive.

The other drawback was the age of the hotel. It was old. Although the rooms were kept clean, they were small. Mattresses that should have been replaced eons ago, were lumpy, and the springs on the bed sang a squeaky tune each time you moved.

Light bulbs were of the 40-watt variety and the walls were paper-thin. Nothing like hearing what was going on in the next room, whether it was the television program or, a bed banging against the wall, and hearing those moans and groans that went with it.

Most of our layovers at Ed's Beds led to early morning wake-up calls, such as at 4 a.m. Once dressed, you would head down to their kitchen where they offered a free continental breakfast. You know coffee, Danish, juice, cereal.

One morning, while sipping coffee and munching on a Danish, out of the corner of my eye I had caught a glimpse of a furry animal scurrying across the kitchen floor and disappearing into the next room.

"Billy," I said. "I didn't know you had cats here."

"We don't." He answered.

The next thing I saw was him chasing this rat around the room with a broom and banging at it until one final blow put the rat into its next world. Then he picked it up by the tail and deposited it into a trash can. This performance was followed by the 80-mile-an-hour ride back to the airport.

Eventually, Ed's Beds were out and the hotels near the airport were in. Long layovers were in downtown Chicago.

Unfortunately, some years later, I heard that Billy died in an auto accident during a heavy rainstorm. So did a couple of aircrew members from another airline who were with him. I'm not sure if the accident was caused by his pedal-to-the-metal attitude or something else. He was one hell of a driver.

DEALING WITH MOTHER NATURE

All through the years, I never got tired of seeing beautiful sunrises and sunsets. Looking down at mother earth, America, or flying over the Atlantic Ocean, The Gulf of Mexico, or The Caribbean Sea.

At night, full moons, solar and lunar eclipses, and billions of stars were punctuated by the brilliance of shooting stars and meteor showers.

Then there were those days and nights when Mother Nature decided to turn against you.

The kind of weather when even the birds stopped flying.

The kind when your approach to landings required your full attention, eyes glued to your instrument panel.

The kind when your heart rate went up a notch when the ceiling was less than a hundred feet and the Runway Visual Range (RVR) was no more than 700 feet.

The kind when you break out of the clouds and saw those beautiful green threshold lights come into view, then the row of white centerline lights, dimly visible, leading the way as you touched down. The heart rate goes down a notch because you made it.

Speaking of landing in heavy fog and near-zero visibility. There was an incident while landing at the Atlanta Hartsfield Airport when they were in the process of upgrading their runways and terminal during the 1970s.

We had just landed on runway 9R and were turning onto a taxiway when from out of the fog came a semi-tractor trailer toward us. The captain immediately jammed on the brakes and applied full reverse on the engines.

The tractor-trailer driver made a sharp right turn and nearly flipped it on its side. A call to ground control brought out a follow-me truck which led the lost driver back to a service road. Thankfully, a head-on collision was averted.

There were the fun times when you had to land in heavy and gusty crosswinds on snow and ice-covered runways that were trying to push your aircraft sideways off the runway.

Counteracting them by co-coordinating the use of rudder and ailerons with hands and feet, and at the same time, jockeying throttles at Mother Nature's bad attitude. It is something you learn when you first start flying.

Wet and icy runways. Landing on runways under those conditions is usually smooth because of the slickness of the surface. It also meant there was always the possibility of hydroplaning when the tires go from zero spin to 140 miles per hour in seconds.

What about hurricanes? With our weather radar, you could see the circle of its eye as we flew over high above it. The damage the tornadoes left behind and the heavy rain that comes with them.

Swollen rivers overflowed their banks, flooded farmland, towns inundated, and washed-out bridges, and shorelines devastated by ocean surges.

Downed trees and power lines, miles, and miles of raped landscape, destroyed homes, un-imaginable destruction. Viewed safely from being miles high in the sky.

Thunderstorms:

At night it was like watching a fireworks display all around you. As much as you try to avoid them, there were times when you had no choice but to come close to the cloud-to-ground and cloud-to-cloud lightning and experience the heavy rain and turbulence that comes with them.

If you were flying under instrument conditions, St Elmo's Fire would be dancing across your windshield or off the nose of your aircraft like a white probe that I called, King Arthur's Lance.

Push the throttles forward, the probe would increase, reduce power and it would retract. Several times during my career, the aircraft I was flying was struck by lightning. Afterward, it had to be taken out of service and demagnetized.

One phenomenon that caught my attention when I first started flying the 727, was called the Pilots Halo. We were descending through some cloud layers and had broken out and were just about to enter another.

The sun's rays were coming from the left side of the 727's nose. I happened to look out my right-side window and there it was. The Pilot's Halo.

I could see the silhouette of our aircraft on the cloud deck and the halo was following us. It was a huge multi-colored circle that surrounded the nose of the 727. Inside the circle was a cross, much like that of a gun-sight.

It stayed there until we re-entered another layer of clouds. The halo, so I'm told, is caused by moisture particles in the air, along with the sun's rays hitting the angle of the aircraft just right. It's an amazing sight, but then again, most of what I saw in the air was amazing.

FLYING WITH HERO'S

As a kid growing up, my longing to fly came from a lot of those World War Two movies I had snuck into. In those films, the hero always seemed to be 6' 4" with thick black wavy hair, straight teeth, a crooked smile, rugged looks, and no fear of danger.

Of course, in the real world, most of those pilots who flew those combat missions were just average Joe's doing their job. Fortunately, I had the privilege of flying with many of them. Most of all, I would learn never, never, never, judge a book by its cover.

This brings me to August 27, 1966, when I first flew with Captain Fred Wesche III, several days after the end of the IAM strike.

My first impression was that he was not a Hollywood-looking type of pilot. He was shorter than most of the pilots I had flown with. A little stocky, thinning grey hair, wore glasses, went by the book, as it should be. I would find over the years he was a pleasure to fly with.

The first thing I learned about Fred, during that sequence of flights, was his love for music. He played the trumpet, French Horn, and some piano and wrote musical arrangements for his band that he called, "Fred Wesche's Big Band: The Million Dollar Sound." It was well known in southern New Jersey.

In the world of airline flying, throughout one's career, you would fly with the same cockpit group for an entire month. The three-man crew, such as on a B-727, consisted of a captain, first officer, and second officer. The two-man crew, as on a DC-9, would be a captain and a first officer. Depending on your seniority, you might not fly with any crew for months, possibly years.

Whenever I did have the opportunity to fly with Captain Wesche it was the usual chitchat about music, ALPA, contract negotiations, or subjects that would pop into our conversation

During our conversations, he never spoke about his flying B-17s during WWII. That is, not until many months later when I flew with him again.

As I entered our Newark flight operations room, I had glanced at our pilot bulletin board. Posted on the board was an article that had been cut out of a local newspaper entitled, "The Rabaul Raider." I then spotted a photograph of Fred next to it. I read the article. "Holy cow!"

When I found out Fred had posted the article, I couldn't wait to talk to him about it, if he was willing. I was surprised he never mentioned it before.

Our route for the day would take us from Newark to Detroit via Greensboro, and Charlotte before laying over in Detroit.

The following day we would do the reverse. By the time we returned to Newark, we would log over fourteen hours of flight time.

That doesn't sound like much, but it is when you are dealing with nasty weather.

After leaving Newark we climbed to our cruising altitude of 31,000 feet and leveled off. Fred engaged the auto-pilot and rang for one of the stewardesses to bring us coffee before serving their passengers.

As we settled into the routine of monitoring the flight, I had asked him about the article. Before he got to it, he gave me some of his background.

He went to Rutgers University and graduated in 1939. He joined the Army Air Force in August of 1940, received his wings in April 1941, then trained to fly the famous B-17 Flying Fortress.

When World War II started, he flew anti-submarine patrols out of the Boston area. Then was transferred to the west coast, and later to Hawaii.

From Hawaii, he was sent to Midway Island in May of 1942, arriving shortly after the Battle for Midway Island.

He told me an amusing story that happened to him and his crew while there. Maybe not at the time, but now, some twenty-five years later, as he reminisced.

He said the flight crews were always on alert in case of an enemy attack. On this one day, he and his crew were relaxing near their aircraft. Because of the extremely hot tropical conditions, he was only in his shorts and shoes resting underneath the wing of his B-17, while half of his crew were swimming naked in a lagoon close by.

Everything was fine, he said, until the air raid warning horn sounded, which was much like the blare of a Greyhound bus horn.

When that happened, he said a white ball would run up a flagpole next to the control tower. That indicated a possible enemy attack approaching some 200 miles away.

When a second ball was posted, it meant a definite attack with the enemy about 50 miles away. A red ball meant an attack was imminent. This time, no white balls, only one red one appeared.

Fred said that he and his crew jumped into the B-17, took off, flew to their assigned area, and circled, waiting for the enemy. Wearing only his shorts and shoes as were his other crew members.

The guys who had been in the lagoon were flying naked, wearing only shoes. To top, that off, all the hullabaloo turned out to be a false alarm.

According to him and from what I had gathered from reading the article, his bomb group was eventually sent to Port Moresby, New Guinea.

While there, his group made raids on Japanese warships that lay in the harbor of Rabaul. His bombs sank a Japanese troop transport ship. Thereby earning him being called, The Rabaul Raider, by the newspapers.

He told me that there were other raids carried out in the Pacific by his group, and more ships were sunk.

On one of his raids, flack had crippled his aircraft and some of his crew were wounded. They were lucky to get the aircraft safely back on the ground. During his time there, there were more raids and more ships sunk.

According to the newspaper article Fred received the Air Medal for his gallant actions. That was something he didn't mention during our conversation. Instead, our chat then turned to his music. He put his war record aside.

I would fly many times with him after that. Not once did we ever speak about the newspaper article or his experiences during the war again. Music, yes. That was the kind of man he was.

After flying with him, I got to thinking about my time in the Navy and the enlisted men and Navy pilots I had worked with. It never entered my mind that most of them must have fought in battles during the war. Especially those who were on aircraft carriers.

I surmised that it was probably because of my youth, being an enlisted guy, and not in the same circles as officers. Now, as an airline pilot, flying with guys like Fred and Karl, and others, I could relate to them. They were, and always will be, in my opinion, the real heroes, I always felt privileged flying with them.

IT'S BACK TO MIAMI FOR A PHYSICAL AND SIM TRAINING AND MURDER

As a first officer, you would have to take a yearly physical and a proficiency flight check on the aircraft you were flying. This would take place most of the time in Miami. It included reviewing aircraft systems, ditching, hijacking procedures, and written tests.

Followed by four hours of flying the simulator and reviewing emergency procedures such as. Engine fires, hydraulic failures, high-altitude decompressions, emergency descends, and so on.

The motel we stayed at was located on N. W. 36th Street. It was convenient because it was across the street from our training site and the Eastern employee's cafeteria. A block away was the main headquarters for Eastern Air Lines, which we pilots referred to as the Taj Mahal, and, depending on whom you talked to. The Ivory Tower.

Not far from the hotel, and within walking distance, was the quaint town of Miami Springs. The town was founded in the 1920s by world-famous Naval Aviator, Glenn Hammond Curtis and James Bright.

The main street was called the Curtiss Parkway. It was also the main road from Miami Springs which crossed over the Miami River into Hialeah by way of the Curtiss Parkway Bridge and the Hook Square Bridge. Each was one-way and was also used for pedestrian traffic.

For whatever reason, several incidents had occurred when I went to Miami for flight training. Two took place in the Springs. None of them were good.

While out jogging one day, I crossed over the Hook Square Bridge into Hialeah and had looked down at the river. Alongside it were emergency vehicles, and where dozens of people had gathered.

In the water, lying face down, tangled in the weeds, was the body of a young boy who appeared to be around eight or nine years old.

Puzzled why everyone was standing there, I ran down to the bank and asked one police officer why they didn't get him out and perform CPR. He responded saying that every indication showed the boy had been in the water a long time and there was nothing they could do for him.

He also said they had to treat it as a crime scene, their standard policy. Even though they believed it was an accident. On the bank was an over-turned grocery cart that had aluminum soda and beer cans in it. More cans had spilled out and were scattered on the bank and in the water.

They surmised that the boy was picking up the aluminum cans to turn them in for money, lost control of the grocery cart and it over-turned dumping some of the cans into the water.

When he reached over the bank to retrieve them, he presumable had lost his balance and fell in head-first. Got tangled in the weeds, and drowned.

My only thought at the time was. I hoped his parents didn't come by and see their son still face-down in the water. It was hard enough for me to see him like that.

Another time while in Miami for my yearly proficiency check, came another incident in the Springs.

I was the only customer in a men's clothing store and had picked out a shirt and taken it to the clerk to pay for it. As I did, two men walked into the store and went over to the clerk. One said, "You're under arrest." Both men then showed their police badges.

"Can I take care of my customer first?" The clerk had asked. He meant me. The officer in charge told him it was okay. I paid for my shirt and walked out the door, with the three of them right behind me. The clerk locked the store door, got into the backseat of the unmarked police car, and off they went.

The following day I read the local newspaper about the arrest. It seems the clerk murdered his girlfriend, stuffed her into a fifty-five-gallon drum, filled it with cement, and threw it in the Miami River. Where it was eventually found. I could not get over his being arrested before my eyes.

EASTERN BUYS MACKEY AIRLINES AND SENIORITY BECOMES AN ISSUE

January 8, 1967. Another airline merger. Eastern absorbed Mackey Airlines, and more importantly, their Caribbean routes and their pilots. Merging their pilots into our seniority system became an issue.

When a merger takes place, depending on what is agreed upon, pilots of the acquired airline are usually structured into the takeover airlines pilot seniority list.

Their seniority was based on their date of hire with Mackey Airlines. It also depended on whether the pilot was a captain or a first officer.

Mackey had very few pilots compared to the 2,700 pilots Eastern employed at that time, but even the loss of one seniority number caused grumbling from us Eastern pilots.

One number may seem a trifle, but it isn't, and as I had explained before. Seniority isn't everything. It is the only thing!

While the tussle over seniority rights was ongoing, there was other good news. On June 13, 1967, the Civil Aeronautics Board (CAB) awarded Eastern new routes to the cities of Seattle, Washington, and Portland, Oregon, via, Orlando, Melbourne, and St. Louis.

These additions meant more aircraft, more pilots, stewards and stewardesses, agents, baggage handlers, reservation people, and mechanics needed to be employed. It also meant new cities and new adventures for me.

During that year, another well-known aviation personality, Scott Cross-field was brought on board. He was of X-15 fame. Noted for surviving a catastrophic explosion while ground-testing an LXR-99 jet engine.

As an executive for Eastern, he helped in developing technological applications, new aircraft specifications, and flight research programs.

He left Eastern in 1973, but continued his career, working for other companies. Many years later at the age of 84, while flying alone in a Cessna 210A from Prattville, Alabama to Manassas, Virginia, he encountered severe thunderstorms over mountains in northern Georgia.

According to the official reports, the aircraft broke up in flight due to the severity of the thunderstorms. Unfortunately, he lost his life.

His years of knowledge and dedication to aviation made flying a lot safer for us, pilots.

BARBARA, KIRK DOUGLAS, AND WORRY

Eastern Air Lines had its perks. It was called pass-riding, and it was available to all of its employees.

If seats were available on any Eastern flight, you and your family could fly free. It was something my family and I did quite often.

On several occasions, I would bring my wife Barbara along. One of those times was when I had an eighteen-hour layover in New Orleans.

At that time, Eastern crews stayed at the Royal Sonesta Hotel. The hotel was on Bourbon Street and in the heart of downtown New Orleans.

The layover had given us enough time to tour the city and enjoy the atmosphere of the French Quarter and its restaurants. Where we enjoyed Creole dishes of succulent oysters and shrimp. We then made our way to enjoy Dixie Land Jazz at Preservation Hall.

For those who have never been to New Orleans, which was Barb's first time, there was another treat called Cafe' DuMonde.

They were noted for their beignets, and their famous coffee, which was a blend of milk and chicory. According to their folklore, if it was one's first time, there, you were supposed to make a wish and it would come true.

Even after that enjoyable layover with Barbara, it was the flight back to JFK that still stands out in my mind.

The following morning our flight EA66, which I had flown numerous times, lifted off from MSY for the two-hour forty-five-minute flight to JFK.

While en route our senior stewardess came into the cockpit and informed the captain that we had a major movie star sitting in first class, Kirk Douglas. He was known to be quite a ladies' man, at least in the movies. Which was where my wife was sitting, but in a different row.

The captain, who was a great fan of Douglas, said he was determined to get his autograph once we landed at JFK. During the flight, he must have related to me every film the star ever made. That didn't make me feel any better about having them both in first class.

My wife is a wonderful, very attractive woman and could pass for being a movie star herself. The more the captain talked about Douglas the more it seemed to make our flight a lot longer. JFK couldn't get here soon enough.

After we parked the aircraft, the procedure was to hook up to a ground power supply. That meant keeping the number one engine, the left engine running. While we waited for the hook-up, the passengers were deplaning.

The captain, in his haste to get his autograph, left his seat but was too late. Douglas had already left the aircraft. Somewhat dejected, he grabbed his suitcase and flight bag and hurried out of the cockpit. The flight engineer and I followed.

As we were about to leave the aircraft, the maintenance team arrived to see if there were any items in the logbook to be repaired. One of them had asked the captain what was wrong with the number one engine. His answer. "Nothing is wrong with it. Why?"

His reply. "Because it is still running."

In our haste, we forgot to shut the engine down. So much for the securing checklist. Thank goodness the parking brake was set, and the wheels chocked. Had they not been, who knows what might have happened? That never happened again.

Read the secure checklist first, then leave the cockpit even if you want a movie star's autograph.

I asked Barbara if she had the opportunity to talk to the movie star. Her answer was, "What movie star?"

"Kirk Douglas. He was sitting in first class." She said she didn't know he was there. The senior stewardess then told us he spent most of his time reading what she thought was a script and had kept to himself during the flight.

All through those years of airline flying, many well-known celebrities had been on my flight, but none had the strong charisma of Kirk Douglas.

WRONG RUNWAY-WRONG AIRPORT

August 4, 1967. The Captain was Art Senderoff whom I had flown with before. It was also the second day of a three-day sequence. The previous day I had been the first officer, and since we were still seat-swapping, I was now the second officer.

In the right seat was one of our new first officers who had been with the airline for only a short period.

At the time we had been on our way from Chicago to JFK, with stops in Indianapolis, Louisville, Atlanta, and Jacksonville, before arriving at JFK.

It was early morning, and the sun was just rising on a very hazy day. Due to the haze level, and having to stare directly into the sun, our forward visibility was less than a half-mile as we made our easterly approach to Indianapolis.

Art was flying the aircraft on instruments because of the poor visibility. He told the new first officer to let him know when he sees the runway we were to land on.

A few minutes later the first officer called out that he saw the runway and pointed down to it. At the same time, I was having pressurization problems and was focusing my attention on controlling it, so I was not looking out the window.

Art had transferred his attention from flying on instruments to a visual approach. Not to overshoot the runway. He dropped the landing gear and went to full flaps to get the aircraft into a landing configuration.

Then realized the first officer had mistaken an airport that was in line with our approach path to Indianapolis. Which was still five miles away.

113

Art immediately went from landing mode into go-around mode.

When he did that, I glanced out the window and looked at the runway we almost landed on. It had a big white X on it, indicating it was closed and the wrong airport.

Art climbed back up to our normal approach path altitude. made the necessary adjustments, and we landed without incident. His only comment on this short fiasco. "So much for noise abatement."

Because of the distance and the visibility, the control tower personnel weren't aware of what happened and we were not about to tell them. Once we were on the ground and parked, Art told me to leave the cockpit. He wanted to talk to the first officer, alone.

Our flight sequence for the rest of the day was uneventful.

Art, like many of the older captains I flew with, was a veteran who was engaged in combat missions during WWII. Some would relate their combat experiences to me. When they did, you tuned in and kept your mouth shut, and listened.

Art once told me he was a concert violinist who would occasionally play with the Hugo Winterhalter Orchestra. Then he made another comment about an experience he had during the war.

I knew Art was a Navy pilot who flew combat missions off an aircraft carrier in the Pacific. According to him, I'm going by what he told me. While on leave, he had gone to a movie theatre.

As usual, between the double feature, a war newsreel was being shown. As he sat watching, the reel showed a plane landing on an aircraft carrier. Suddenly, it veered to the right. The right wing came in contact with the superstructure. The plane spun around and began to disintegrate, leaving only the cockpit intact. The pilot was unhurt.

I'm sure anyone who has seen a war movie, or film clips of aircraft landing on aircraft carriers, has seen that film clip. The pilot? Art Senderoff.

He told me his aircraft had taken enemy fire, one bullet grazing the right earpiece of his helmet. Upon landing, his aircraft drifted to the right on touchdown. The right brake locked, which pulled him further to the right and into the superstructure. He said he was not hurt in the crash. Just shaken.

I realized it was an incredible stroke of luck to fly with someone I admired. In my career, I was fortunate to know and work with such brave people.

THE LOVELY JULIE

A week later, on August 12, it was a dark and stormy night as we made our approach to the Pittsburgh International Airport. The captain was Skeets Grubb, because we were seat-swapping, I was the second officer.

With the use of our weather radar, we were able to dodge several large active thunderstorms that were in the area. Just as we began our ten-mile ILS approach to runway 28R we had taken a lightning strike to our number one engine.

The force from it knocked out our number one generator. That supplied electrical power to some of our flight instruments. I immediately switched to our backup system to recover them. Followed by a normal landing.

Upon inspection of the engine, we found a scorched ten-inch round hole in the cowling where the bolt had struck. A badly damaged generator and melted wiring. We were very lucky.

Summer drifted into autumn and autumn into winter. Along the way, I would get to fly with another World War Two pilot.

November 20, 1967. The captain was Phil Stahlman, and it was the first time I flew with him. The next time would be eight years later on August 26, 1975.

As I had mentioned before, even though Eastern had over 4,600 pilots, they were spread throughout the seven crew bases. You might fly with one group of pilots for months at a time. Then not fly with them for many years, or, ever again.

Our schedule on that November day was one sequence southwest

116

bound that took us EWR-ATL with several stops in between. It was an enjoyable day of flight with a down-to-earth captain who flew the B-727 so competently and with such ease that many passengers would not deplane without wanting to shake his hand.

For those two days, it was just small talk as we focused our attention on our in-flight duties. Nothing of note, and no mention of past flying experiences. Just an enjoyable two days of flying.

It was what I would find out about him years later from other Eastern pilots that I found noteworthy. Their information came from those who flew combat missions during WWII and knew him.

I mentioned that other captains would tell me about some of their experiences during World W II. As much as they were in harm's way, none of their combat missions compared with the crew of a B-17 named The Lovely Julie.

October 15, 1944. For the 398th Bomb Groups 601, 602, and 603 squadrons of the 8th Air Force, this was mission number 98. Their target was Cologne, Germany.

The group of B-17s left North Hampstead in the early a.m. Tragedy struck immediately as one of the group crashed on take-off killing all aboard. Still, the group headed toward Cologne.

Aboard the Lovely Julie was Command Pilot 1st Lt. Larry Delancey, and the co-pilot was 1st Lt. Philip H. Stahlman. It was Stahlman's twenty-fifth and final mission before being rotated back to the United States.

Most combat pilots flew 25 missions before being rotated. Many volunteered to fly additional missions, even though they were not required to do so.

Lovely Julie was flying at 27,000 feet in a tight formation with hundreds of other B-17s. As they approached their target, the flak that they encountered was exceptionally heavy.

Once over their target, it was bombs away. No sooner were the bombs released, than came a sudden violent explosion. The nose section of their bomber peeled back over the cockpit blocking their view. Their instrument panel disintegrated from the blast, showering the crew with quilted batting.

The direct hit from the German anti-aircraft shell killed their bombardier. Other crew members were momentarily knocked unconscious. DeLancey and Stahlman struggled to maintain control of the aircraft which by all rights should have been spinning downward out of control.

Heavily damaged, and because the nose of the aircraft was peeled back and open, they were subjected to the elements. The blast destroyed their radios, their oxygen supply, and their hydraulic system. At their altitude, the temperatures were -30 degrees below zero.

The force of the wind whistled through the gaping hole. Their airspeed of over two hundred knots made it even colder. They were freezing. They soon realized they were a menace to the B-17s that surrounded them. They dropped down out of formation and began their descent to a lower altitude before they passed out from oxygen starvation and leveled off at 2,000 feet.

Fortunately, their four engines weren't hit and were running normally. As they spent their energy on flying a nearly out-of-control aircraft, they slowly banked back toward North Hempstead. Navigation became a problem.

They had no instruments except for an altimeter and a magnetic compass. No maps and no radios. Their navigator, Lt. Raymond Le Doux told DeLancey to fly a southwesterly compass heading. Once they crossed over the Belgium-Holland and France borders, Le Doux was able to pick up landmarks which led them back to England and their base.

At North Hempstead, tower personnel who were waiting for the squadrons of B-17s to return said they heard what sounded like the wail of a Banshee coming toward them.

What they saw was unbelievable. The B-17's engines were at full throttle. The wind that shrieked through the damaged nose made it sound as if the aircraft's spirit was howling in terrified relief as it approached the runway.

Lovely Julie was coming home. Critically injured, barely able to fly, she touched down safely. Mission number 98 ended.

The crew of the Lovely Julie received decorations. Lt. DeLancey received the Distinguished Flying Cross and Silver Star. Lt. Philip Stahlman, the Distinguished Flying Cross. Lt. Le Doux the Distinguished Flying Cross for his navigation.

Photos and articles about thcir damaged B-17 hang in the National Air and Space Museum in Washington D. C. for all to see and read about their heroic flight.

At the time my family and I had visited the NASM. While there, I read about his commendable story. It was an amazing feat.

As I look back, it seemed that in a very short period, I flew with several pilots I would emulate playing a game of war with other neighborhood kids. Never thinking that one day I would fly with some of them as their co-pilot. It was a genuine honor to serve with them.

MORE ICING CONDITIONS: BUT ON THE GROUND?

Low overcast skies and a hint of approaching precipitation loomed over Newark International Airport on the morning of January 14, 1968.

I would be flying with Captain Fred Wesche again. Our destination was Miami, along with several stops before we would get there. It was also Super Bowl II day in Miami.

In those days, some captains would leave the cockpit door open while passengers were boarding and would welcome them to take a peek inside the cockpit.

A group of passengers who were going to the game inquired about arriving on time in Miami. Fred assured them, even though we were making two stops, we would land in Miami on schedule, and long before game time.

Before we started the engines the temperature was hovering several degrees above freezing. The wind was out of the northeast which meant our take-off would be from 4R.

Even though there were low ceilings, we thought we would break out into clear skies above 5,000 feet. All of which were part of our weather briefing with our dispatcher and meteorologist. Unfortunately, Mother Nature had other ideas.

As we began our taxi to 4R, we fell in behind a TWA four-engine Convair 880 jet. Halfway down the taxiway, a light mist began to fall, along with an increase in wind speed. At the same time, ground control informed us about a sudden drop in temperature. With their warning, we knew trouble might be coming our way.

When the temperature dropped, the light mist turned to super-cooled droplets of freezing rain. The taxiway being colder than the air was soon covered with a sheet of glazed ice as was our aircraft.

The increase in wind speed and the icy taxiway rapidly became significant factors. Ahead of us, the TWA Convair 880 began sliding sideways on the ice-covered taxiway. Then it did a complete 180-degree turn to its left and was pointing at us, and it was not stopping.

At the same time, we felt the effect of ice and wind. Then our aircraft began an uncontrollable 45-degree turn to our left.

Although Fred was immediately on the brakes we couldn't stop because of the icy surface. As we were about to slide off the taxiway into the grass Fred went into full reverse on all three of our engines which stopped our slide.

It also had appeared that the 880's captain had done the same thing, full reverse to bring it to a stop. We sat facing one another with less than a hundred feet separating our noses. I know we were glad to have control of our aircraft again. We were certain the cockpit crew of the 880 felt the same.

After this close call, Newark's control tower stopped all aircraft movement. Runways and taxiways were closed as was the airport.

Those aircraft that had been making their approach to land at Newark were routed to other airports that were still operating.

It's interesting to note that no matter how much an aircraft weighs, (the B-727-100 has a take-off weight of 169,000 pounds. The Convair 880 has a take-off weight of 193,000 pounds) can become vulnerable to icy runways and gusty winds.

It wasn't long before airport maintenance trucks began spraying the runways and taxiways with de-icing fluid. Salt is never used because of its corrosive nature.

Forty minutes later the work was completed and the airport reopened.

Both the 880 and we were then cleared to return to our respective gates to re-fuel and begin the process of de-icing the aircraft.

After it was completed, it wasn't long before we were airborne. Then it was pedal-to-the-metal. We did quick turns at Greensboro and Charlotte, off-loading and boarding passengers at a record pace. We landed in Miami a little over an hour behind schedule.

Those passengers who were going to the Super Bowl game could not thank us enough knowing that they were not going to miss it.

The Green Bay Packers beat the Oakland Raiders, 33 to 14.

WESTWARD HO!

April 4th, 1968. it was westward ho! The Captain was Ron Lebo and the First Officer was Joe Lombardo. Because we were still seat-swapping, I would be, you already guessed it. I was okay with that because the following day I would be in the right seat and Joe would be the flight engineer.

But that wasn't all I was looking forward to. It was a two-day trip. LGA-STL-Portland, Oregon (PDX)-Seattle, Washington (SEA) with a layover in Seattle. Then fly the reverse schedule back to LGA.

As we crossed over the Adirondack Mountains, those same mountains I flew over while flying the DC-7B in November of 1964 when all four engines quit, I made a mental note to compare them with the Rocky Mountains. In our favor, the weather was forecast to be CAVU on both days.

It would be my first time to see America west of St. Louis. I was looking forward to it. All the flying I previously had done, was east of the Mississippi River.

At St. Louis, we had fueled to our maximum and boarded our passengers. Those flights from St. Louis to Pacific Coast cities took nearly five hours. Some 1,175 air miles ahead of us lay Portland.

It was also close to being the aircraft's max flight range. Spring and summer did not create fuel problems, but winter was another story. The main culprit was the Jet-Stream.

Polar jets or sub-tropical jets are usually found at altitudes between 30,000 feet to 39,000 feet. Wind speeds can range anywhere between 150 to 225 miles per hour. When you have that kind of airstream on the nose of your aircraft, it has a dire effect on your ground speed. As in making the flight much longer.

In winter, the winds are known to sweep down from North Western Canada, loop their way over the southwest portion of the United States, then flow upward on a northeasterly track toward New England.

On the other hand, having a Jet-Stream on your tail is another story. Several years later, in November 1970, I would be flying with another captain and second officer in our attempt to set a world speed record by using the Jet-Stream.

As we flew westward, movies about Cowboys and Indians, covered wagons, Pike's Peak, Devil's Tower, the Oregon and Bozeman Trails. Had come to mind. As did reading about American history while in school.

At the time they were just words on paper, but they always sparked my imagination. Now I was about to see it from 31,000 feet.

Some one-hundred-and-five-plus years ago, President Thomas Jefferson commissioned two men to find a pathway to the Great Northwest and the Pacific Ocean.

The men, Meriwether Lewis, and William Clark were chosen to find that pathway. What followed were some 400,000 settlers with a dream. They had left family, friends, and jobs behind, each in search of their Shangri-La.

Their jumping-off point was Independence, Missouri. Before them, lay 2,200 miles of wandering and hardship. Wagon trains by the hundreds, mostly made up of immigrants, began the four-to-six-month trek. Little food, limited water, Indian raids, and death, stalked these travelers. Still, they persevered.

Because of their courage, the West attracted others and it still does. Except now, the travelers, our passengers, were in an aluminum tube cruising along at 500 miles an hour. Being served hot meals, cold drinks, hot coffee, pillows, and blankets. All for their comfort over the next four-and-one-half hours.

As we settled into our normal flight routine, ATC informed us that off to our right, slightly behind us, and 5,000 feet below us, was an air force

KC-135, Boeing 707.

The KC-135 was used to do mid-air refueling. It was flying block altitudes and was in the process of doing one. Block altitudes are altitudes where an aircraft can vary altitude for several thousands of feet, without penalty.

When aircraft are trying to hook up to be refueled, they're subjected to wind currents, clear-air turbulence, and jet wash from the refueler's four engines.

Refueling is not an easy thing to complete while trying to control an aircraft that is constantly rising and falling. Then might have to break away because of the turbulence, and start the process all over again.

As I looked down, the captain, unable to see the KC-135 from his position, informed our passengers of what most people will never have the opportunity to witness.

There were two, what appeared to be air force F-4 Phantoms, which were probably out of McConnell Air Force Base, Kansas, practicing for Viet Nam.

Both were snuggled in tight, receiving fuel from their in-flight gas station. A beautiful sight to witness. When they were finished, they broke away probably to do a war-training mission.

I would get to see many of those mid-air refueling experiences, especially when the Viet Nam War was at its height. Each one was still awesome.

Long before we were to cross over the city of Denver, the panoramic view of the snowcapped Rocky Mountains loomed ahead. Their ruggedness and enormous mass that stretched for hundreds of miles are quite spectacular.

As we crossed over the Rockies, 17,000 feet below us was Pike's Peak. Which stands 14,114 feet above sea level and is 10,000 feet higher than the Adirondack Mountains. Just hills, comparatively speaking. As one captain I flew with said, "No one joins the mile-high club camping in the Adirondacks."

THE SUN AND ITS ULTRA-VIOLET RAYS

There was something else that was quite noticeable as we continued to fly on a westerly heading that we could not ignore. The sun.

It was getting late in the afternoon and the sun was beginning to set. Except, it didn't. At least not right away. Partly because of the three-hour time difference from the east coast to the west coast and flying at such high airspeeds.

The glare from it reduces your forward visibility, and as was the habit, you tend to slouch in your seat to avoid it. Or, occasionally look away to keep it from damaging your eyes. Wearing sunglasses helped, as did the tinted plastic glare shields we used.

There were times when ATC would point out approaching air traffic that was coming toward us. They could be 1,000 feet above or below and we would not see them as they passed.

There were other concerns about the sun. Flying at such high altitudes, there was little protection from its ultraviolet rays, the sun's radiation. For some of those flight crews who were exposed to decades of those rays, skin cancer was a definite concern.

I always used some sort of balm, or sun lotion to help prevent it. To protect my eyes, I wore Ray-Ban Aviator Sunglasses. I chose them because they were polarized and blocked 100 percent of the sun's ultraviolet rays. Fortunately, I never had a problem.

126

MORE AMERICAN HISTORY LIES AHEAD

As mentioned before, we fly highways in the sky. Flying in a straight line from point A to point B was not always possible. Those highways brought us over to Fort Hall, Idaho, a well-known settlement one-hundred-and-fifty years ago, and more American history. It was where the Oregon and California Trails met.

Most settlers that left Independence, Missouri, who were on their way to California, followed the Oregon Trail to Fort Hall and then took the California Trail. Another group on its way to California had heard about a shortcut.

Whenever my flights were out of Reno, Nevada, to cities in California it would bring me over the rugged Sierra Nevada Mountains.

Whenever I would look down at them, it would remind me of the group that took the shortcut.

In 1846, the leader of a group of 50 covered wagons heard about that shortcut to Sacramento. It was called Hastings Trail and broke away from the Oregon Trail at Fort Bridger. The group was led to believe that following that trail, would cut their journey to California by many weeks.

Their leader, George Donner, and co-leader, James Reed, decided it was the right decision believing they could cross over the rugged Sierra Nevada Mountains before the first snowfall. They were wrong.

Snowbound, with little shelter, and no food for months, the party resorted to cannibalism. Of the 83 members of the Donner Party, only 43 survived to reach California.

Flying above this trail, I could not help but be thankful I was not on that fateful trip.

After landing at Portland and refueling, it was on to Seattle. En route, I got to see a beautiful snowcapped mountain called Mt. Saint Helens.

In 1968, it was a sleeping volcano, resting quietly. Then on May 18, 1980, St. Helens erupted in all its fury. I was glad I wasn't flying over it on that day.

Flying from the east coast to the west coast made for a long day. Even though, I was always ready for those eighteen-hour layovers and looked forward to seeing the sights of Seattle. There was one problem. It's called jet lag.

The three-hour time difference from the east coast to the west coast, may not sound like much, but it could be. Especially when you're up at 5 a.m. eastern standard time.

It may be 6 p.m. arrival time in Seattle, but it's 9 p.m. body time. Regardless, Fisherman's Wharf and the Space Needle were always beckoning.

Although I enjoyed laying over in Seattle, there was one hotel that wasn't top-notch. It was called The Heart of Seattle. I had several incidents happen while staying there. One was with a captain who had somewhat of a short fuse.

This captain had called the front desk to complain about the loud noise of a party going on in the room next to his at 3 a.m. He had asked the manager to have them tone it down.

When the manager failed to stop the racket, the captain decided to take the matter into his own hands. He had knocked on the party door and then got into an argument with one of its occupants who promptly punched him in the jaw which led to security being called.

Shortly after that, it was, All Quiet on the Western Front. Although I couldn't prove it, the occupants were part of a boxer's convention. Maybe, maybe not?

Another time, it was 3 a.m. This time the loud party was next to my room. A call to the front desk. Nothing. That party lasted until 5 a.m. Again, very little sleep.

I found out later that morning, that it was a group of businessmen from Japan. For those two hours, they only spoke Japanese, loud Japanese. Maybe if I understood their language?

The last time I stayed at the Heart of Seattle was in the summertime. The air-conditioning unit in my room wasn't working which left me no choice but to keep the window open for fresh air while I slept.

At 2 a.m. I had awakened to the sound of, whoosh, whoosh, then bottles smashing. Thinking I might be dreaming, I turned over and tried to get back to sleep.

Then I heard that whoosh, whoosh, sound again, followed by more shattering of glass. I got up and went to the window and looked down.

Several floors below me, laying on a blanket on the roof that overlooked the hotel's alley, were a man and a woman, naked, having sex.

In between their activities, they had been drinking beer. They were tossing the empty bottles out over the alley, where they crashed onto the concrete and shattered. The whoosh, whoosh, sound came from the empty beer bottles as they tumbled through the night air.

At the time, I thought that their air-conditioning unit must not be working either. I also thought that if they roll too far on the small roof, they would have an enjoyable five-second drop to the concrete alley below. After that?

I just shook my head and went back to bed. Another Sleepless Night in Seattle.

MORE CITIES, MORE ADVENTURES

As Eastern kept adding new cities to its route structure, it afforded me more opportunities to see the heart of America, not only from the air but from the ground. Sightseeing became part of many of my layovers.

Boston. The Boston Tea Party, the American Revolution, "One if by land, two if by sea." The Battle of Bunker Hill.

Richmond, Virginia. Home of the capital of the Confederate States of America. Jefferson Davis, General Robert E. Lee.

Fort Sumter, Charleston, South Carolina, the beginning of the civil war between the states. Brother against brother.

San Antonio, Texas. The Alamo and thirteen days of Glory.

Many other cities had history-making events and I considered myself fortunate to be able to enjoy them all.

Summer, 1968. I was the second officer on a flight from Newark to West Palm Beach. One that had started as a ho-hum day.

An hour and a half into our flight our senior stewardess had entered the cockpit. She complained to the captain about an irate woman in first class who was making nasty comments to the man sitting in front of her.

The captain told the attendant to calm the woman down. If she couldn't, he would take care of it. She left the cockpit and three minutes later she was back. Same problem. That was when the captain turned to me and told me to handle it.

As I stepped out of the cockpit, the woman in question stood up and dumped her food tray on the head of the man sitting in front of her.

I rushed back and grabbed the woman's hands and forced her back into her seat. I made a quick apology to the man and told him that Eastern would take care of having his suit cleaned. He told me not to worry about it.

My attention then turned to the woman, who by now was in tears, as was the woman sitting next to her. It turned out to be her mother.

I asked the passenger why she dumped the tray on the man. Before she answered, she grabbed her purse and opened it.

As she reached into it, I closed it on her hand, preventing her from retrieving whatever was inside. My first thought was that it was a gun. It wasn't. It was a handkerchief. Then she told me why she dumped the food tray.

She was angry at the man because her husband was in the army, in Vietnam, and had been there for a long time. She wanted him home before he was killed. She then pointed to the man and said, "He was not doing enough about it."

I was puzzled by her comment until I realized the man was Averell Harriman. He headed the U.S. Delegation to the preliminary peace talks in Paris between the United States and North Vietnam from 1968 to 1969. It was a difficult time for all of us.

I informed the woman, if there were any more outbursts, the police would be waiting for her when we got to PBI. That immediately put an end to the commotion.

Back in the cockpit, I told the captain what took place. He told me that I should not have put my hands on her because she could sue Eastern and me for assault and battery. So much for backup.

What truly impressed me was the way Averell Harriman, a gentleman from start to finish, handled the whole episode.

You never know when those little airplane gremlins decide to make their appearance, do their little dance, and make an easy day of flying into something much more intriguing.

PLEASE GET MY BAGGAGE OFF YOUR AIRPLANE!

July 12, 1968. Helmut Hetz was the captain and it was the first time that I flew with him. He was one of several German pilots who flew for the German Luftwaffe during WWII that Eastern had hired.

I would find that he was a gentleman and it was always a pleasure to fly with. We had our flight planned from MIA-FPO-MIA. Each leg was no more than thirty minutes of flying time.

Upon landing in FPO, we deplaned the passengers, then waited for the boarding to begin for our flight back to MIA. Unfortunately, the ground crew could not get the aft cargo door open to offload our passenger's baggage. Now what?

After thirty minutes of trying to open the door, our efforts were useless. A broken latch? A jammed handle? Captain Hetz contacted our maintenance department in Miami and was told the only way into the cargo compartment was through the floor of the aft cabin. He elected our second officer and me for the task.

Our first thought was to grab the crash ax that was kept in the cockpit and hack away. Helmut and our maintenance department had a better idea. Rip up the carpet, grab screwdrivers, and start unscrewing the hundred-plus screws. This would allow us to remove the fiberglass hatch and let us enter the compartment.

An hour and a half later, after we had gained access we had found a large suitcase had jammed the handle preventing the door from opening.

It was a job well done and all the luggage was offloaded. Just before we were to board our Miami-bound passengers was when we found out that things weren't so great after all.

The reason. Fire protection in the cargo compartment was compromised. All the passengers' luggage had to be loaded into the forward cargo compartment.

Without going into the five classes of fire protection required by the FAA (A.B.C.D.E) for cargo compartments, I will refer only to the B-727 cargo compartment Class D.

It had to be relatively small and sealed so that a fire in the compartment would quickly expend the available oxygen, and not be able to threaten the rest of the aircraft.

The compartment was pressurized as was the entire aircraft. The exceptions were the nose radar dome and aft of the rear bulkhead door.

The compartment had enough airflow to allow the carrying of animals in the rear cargo hold. Once we broke through the hatch it was no longer a Class D compartment. This meant it had to have a fire compression system. Such as an automatic fire extinguisher that would sense a fire.

On May 22, 1996, a Valujet Airlines flight 592, a DC-9, departed MIA-ATL, only to crash into the Florida Everglades with the loss of 105 passengers and its 5 crew members.

The NTSB found that the probable cause of the accident was approximately 144 chemical oxygen generators being improperly carried on the flight.

The oxygen generators were being carried in a Class D cargo hold. Since that accident, Class D cargo compartments are required to have smoke detection and fire suppression systems.

WHAT HAPPENED TO OUR CLOTHES?

Mother Earth had traveled another quick six months in its orbit around the sun which brought us into February 1969.

On the 8th of that month, it was a cold and blustery day as we left EWR on what was supposed to be a two-day trip with a layover in STL.

The captain was Tom Dozier, the Second Officer was Larry Mosser, and I was the first officer. We were about to find out that old man Winter wasn't going to give up easily.

The next day, the 9th of February, the New York area got hit with an unexpected snowstorm. It quickly developed into a blizzard producing chaos.

All flights into and out of the New York airports were canceled. Flight crews that were scheduled to fly were stuck in New York hotels as were other crews based in the New England area. Those of us who were able to get to the airport began flying other flight crew's schedules.

Our two-day trip stretched into three days, then four. We flew to eight different cities, none of which were in the northeast corridor.

On the third night, we ended up laying over in Corpus Christie, Texas. By that time our clothes were beginning to smell pretty ripe as we had only packed for a one-night layover.

Tom had a great idea. It was to pool our clothes, underwear, socks, and our uniform shirts and put them in the washing machine the hotel provided. He also suggested that we have dinner and retrieve them afterward. It sounded good to Larry and me.

After dinner, we found out that both the washing machine and dryer were gone, as were all our clothes. When we told the manager of the hotel. He said there were out-of-order signs on both machines and we shouldn't have used them. There weren't.

Apparently, the machines were sent out for repair while we dined. With all of our clothes in them? It was obvious the workmen never bothered to look inside.

By then it was nearly eight o'clock at night and the manager couldn't get hold of the repairmen. Apologies followed, along with a promise to get them back. Fine. Except we were scheduled to leave early the next morning.

Larry came up with a brilliant idea. He told the manager when the clothes were retrieved to send them all to his home in New Jersey. He would then send our clothes to Tom and me.

When we boarded our flight the next morning, we were wearing our black uniform coats and pants, and black shoes. Our shirts were of the multi-color variety with no black uniform ties. Our passengers eyed us curiously until Tom told them what happened. They just laughed.

As for the blizzard? On those two days, it had dumped 15.3 inches of snow along the east coast. The mayor of New York was John Lindsay. He took a lot of flack because it would take more than a week before many of the streets were plowed.

A week later, I received a package in the mail. It was from Larry. It contained all my clothes that were clean and neatly pressed, including my underwear. A present from Larry's wife.

WE HAVE A BOMB ON BOARD?

May 29, 1969, was the beginning of a two-day sequence. The captain was Vince Rush whom I had been flying with for the whole month. The first day was rather short. Newark to Charlotte then layover.

The following day was much longer. With us having to fly to four different cities before returning to Newark. Of course, we took turns as to who would fly each leg. One portion of mine had me flying from Baltimore to Miami.

We crossed over Wilmington, North Carolina, at 31,000 feet on Atlantic Ocean Air Route 7. Another one of those highways in the sky. It would bring us some two-hundred miles off the coast of Florida.

From Wilmington, our flight plan called for us to fly direct to the Freeport, Bahamas' VOR, a navigation aid, then to Miami.

For once, there was no building of those cauliflower-looking clouds we often called nympho-cumulonimbus. Although ATC had advised us that all warning areas were hot.

All along the east coast of Florida, there are hundreds of miles of air space reserved for Uncle Sam's military to play war games. This meant you can't enter any of them no matter what.

Since the visibility was unlimited, we could look down at the ocean and see the sight of ships sailing southeastward toward the Caribbean.

The sea appeared calm. The water was a deep blue, a good day for sailing. For us, our flight had been smooth. A good day for flying. Even the crew meals seemed to be a lot tastier than usual.

As I was downing the last sip of my coffee, we received a SELCAL from the company. SELCAL stands for selective calling. It is used by air carriers as a way of communicating by radio between the company and an aircraft. Normally, when you received a SELCAL, it would be about changes in the weather, runway conditions, or in-flight delays at your destination. This call wasn't for any of them. It grabbed our attention right away.

Eastern had received a telephone call from an unidentified person who said he had put a bomb on board our flight while in Baltimore

Here we were more than 200 miles off the coast of Florida. The warning areas were hot so we couldn't penetrate any of them to divert to other airports such as Jacksonville, Daytona Beach, or West Palm Beach.

Vince had decided that we had no choice but to continue and land in Miami. What was remarkable was how the three of us approached the situation in a very calm and professional manner.

We notified ATC of our predicament and at the same time had squawked 7500, then 7700 on our transponder. This meant we had an in-flight emergency. We then requested to descend to 10,000 feet, and possibly lower.

Vince had chimed for the senior stewardess to come to the cockpit. Luckily, the meal service had been completed and the cabin crew was in the process of stowing passenger food trays.

He had informed her of what was taking place and told her to quietly advise the rest of the cabin crew of our dilemma and our plan of action once we landed.

Then added. "Do not tell our passengers. We don't want an in-flight panic on our hands." She nodded, then left the cockpit.

During our descent to 10,000 feet, we began to de-pressurize the aircraft. By de-pressurizing the aircraft the idea was, if a bomb did detonate it might blow a hole in the fuselage, but hopefully, it wouldn't bring the down the aircraft.

We descended below 10,000 feet and leveled off at 2,000 feet, but we were still twenty-five minutes from landing. Due to the nature of our emergency, other aircraft ahead of us were being vectored out of our way. Speed was of the essence.

We were still doing 350 knots when we crossed over Miami Beach before we began to slow the aircraft for a landing on runway 9L.

Vince then made announced to our passengers that we had received a report that a device may have been put aboard our aircraft. Adding, that after we land, we will stop on a taxiway and take precautionary measures and evacuate everyone on the taxiway.

Upon touching down, it was full-reverse and max braking. We made the second turn-off and cleared the runway with the airport's emergency vehicles right behind us. When we stopped, Vince made one final announcement. "Evacuate! Evacuate!"

When both the forward air-stairs and rear air-stairs were lowered, our stewardess immediately began a calm and orderly evacuation.

Then led their passengers out and away from the aircraft. All of this was done in less than 90 seconds. Remarkable, especially under dire circumstances.

As for us, the cockpit crew, we shut down all three engines and made a quick inspection of the cabin making sure no one was left on board. Then we made our hasty exit. The flight was over.

By then, the emergency vehicles had surrounded the aircraft and stood by in case there had been a bomb on board and it exploded.

What happened next came as a complete surprise. The fire battalion chief, who was in charge, came over and stood next to me. I had asked him what his plans were as far as checking for a possible bomb. He told me that they had never had to handle a bomb threat before. I surely thought it would have been part of their training.

No one went aboard the aircraft to inspect it, nor were any cargo doors open and inspected. Passengers began to complain and were asking if they could walk to the terminal. The battalion chief answered a terse. "No!"

"What about our luggage?" A passenger asked"

"You'll have to wait until they inspect the aircraft." He answered.

Some of our passengers were getting upset. Not because of what just took place, but the delay in getting their bags, and the possibility of missing connecting flights.

Finally, coming toward us were our aircraft mechanics riding an Eastern aircraft tug. They promptly attached a tow bar and began towing the aircraft to the terminal. No inspection. Vince and I were appalled.

Fifteen minutes later, two buses arrived. Then we, the flight crew, along with our passengers boarded and were dropped off at the terminal. But by that time Vince and I were about to throw a fit at what took place.

We met with our station manager whose nose was bent out of shape because he had to order the buses. That cost Eastern some hefty dollars.

He wanted to know why Vince didn't just taxi to the gate. More or less, second-guessing the captain's decision to evacuate. That was when I had to step in front of Vince before he punched our station manager in the nose. I felt the same way.

After a few well-chosen words, Vince explained his decision.

After a lengthy delay, the aircraft went through an entire inspection at the gate. All of the passenger's baggage were removed and inspected. No device was found. Afterward, they were happy to be free and on their way. I am sure they will never forget that flight.

As for our crew, it was off to flight operations to prepare for our flight to Newark.

A CATASTROPHIC ENGINE FAILURE

Several months later, September 19, was the last day of a long three-day sequence. The captain was Bill Fisher whom I had flown with many times before.

Bill was one of those guys who was quiet and reserved. He did not talk much and was somewhat of a heavy chain smoker.

We had started our morning in Houston on our way to Boston. Then it would be my turn to fly from Boston to Washington D. C.

In Boston, as I was preparing to board our aircraft for the flight to DCA I noticed the flight crew of a B-727 parked at the next gate staring up at their number three engine and pointing to its cowling. Curiosity took over and I went to see what the mystery was.

The cowling was torn in half. The engine, a Pratt Whitney JDT8D that was used on our B-727s, which has the capability of producing 12,000 to 17,000 pounds of thrust, needed to launch more than 160,000 pounds of aluminum airborne, had a catastrophic failure at the most critical phase of flight, the take-off.

Its second officer had invited me to come with him and take a look inside the aft air-stairs entrance and pointed to an open-access door. Inside there were two Freon engine fire bottles that are used to extinguish a jet engine fire.

Both lines coming from them to the engine were severed. Had the engine caught fire, there would have been no way of extinguishing it.

He then pointed to the bulkhead frame of the aft cabin door. It was made of metal and a good three inches thick. Embedded in the frame at head level, was part of the fan blade of the number three engine.

When it disintegrated, the fan blade whirling at thousands of rpm had flattened out, cut through the Freon lines, and sawed itself halfway through the frame.

Another two inches to the right, the blade would have sawed through the passenger bulkhead and possibly decapitated the passenger sitting next to the door.

It was astonishing to see that kind of damage and more importantly, realize what might have been. Strange things do happen when you least expect them. Then it came to my turn to fly from Boston to Washington D.C.

As we raced down the runway and reached our rotation airspeed of 140 knots, I eased back on the control column and we lifted off. Making sure that we had a positive rate-of-climb, called for gear up.

No sooner were the wheels stored in their wheel wells came the loud and awful sound of metal grinding against metal. The number one engine was starting to come apart. The aircraft began to shake violently. The instruments were a blur.

As trained, the pilot flies the aircraft while the other crew members focus their attention on the emergency. The captain and second officer did exactly what they were supposed to do. Shut the engine down, followed by a quick return to the airport and landing.

Afterward, it was up to our mechanics to find the reason for the engine failure. In the meantime, dispatch notified us that another aircraft would be available within an hour.

Captain Fisher then took it upon himself to explain to those who were aboard our flight, the reason for the precautionary shutdown of the engine. Not the reason for the engine failure, for at that time, we did not know the cause. It was interesting to note that not one of those passengers canceled their flight to Washington.

Two hours later, the aircraft we were awaiting arrived. Just before our departure to DCA, the mechanics who had investigated our engine failure told us what they thought might have caused it.

They believed our engine failure was related to the engine failure of the other B-727 whose number three engine came apart. Their engine had spread debris all over the runway.

Even though the airport ground crews had inspected the runway and said that they had cleared the debris, they may have missed some of the shrapnel.

They also surmised that during our take-off our left main tire may have struck a piece of a remaining fragment. They said they had found a deep cut in the tire tread.

Whereas, a scrap of metal may have flown up and got sucked into our number one engine's fan blades. Of course, this was speculation. We never did find out the real reason. It was a strange event and could have been a disaster.

SOUTH OF THE BORDER DOWN MEXICO WAY

On September 7, 1969, I was about to get my first taste of what it was like to fly into another country. It was South of the border down Mexico Way. The captain was Tom Lamborn.

Our flight took us from Newark to Mexico City. With two intermediate stops along the way. Those being Atlanta and New Orleans Then do the reverse the following day.

Flying to other countries can sometimes be a challenge. To start with, all air traffic controllers throughout the world must speak and understand the English language. That requirement can be debated.

Many foreign controllers speak with heavy accents and at times, may not be fully understood. Their directions often need to be repeated several times.

That can have serious consequences, especially in mountainous terrain. Unfortunately, some of those misunderstandings have led to disastrous results such as burying an aircraft into the side of a mountain.

The leg from MSY-MEX brought us out over the Gulf of Mexico and hundreds and hundreds of miles of empty ocean. Except for seeing an occasional cargo ship or ocean liner.

During the winter months, the skies are mostly clear. Summertime could be another story, especially if it's hurricane season. Lashing winds, violent seas, and a handful of airplane when making approaches in nasty marginal weather.

Laying over in Mexico City, a beautiful city on a nice day, was always a pleasure. Other days, not so much since the city lies in somewhat of a bowl because of the mountains that surround it.

Since Mexico City is situated at a high altitude, approximately 7,380 feet above sea level, where the sun is stronger than it would be at sea level. Pollution becomes a problem.

About 75 percent of their air pollution is caused by toxic gases, such as carbon monoxide, and sulfur dioxide, emitted by hundreds of thousands of vehicles. All of which create limited visibility in mountainous terrain. As in. Stay on course when making an approach to land.

The people I had the pleasure of meeting and working with, and the employees of the hotels where we stayed, couldn't have been nicer.

There were many times when they would direct me to some of the finest restaurants in the city. One of them that I do have to mention. It was called. Anderson's.

The first time I ate there, my waiter tapped the back of my hand as I was about to eat my Caesar Salad with a knife and fork. He handed me the menu which had a history of the famous salad. Followed by a short history of its origin by reading the back of the menu that the waiter had handed me.

Believe me, I am not a gourmet of fine foods. Although I have eaten many Caesar Salads, as I am sure many of you have. The wrong way!

According to Mexican legend, as recorded on the menu. On the 4th of July, 1924, Italian-American, Caesar Cardini, became the originator of the famous salad, and not Julius Caesar. He hated anchovies.

Cardini was short of food at his restaurant in Tijuana, Mexico when an inspiration came to him. He threw together a conglomeration of Parmesan cheese, lemon juice, olive oil, egg, Worcestershire Sauce, anchovies, and garlic. It was presented on a Romaine lettuce leaf which was to be eaten by hand, not with a knife and fork, as I was about to do. It was such a great success, his customers clamored for more. Enough said.

As much as I always like flying to Mexico City and enjoying the sights, there were some sights I didn't like seeing.

Our second officer, Jim Geraghty, and I had just finished dinner and had been on our way back to our hotel called the Maria Isabella. As we rounded a street corner, I had accidentally stepped on the leg of a man lying on the sidewalk and jumped back startled. Then realized the man was dead.

Standing next to the body was a policeman who seemed unconcerned. Others stopped by, but only to briefly look down, and continue on their way. It was as though it were an everyday event.

The policeman, Federales, told us that the man may have had a heart attack and died. He said he was waiting for an ambulance to arrive. Jim and I looked at one another, shook our heads in disbelief, and continued to our hotel.

Jim was one of my Seaton Hall ROTC flight students while I was instructing at the Wings of Morristown flight school in the summer of 1963.

He, like many of my other Seaton Hall University's ROTC flight students, ended up at Fort Rucker, Alabama. He was trained to fly the Army's L-20. Ending up in Viet Nam flying as a forward air reconnaissance pilot. I was happy he got through that war unscathed.

DUCKING UNDER A LIGHTING BOLT

On January 13, 1970, the winter weather was coating the northeast with snow flurries. It was a two-day sequence of flights with Captain Walt Brady, who was our chief pilot in New York.

Seat-swapping was still in effect. Normally I was supposed to have been the first officer on that day as I was senior to our second officer. The following day, I would be the second and he would become the first officer.

The sequences of flights had us going from Newark to Miami and layover. On the second day Miami to Freeport, Bahamas, then to West Palm Beach, and back to Newark.

Before the flight began, Captain Brady had asked me to be the second officer for two days. The reason. He wanted to give the other pilot a two-day proficiency check as a first officer.

The first day was uneventful. The second day became a little more exciting. Almost too exciting.

Even though it was snowing in the northeast, there were thunderstorms off the coast of Florida.

The flight from Miami to Freeport had been a little choppy due to the storms. Even so, with our Dopler weather radar, we were able to skirt around the build-ups without any problems. Freeport to West Palm Beach became a little more exciting.

We were cruising along at 15,000 feet and had just broken out of a cloud deck into an open sky. Ahead of us, was a nasty-looking build-up of clouds, and as we were about to skirt around them. Trouble.

Suddenly, from out of the cloud, snaking its way toward us was a jagged, cloud-to-cloud bolt of lightning, and we were in its way.

All three of us attempted to duck under the instrument glare shield knowing we were about to be struck, and it was going to be violent.

Unbelievably, the bolt passed directly over the top of the cockpit for what seemed to be mere inches. Then I thought it was going to hit the vertical stabilizer. It didn't.

Cloud-to-cloud lightning happens quite frequently. The trick is not to be in its way.

Many years later, as a captain on a flight from Bermuda to Baltimore, my crew and I would experience one of the most damaging lightning strikes I ever encountered.

EASTERN SHUTTLE FLIGHT 1320

Tuesday, March 17, 1970, was St. Patrick's Day, and celebration time throughout the world. Irish eyes were smiling. Except on Eastern shuttle flight 1320.

Flight 1320 was a DC-9 bound from EWR-BOS. It consisted of a two-man cockpit crew. Captain Bob Wilbur Jr. was in command and First Officer James Hartley assisted him.

Attending to its passengers, were Senior Flight Attendant Christine Peterson, Flight Attendants Arlene Albino, and Sandra Kay Saltzer.

All was well as the flight attendants went about their business collecting the airfare from their passengers. That was until Flight Attendant Saltzer asked the gentleman sitting in seat 22D for his airfare.

At that time, airfares were collected in-flight on all of Eastern Shuttles.

He handed Saltzer eighteen dollars, stating that he was a student. That was the student rate at that time.

Saltzer thought that was rather odd because he looked much older than most students would be so she had asked him for some kind of student identification.

Instead, John Joseph Divivo Jr. took out a gun, which was later found to be a .38 caliber pistol, from his shaving kit, pointed it at her, and told her he wanted to see the captain.

Saltzer then told Divivo to put away the gun so it wouldn't scare other passengers. Oddly enough, he put the gun in his coat and they both went forward toward the cockpit door.

Seeing this, Senior Flight Attendant Christine Peterson followed them.

148

Saltzer told her Divivo wanted to see the captain, so she let Saltzer ring the captain.

At that time, flight 1320 was approximately thirty nautical miles southwest of the Boston VORTAC descending for their approach and landing.

At first, when told that a passenger wanted to see him, Captain Wilbur told Saltzer they were too busy and would talk to him on the ground. When told the passenger was armed, First Officer Jim Hartley opened the cockpit door and Saltzer and Divivo entered.

When Captain Wilbur realized this was a hi-jacking, he told Saltzer to go back and take care of the passengers.

From that moment on both pilots tried to minimize the situation. They had offered him the jump seat and made casual conversation with him. Then soon realized that there was indeed something wrong with him. While Divivo was distracted, Hartley was able to squawk 3100, today it's 7500, on the transponder. The code that said a hi-jacking was in progress.

Unfortunately, ATC was unsure which aircraft was in duress as there were many aircraft in the traffic pattern even though they were in contact with Flight 1320 throughout the entire event. All of these calls were recorded by both air traffic control and Flight 1320's cockpit voice recorder.

Shortly afterward, Divivo told them he didn't want to go to Boston. When questioned about where he wanted to go, he told them to fly east and out over the Atlantic Ocean then let him know when they were two minutes from running out of fuel.

It was obvious the crew could not allow that to happen. Doing so would mean crashing into the Atlantic Ocean and killing all passengers and crew. After ten minutes of the flight, and five miles out over the Atlantic, Captain Wilbur asked Divivo if it would be okay to turn back. Strangely enough, he said yes.

As Captain Wilbur banked left back toward Logan Airport, the sound of a muzzle blast filled the cockpit. As he spun to his right, he looked straight into the barrel of the still smoking .38 Divivo was holding.

Instinctively, as Wilbur raised his right arm for protection, a second blast occurred. The bullet tore through his right forearm and penetrated his upper left bicep, shattering the bone. The pain was unbearable. Another blast could mean the end.

Miraculously, Hartley, who had been shot in the back at point-blank range, and was mortally wounded from the first bullet, lunged at Divivo, overpowered him, grabbed his gun, and shot him twice. He then beat him to the cockpit floor where he lay semi-conscious. Hartley then slumped in his seat dropping the gun on the center console between him and the captain.

Captain Wilbur now bleeding profusely from his gunshot wounds, with his first officer dying, had only one thought, and that was to get medical care for his first officer and get the aircraft on the ground safely and as soon as possible.

Three miles from touchdown, the dazed hijacker managed to get to his knees, grabbing and clawing at the captain.

Captain Wilbur saw the gun lying on the console, grabbed it with his right hand, and repeatedly smashed it over the hijacker's head until the gun shattered into four pieces. The hijacker again collapsed to the cockpit floor and lay there.

Captain Wilbur landed the aircraft, taxied to the gate, and was in the process of shutting down the engines when law enforcement officers came aboard. By that time, the hijacker began regaining whatever senses he had and was forcibly dragged off the aircraft kicking and screaming.

Unfortunately, First Officer Jim Hartley Jr. would succumb to his wounds.

In the aftermath, two heroes were recognized. One was Captain Robert M. Wilbur III who received many accolades from all over the country, including a telephone call from then-President Richard Nixon.

It would take many months for him to recover from the wounds he received before he was once again flying for Eastern Air Lines.

First Officer Jim Hartley Jr. also received many accolades and eventually would have our new training center in Miami called The James E. Hartley Training Center after him.

The hijacker, John Joseph Divivo, was charged with murder, then sent to the Bridgewater State Hospital for a mental evaluation, and then to Suffolk

County Jail at Charles Street.

On October 31, 1970, while awaiting trial in jail, Divivo hanged himself by tying a neckerchief to his cell bars at 3:00 in the morning.

To understand fully what took place that day in the cockpit, one needs to realize how cramped a DC-9 cockpit is.

Picture yourself sitting in an oversized clothes closet that is approximately ten feet across and seven feet deep. There is only room enough for two pilot seats and in between them, a center console containing navigation/radios and auto-pilot aids.

The control column is a mere 18 inches in front of the pilot's adjustable seat. The instrument panels are less than a foot beyond the control columns. Some two feet behind the seats are the bulkheads that hold row upon row of circuit breakers.

The entire cockpit is designed so that all necessary flight instruments are within easy reach of the two pilots. Let's not forget the jump seat just aft of the center console, which has barely enough room for a rider to sit upon. It is one of the most uncomfortable seats you can imagine.

Envision those two pilots fighting with a deranged hijacker trying to kill them, their passengers, and their cabin crew. Hopefully, you can understand the incredible courage shown by Captain Wilbur and First Officer Hartley.

Sadly, Flight 1320 was not the first hijacking that occurred with a crew member killed while in flight.

On May 7, 1964, Pacific Southwest Airlines Flight 773 departed Reno-Tahoe Airport bound for San Francisco.

While in flight a deranged passenger had entered an unlocked cockpit door and then opened fire on both Captain, Ernest Clark and First Officer Ray Andress, killing them both. He then turned the gun on himself, committing suicide. The aircraft crashed near Danville, California, killing all 41 passengers and the lone Flight Attendant, Margaret Schafer.

The NTSB concluded, with the aid of taped conversations between the pilots of Flight 773 and ATC, and the recovery of the cockpit voice recorder, that the hijacking was a case of murder and suicide.

At that time, the FARs allowed, on certain aircraft, that the cockpit door did not have to be locked. In this case, the aircraft was a twin-engine Fairchild F-27 and the door was unlocked.

After the hijacking of Flight 773, the FAR pertaining to requiring the cockpit door to be locked was amended. It became known as the Clark Act, named after Flight 773 Captain, Ernest Clark.

Another hi-jacking where an airline employee was killed comes to mind. On October 24, 1972, four men entered an Arlington, Virginia bank. They shot and killed 2 people and escaped.

On October 30, 1972, the four entered the Houston International Terminal. They turned their attention to Eastern Air Lines ticket agent Stanley Hubbard, who they shot and killed. Then they shot another ticket agent four times in the arm. Thankfully, he survived.

Then boarded an Eastern Air Lines flight and ordered the crew to take them to Cuba. Were they were arrested.

Unfortunately, the Cuban authorities gave the hijackers sanctuary. Later, they made their way back to the United States. It took nearly twenty years before the four were captured and brought to justice.

June 17, 1970. Thunderstorms, lightning, heavy rain, and flight delays became the norm. On that day Len Finely was the captain and I was the first officer.

Our flight started from Seattle, Washington, with stops at Portland Oregon, St. Louis, Philadelphia, Bradley Airport in Windsor Locks, Connecticut, and then Boston. As we taxied out for takeoff from PHL a line of thunderstorms started coming through. The airport was closed.

We, along with other airlines, had parked on a taxiway waiting for the storms to pass. After a three-hour ground delay, we continued to Bradley and then to Boston, followed by a much-needed layover.

What should have been less than an eight-hour day became eighteen hours of duty time. Our flight time should have been less than eight hours, which became eleven hours and forty-two minutes.

I thought at that time there would be no way I could ever log more flight time in one day than that. How wrong can you be?

LOST OF THE BALLOON, FREE LIFE

T here have been many cases when an aircraft flying over open water, calls a Mayday. Then disappears forever. It is usually caused by pilots exceeding their capabilities.

September 20th, 1970. The captain was Ed Hill and I was the first officer. Our flight from Bermuda to Baltimore had been uneventful, although hundreds of miles to our north-northeast position were squall lines. Very bad weather.

En route, New York's ATC asked us if we could contact N2079. At first, I thought they were talking about a lost aircraft. It wasn't. It was a seven-story hot air balloon called Free Life.

After several attempts of trying to contact the balloon, and searching the skies above and the seas below, there was no communication.

That seemed logical because they should have been far north of our position. Then again, their balloon was at the mercy of the winds and could be anywhere, especially with the squall lines north of us.

Several days before its launching, the headlines were all about this crew's fourth attempt to be the first hot air balloon to cross the Atlantic Ocean.

It had taken off from a farm field in East Hampton, New York. Onboard were pilot, Malcolm Brown, his wife Pamela Brown, and Rodney Anderson. The 70-foot-tall balloon was filled with hot air/helium, and packed with ping-pong balls, in case they had to ditch. Think DickMerrill.

Merrill was a famous aviator who made headlines in 1936. He had stuffed 41,000 ping-pong balls in the wings of his airplane on his round-trip transatlantic flight. Which was dubbed the Ping-Ping Flight. The thought being if he went down in the ocean, the balls would keep the aircraft afloat long enough to be rescued.

Unfortunately, 30 hours after launch, according to authorities who were monitoring the flight, a hot air mechanism designed to maintain the balloon's altitude failed.

Evidently, the balloon encountered a high-altitude cold front and a severe rainstorm. Soon after, they were forced to ditch in the Atlantic at night, about 600 miles southeast of Newfoundland.

Their message was, "We are ditching." They then added, "We are requesting search and rescue." Unfortunately, after two weeks of search and rescue, only small pieces of wreckage from the balloon were found.

In October of 1970, Eastern made a public offer for a small Caribbean airline called Caribair. Caribair's main competition was another Caribbean airline called Prinair Airlines.

Had Eastern not kept Caribair viable with loans, it would have failed. With objections from Prinair on an Eastern takeover and nearly three years of objections, Eastern won its battle. The tiny airline was merged into Eastern on March 15, 1973.

For Eastern, it was a plum, and the gateway to more Caribbean islands. I liked what would lie ahead, island hopping. Montego Bay, Kingston, Port-Au-Prince, Santo Domingo, St. Croix, St. Thomas, St. Maarten, Antigua, Pointe-a' Pitre, St. Lucia, Barbados, Port of Spain, Curacao, and Aruba.

SETTING A WORLD AIRSPEED RECORD

S erendipity! According to Webster's Dictionary definition is, "The faculty of finding valuable or agreeable things not sought for."

November 4, 1970, was just one of those days when you would drive to the airport, check the en-route weather to your destination and expect a normal day of flying.

On that day, a Newark to Houston flight with one stop at Atlanta, was on the schedule. Then came a four-and-a-half-hour layover in Houston before returning to Newark.

The captain was John Brady, the second officer was Dave Claire, and I was the first officer. The weather, CAVU. The only problem with the flight was having to deal with a two-hundred-mile-an-hour Polar jet stream.

The stream had swept down from Canada and looped over the southwest portion of the United States. Then flowed upward on a northeast track toward New England. Which meant headwinds to Atlanta and Houston.

I flew the first leg to Atlanta at several thousand feet below our normal cruising altitude, due to the headwinds. The headwinds had a profound effect on our ground speed, meaning the flight was going to take much longer than usual.

Captain Brady was flying the next leg of our flight from Atlanta to Houston several thousand feet below our normal cruising altitude for the same reason.

While en route to Houston, an idea popped into my mind. If we have this

155

kind of headwind going southwest bound, our flight northeast to Newark was going to be a hell of a lot faster.

I looked at John and kiddingly said. "If we have this jet stream on our tail going back to Newark, we could set a world airspeed record." Of course, I thought he would just laugh at the idea.

Then again, you would have to know Captain John Brady. He was one of Eastern Air Lines' best. To me, he was one of those gregarious individuals we so seldom see or get to know.

Before Eastern, he was a pilot from the old school. You know. Helmut and goggles, navigating those Adcock Radio Range's listening to the dots and dashes of Morse Code to ensure that you were on course.

Then having to make approaches to landing fields at night guided to the runway by lighted kerosene pots.

John also flew B-24s and B-29s for the Army Air Force during WWII, so I wasn't all that surprised when he said. "That's not a bad idea. I'll check with dispatch when we get to Houston."

In Houston, Dave and I went to the hotel the company provided.

Whenever there was an intermediate layover of over four hours, and having to fly another route that same day. A hotel room was provided.

In the meantime, John had stayed at flight operations making telephone calls. Not only to our dispatcher but to the Ivory Tower in Miami for permission to attempt the flight.

While John remained at the airport. Dave and I enjoyed the hotel's swimming pool, ate lunch, and waited those several hours for an answer. Would it be a go or a no-go?

The answer from the Ivory Tower: "Go for it!"

Whoa! Not so fast. Other factors had to be considered. You can't just jump in an airplane and declare. "I'm out to set a world airspeed record." It requires a lot of planning in a very short period.

It needed the FAA's approval. One caveat was to be able to fly off airways and directly toward Newark. If the Air Traffic Control Centers deemed it okay and did not interfere with other air traffic. Which they approved.

Then there was the National Aeronautics Association (NAA.) They were the ones who decided whether or not you could do a speed run.

If they allowed you to do it, they would have to have NAA associates stationed in both Houston and Newark's control towers. This is to log the official time of lift-off and landing. The moment finally arrived. Would the NAA let us do the speed run?

Their answer was also. "Go for it!"

Our normal scheduled flight time from IAH-EWR was three hours and five minutes. One last-minute check of the winds, at the altitude we intended to cruise at was two hundred miles an hour, and right on our tail.

Before starting the engines, John made his usual announcement to our passengers but made no mention of our attempt at a speed run. Nor did he inform our cabin crew of what we would be attempting.

This was done for two reasons. One was the possibility of our passengers being too apprehensive. On the other, our flight attendants might have a slip of the tongue.

At 7:25 p.m. Central Standard Time, our flight, EA592, taxied out for takeoff. I had assumed John would be doing the flying. Not so! He told me, "You thought of it. You fly it." I was surprised.

Most captains, I believe, would be the ones who would want to set the record. Regardless of who flew it, it was a cockpit crew attempt.

As we rolled onto the runway in take-off position, the tower cleared us for immediate take-off. Once airborne, they told us the exact time of our lift-off.

As we climbed to 35,000 feet, ATC gave us a radar vector heading directly toward Newark, allowing us to bypass the normal airway routes.

At altitude, we began to feel the effects of the jet stream almost immediately. The air was smooth, the night sky filling with those diamonds we call stars. Mother Earth was moving swiftly below us. Towns and cities came and quickly went.

At several points along our route, we had flown directly toward our normal navigation aids, called Visual Omni Ranges. Which has Distance Measuring Equipment, VOR/DME.

These aids provide a readout as to how far you are away from their stations. Normally their readout was up to 200 miles away. By timing the distance flown in one minute, gives you your ground speed.

At several points en route, we covered more than ten miles in one minute. Ten miles in one-minute times 60 seconds is 600 miles per hour.

As were being handed off from one ATC to another, we could hear the enthusiasm in the voices of the controllers. They were also involved in our attempt to set the record. Even cockpit crew members from other airlines, who were listening in on the same frequency, shared the encouragement.

All was well until we were one hundred miles south of Gordonsville, Virginia. That was when we began to encounter light turbulence.

At the same time, Washington ATC told us we had to get into the flow of regular air traffic and fly the normal airway routes. This happened so we would not disrupt the regular flow of airline traffic.

That was a big disappointment. We had thought we would be number one all the way to EWR because we were attempting to set a world record. Unfortunately, having to do that added more flight time.

Light turbulence became moderate as the jet stream collided with other winds and cold fronts. Having to slow down to an airspeed of 280 knots because of the turbulence didn't help. Neither did changing altitudes, trying to find smoother air.

When we finally landed at EWR, our official flight time was recorded as two hours, 29 minutes, and 30 seconds. We averaged a ground speed of 561.85 mph, knocking off thirty-six minutes of the actual scheduled flight time.

Had we not had to slow down because of turbulence and other air traffic, I believe we would have shaved another ten minutes or more off our flight time. Either way, we set the airspeed record for a flight from IAH-EWR. A record, that still stands.

The following day, November 5, 1970, our flight made the local headlines in Miami. That same day the Newark Star-Ledger, a major newspaper in New Jersey, also ran an article about our record-setting flight.

According to the NAA representative, the old Houston-Newark record time was set in 1947 by an Eastern Air Lines Super Constellation.

At that time no one bothered to pay the required $75 to have NAA officials man timers at the airports in both cities. That made the flight unofficial.

As for us, Eastern paid the $75. plus another $5. The $5 was for Captain Brady to have a Sport License required to make the run.

Something else about setting the record. There were no guarantees we would be able to do it. Had we encountered bad weather or a mechanical problem, we would have had to divert to an alternate airport. That would have canceled our attempt. We were lucky nothing happened.

Shortly after we set the world speed record, other airlines attempted to make their own headlines by trying to set airspeed records.

When that happened, the FAA stopped all attempts by any airline of trying to break world records, citing the disruption of airway corridors. They claimed that this activity made too many airline passengers apprehensive and offered numerous other reasons. Too bad. I know there are other records to be broken. To this day our record still stands.

Shortly afterward, our airline reservations went up. Some say it was because of our flight. Others say it was the beginning of the winter season that would bring our passengers to the warm climate of Florida and the Caribbean islands. I still believe our flight contributed a lot to Eastern Air Line's great image.

ENTER CAPTAIN W. LAIN GUTHRIE

This was not the end of the story of why Eastern had let us do the speed run. Starting in August 1970, Eastern had several months of turmoil having to deal with what one might call, bad press. This was about environmental studies concerning an aircraft's Pressurization and Dump valves, (P&D valve).

The P&D valve is located on jet engines and it is associated with engine fuel controls. After an engine is shut down, the valve opens and relieves pressure in the fuel control and manifold while the aircraft sits.

Sometimes, a quart or so of fuel, kerosene, would vent overboard and land on the ground. Eventually, modifications were made where the fuel would vent into the engine tailpipe and then vent overboard as the aircraft took off.

This improved venting would take place some three hundred feet after lift-off, and according to airline officials, the kerosene would dissipate harmlessly into the air before it struck the ground.

Before those changes, an incident took place on August 1, 1970, that sparked an uproar between Eastern Air Line officials and one of our Miami-based captains.

Captain W. Lain Guthrie would make local, and international headlines for several months. On that day, Captain Guthrie refused to fly his DC-8 until the waste fuel was removed from the engines, and not by the P&D valve. He believed that it was creating an environmental impact on the ground and in the air.

The battle between the captain and Eastern began. Two months later,

Eastern dismissed him for insubordination, saying he had caused frequent and long delays. More headlines.

When he was grounded, other Eastern pilots rallied around him. The resulting outcry forced Eastern to reinstate him with full pay and the industry to cease ground dumping. Thanks to Captain W. Lain Guthrie and other Eastern pilots.

I truly believe, because of all that bad press, Eastern was looking for something to show the public a better image. When we requested to make that speed run, Eastern management saw a golden opportunity to turn bad media into something more positive and allowed us to do the record flight.

I would find it ironic years later, that a member of his family would become the first woman ever to race in the famous Indy 500.

Janet Guthrie made racing headlines all over the world in May 1977. She went on to become one of the world's most elite woman racecar drivers of all time. She also followed in her father's footsteps and became a licensed pilot.

Janet's late husband was Warren Levine, an American Airlines captain. Warren was a good friend of Richie Green who introduced me to him when Richie and I were flight instructing for Wings of Morristown in the 1960s. I found him to be a real gentleman.

As I look back and think about all those months of conflict, and the concern about environmental pollution. How peculiar it was she chose the profession of being a race driver.

Tens of thousands of fans sit in racing stadiums, such as the Indianapolis and Daytona speedways, and are subjected to ear-piercing engine noise from race cars whose speed tops 200 miles per hour.

Aren't their lungs being filled with carbon monoxide exhaust for hours on end? Let's also consider the amount of kerosene spilled on the ground as car handlers rush to get their Indy cars back on the track.

These were the same glitches that led to Captain Guthrie's suspension. Oh well.

MAYDAY

February 2, 1971, Atlanta. It was hot and humid. The captain was Johnny Wilson. We were bound for New Orleans, then on to Mexico City.

Our flight was full of passengers and fuel which had made us close to our max take-off weight, which meant a longer takeoff run. The runway we were to use was 27R which had an uphill grade.

Although it was not normally a problem, John had asked the tower if we could do a rolling takeoff. This means, while on the taxiway, you begin to push your power levers up as you roll into position. Except you don't stop. You keep on accelerating, applying full power as you begin to turn onto the runway and commence your take-off. We did that.

Shortly after we were airborne, the control tower informed us that we had blown over a Cessna 172 and it was upside down on the taxiway.

The C-172 had a bent prop, wing, and rudder. Fortunately, no fuel leaked out of the gas tanks, and most fortunately, no one was injured.

It was another incident where a small aircraft got too close behind a much larger one. The jet blast from our engines went under the wings of the C-172 and it ended up on its back.

Knowing no one was injured, I thought of painting a C-172 underneath the captain's side window. It was similar to what happened when we blew over another aircraft while running up the engines on the Connie. Three more and we would become aces.

Several months later more excitement. The captain was Al Egger, and the Second Officer was Jeff Kaffe. We were on our way to New Orleans

162

from Mexico City.

Of course, this brought us over the Gulf of Mexico. While en route over open water, we're required to monitor the emergency frequencies, 121.5 MHz or 243 MHz. This was done in the event another aircraft was in distress and needed help.

About 50 minutes from landing at MSY we had picked up an aircraft distress call. It wasn't on 121.5MHz, and ATC was not aware of it. It was a twin-engine Lockheed Lodestar broadcasting in the blind.

When we answered his call, he told us that he had to shut down one of his engines due to a malfunction. He was at 12,000 feet, descending because he couldn't maintain his altitude with one engine inoperative, and his other engine was overheating.

When I asked him where he was bound, he replied, "Galveston, Texas." That was when I told him to call a Mayday and get help from the Coast Guard. He said that he didn't want to do that. I asked him how many souls were on board and his position.

When we realized he was in our area, we began scanning the area beneath us. We were cruising at 31,000 feet and he was somewhere 20,000 feet below us.

I contacted ATC and told them what was taking place. Al then requested to descend to a lower altitude to allow us to circle the area and look for him.

Incredibly, Kaffe was looking down from the captain's left-side window and spotted the Lodestar almost directly beneath us.

About that time the Lodestar pilot finally agreed to call in a Mayday. He was at 6,000 feet and still descending. Now that he finally declared a Mayday, a Coast Guard aircraft was launched from Galveston and was proceeding in our direction.

After circling for thirty minutes of keeping the Lodestar in sight, our fuel had become an issue and we couldn't remain on station.

Enter an Eastern DC-8, out of JFK bound for MEX. Its crew had heard our communication with the Lodestar and had asked ATC if they could take over. Which ATC agreed.

163

It wasn't long before the DC-8 spotted us circling and the Lodestar below us, and took over. We climbed back to altitude and continued to MSY.

Upon our arrival, we learned the Lodestar made it to Galveston, just barely, and landed safely. The DC-8 continued on its way to Mexico City. That was not the end of the story.

Eastern had a newspaper called The Falcon which kept its employees informed of what was taking place within our company.

One of their articles was about how this DC-8 crew found the Lodestar in serious trouble over the Gulf of Mexico, and how it guided it to a safe landing.

There was not one word of our part in locating, staying on the station, convincing the crew of the Lockheed to call in a Mayday or of the Coast Guard coming out to meet the distressed aircraft.

Nor any mention of us having to leave the area because our fuel became an issue. The next time Al Egger and I flew together, I told him he needed to have a better P.R. man.

A SHOOTING

A s I moved up in the ranks as a senior first officer, I was able to choose the sequences I wanted to fly to and the cities I wanted for my layovers. Tampa, Florida would be a nice change, with its warm weather, and enjoyable restaurants.

In March 1971, I flew the month with Captain John Tulloss. Whom I had flown with many times before. He, like some other pilots, had his own business. His was killing bugs and termites. He did pest control both inside and outside homes and did quite well.

When he first told me about his business. I chuckled.

John was another one of those World War Two pilots that I flew with while with Eastern.

He was a plane commander who flew B-17s during the war and one who did not talk about his combat missions over Germany.

Although there was one mission he flew that was shared with me by another WWII Eastern captain.

The flight took place on May 13, 1944. The target. Stettin, Germany. Thirteen B-17s of the 303rd Bomb Group led by Captain Leroy E. Daub crossed over Stettin at 24,000 feet.

Tulloss's B-17 named Bonnie B, after his wife, was second in the group. The planes dropped their bombs. Flak filled the air, followed by 35 to 50 ME-09s. The German's top fighter aircraft.

According to the B-17's gunners, the enemy were queuing up for an attack on the B-17s. They were thwarted when four P-51 escorts attacked the ME-109s, shooting down five in their first pass. More were shot down as the battle went on.

Thanks to those P-51s the ME-109s left the 303rd Bomb Group and began an attack on another group of B-17s. Unfortunately, one P-51 was shot down. All thirteen B-17s of the 303rd returned safely. John and the rest of his squadron survived the attack and were happy to get back down on the ground safely.

On one of the layovers that month, John, the second officer, and I had gone to dinner at the hotel, where we were staying, in downtown Tampa. While paying the check, the cashier was having problems changing the tape in her cash register. That took about ten minutes.

Across the street was a strip mall. I had asked John and the second officer if they wanted to go with me to a store called Cash and Carry. Just to look around. They declined my invitation.

As I crossed the street and was about to enter the store I heard the blaring of sirens coming up the street. Police cars and an EMS rolled into the parking lot. The police jumped out of their police car. Guns were drawn and they rushed into the store followed by medics.

I raced to the window and peered in. The police turned and ran toward the window I was looking through. They stopped and looked down. I saw the reason why.

A man was sitting on the floor. He had been shot. His shirt was off and his back was bloody. Traces of what appeared to be sinew hung from the large open wound in his back.

While the EMS crew tended to the wounded man, the police came out and asked those of us who had gathered near the window if we saw the holdup or the robbers. No one did. They then asked us to help search for the bullet.

When the man was shot, the bullet had gone through him and had exited out his back. It had struck an aluminum post that held the window in place, making a hole the size of a quarter through the post.

One of the officers stuck a pencil in the hole. It angled upward at about a 20-degree angle.

Twenty minutes later, we gave up looking. The spent bullet could have gone anywhere.

On the way back to the hotel, I started to think. Had it not been for the cashier having difficulty changing the tape, I could have been in the store when the man was shot.

The following week, I was back in Tampa and staying at the same hotel. I went back to Cash and Carry to inquire about the man who had been shot and asked one of the employees who was there that night about the robbery.

He said the robbers had come into the store, each had long hair, wore masks, and had their guns drawn. They walked over to where customer service was located, which is next to the front window of the store.

Behind the counter, was a new assistant manager and it was his first day alone on the job. At first, he said he thought what was happening was part of his training. When the robbers asked him to open the safe, he realized it wasn't, and he refused to comply.

It was then one of the robbers shot him at point-blank range with a 357 Magnum pistol. Luckily, the bullet went through him without hitting anything vital. He was expected to make a full recovery.

The second part of the employee's story was more bizarre. After the bandits made good their escape, something strange happened that would lead to their early capture.

According to the employee, the two men sped away in a car they had stolen earlier. Several blocks after making their getaway, they turned down a side street. They jumped out of the car, discarded the fake wigs they were wearing, jumped into another car they had parked there earlier, and drove off.

They never noticed a woman sitting on her front porch watching their strange behavior. Even though it was nighttime, the woman managed to jot down the license plate of the car as they drove away.

Later that night, while watching the local news, she learned about the shooting and called the police and gave them the license plate number.

The police ran it through their computers and had come up with a name and address, and both men were arrested.

I was grateful the store manager was going to be okay and that I was not in the store at the time of the robbery. It showed me, once again, how life can change in a heartbeat.

A PASSENGER'S PUNCH

For the most part, the rest of the year was normal, despite the behavior of mother nature. Good weather, bad weather, star-lit nights, ice, and snow-covered runways were to be expected. Approaches with low ceilings and visibility were part of the game.

On the other hand, beautiful sunrises and sunsets, oceans with their deep blue, and layovers with sandy beaches nearby were enjoyable ways to mark another trek around the sun. Hello, 1972.

Three months into the new year, things were going well. On March 9, 1972, we were passing through Atlanta on our way to Houston. The Captain was Bruce Mc Dougal.

For whatever reason, this route always required a plane change. Which meant another flight crew was waiting to take over our inbound flight and continue it to its destination. In turn, we had to hustle to our next flight which was located at the end of another concourse.

When we relieved the inbound crew, they had briefed us on what was in the maintenance logbook, etc. The inbound cabin crew remained on board to continue the flight to its destination. As the captain and I went about our cockpit pre-flight, we had left the cockpit door open.

An elderly gentleman came to the door and asked the captain if he could look inside. The captain invited him in and explained some of our instruments to him.

The gentleman then told us how much he and his wife enjoyed their flight from Newark. The captain thanked him and said we were not the pilots but would be the crew flying him and his wife to Houston.

After a few more questions he left and went back to his seat in the coach section. Several minutes later our senior stewardess rushed into the cockpit and said a man just punched out his wife and was in a tussle with other passengers.

As the captain called for security, he told me to go back and try to resolve the problem. When I did, I realized it was the same man who had been in the cockpit.

As I tried to calm him down, I glanced at his wife. Her lip was split, bleeding, and started to swell. By that time, airport security had come on board and the man calmed down.

He and his wife were quickly escorted off the flight. The captain made an announcement apologizing for the man's actions. Tranquility had been returned.

The senior flight attendant then told us what she thought caused the incident. According to her, the wife was angry at her husband because she thought he was flirting with the stewardess while en route from Newark.

She then accused him of doing it while they were on the ground in Atlanta. That was when he smacked her. More letter writing to the chief pilot's office by the captain. Unfortunately, things like this happen and you get involved whether you wanted to or not.

A SNAKE IN A SUITCASE?

Good news had come my way at the beginning of April. I was to be sent to Miami and begin flight training for my Airline Transport Rating (ATR.) Long before I could do that, I had to take an FAA written exam. The exam required knowledge about every facet of flight the FAA could conjure up, and then some. It went on for hours. The long and short. I passed it.

Several weeks before the training was to start, I had flown several flights to the Caribbean. On one of the flights, our crew was required to go through customs in Puerto Rico along with our passengers, before continuing on to Newark.

Like most airports that have custom agents, a separate inspection line was used for flight crew members who had flown the inbound flight.

This allowed the crews to bypass the passenger inspection lines. Normally the inspectors would just wave us through so we could prepare for our next outbound flight.

On this occasion, one of our Eastern flight attendants was pass-riding in her uniform and tried to pass through the crew line with us.

The agent waved us through and then asked her if she was part of our crew. She said no but told him if she went through with the passengers, she would probably miss her outbound flight to Miami.

He asked her to open her suitcase. She hesitated, then reluctantly opened it.

As the inspector began sorting through her belongings, he suddenly pulled out a large wiggling black item and yelled out. "Snake! Snake!" He threw it on the floor and started stomping on it.

Meanwhile, the passengers started scattering. While all this was going on, the flight attendant was yelling at the inspector that it wasn't her snake.

It turned out that it wasn't a snake after all. It was a black vibrating double-edge dildo for women. When the passengers realized what it was, they all laughed. Talk about embarrassment.

MORE TRAINING

On April 10th I got to meet my ATR flight instructor, Captain Warren B. Hill.

Eastern used two Aero-Commander 500B's, 6291X and 354MA, for the training. They were sleek-looking twin-engine aircraft.

The Commander had two 290 hp air-cooled Lycoming engines, a 49-foot wing span, stood 14' 6", and was 37 feet long. Its belly appeared to be only inches from the ground. It held 2 pilots and 4 passengers. Although it had a service ceiling of 19,000 feet, all our training flights were done well below that.

One of the quirks about the Commander, we were forewarned, was that you had to use the rudder pedals gingerly for nose wheel steering while taxing. Larger aircraft have a control wheel that is next to the captain for nose-wheel steering of the aircraft. Thereby having better control of the aircraft while taxing.

Then came the first flight.

I was not the only pilot who was being trained. With me, was an Atlanta-based pilot who had chosen to remain as a second officer where he had super seniority. This meant, though he hadn't flown an aircraft in years, because he was senior, he would be first trained.

Our instructor sat in the right seat, and the ATL pilot sat in the left. The engines were started and we began our taxiing from the ramp to the runway.

The pilot, who had not flown in years, applied too much back-and-forth rudder pressure and lost directional control. Suddenly, we were heading directly toward a parked aircraft.

Warren quickly took control and avoided a collision.

"Gingerly! Apply the rudders gingerly!" He repeated.

As we rolled into position on the runway, the tower had cleared us for an immediate take-off. Another aircraft was on final approach for a landing on the runway we were using for take-off. The pilot went full-throttle on both engines.

I was in the comfortable seat just behind the pilots, but watching intently. We rolled about 100 feet when, unexpectedly, not really, the captain to be, over-controlled the rudder pedals again, losing control of the Commander. This time we were headed for the tulips, grass turf, and off the runway, straight toward the terminal.

I sat up ready to abandon ship. If we busted this up, we had to get out before the plane caught fire. Thankfully, Warren quickly took control again and got us back on the centerline. He then told this pilot it was his airplane and off we went. The rest of the flight went well. Then it was my turn.

When I pushed the throttles forward, it soon became a balancing act with the rudder pedals. It reminded me of my days teaching students to fly a tail-wheel aircraft. Once we were airborne, I found the Commander to be a beautiful bird to fly.

The next four days were like all the other flight training sessions. We practiced engine failures, instrument approaches, go-arounds, stalls, and all the rest that went with training.

On the fifth day, after eight hours of flight training, we took our proficiency check for the ATR certificate. We both passed and returned to our respective bases.

Eastern used the 6291X from June 1965 to November 1975. The 354MA was used from April 1967 to November 1969. Unfortunately, the 6219X had sustained damage to it several times, all taxiing accidents caused by its tricky nose-wheel steering.

Weeks later section 28 was posted. I was not on the to-be upgraded captains list. Disappointed? Yes. That year not many pilots were upgraded. I was more disappointed when I was not upgraded the following year. Nor the one after that, which was at the beginning of 1973.

EASTERN FLIGHT 401

I t was late at night, December 29, 1972. Christmas and festive celebrations were on the menu as the new year approached. At approximately 11:30 p.m. Eastern Standard Time, Eastern Air Lines flight 401, a brand-new Lockheed 1011 Tristar jet 310EA, was making its final approach to runway 9L, some 18 miles west of Miami's International Airport. Onboard were 163 passengers, 3 pilots, and ten flight attendants.

The flight had departed JFK earlier that Friday at 9:20 p.m. In command was Captain Robert Loft with 32 years as an Eastern Air Lines pilot. Assisting him were First Officer, Albert Stockstill, 13 years a veteran Eastern pilot, and Second Officer, Don Repo, 17 years as a veteran flight engineer with Eastern.

Also in the cockpit, riding on the jump seat, was a company employee, Technical Officer Angelo Donadeo, who was returning to Miami from an assignment in New York.

The cabin crew flight attendants, were Adrienne Hamilton, the senior flight attendant. Assisting her were, Mercedes Ruiz, Sue Tebbs, Trudy Smith, Dorothy Warnock, Patricia Ghyssels, Beverly Jean Roposa, Patricia Georgia, Stephanie Stanich, and Sharon Transue. All well-trained flight attendants.

Up until their final approach, everything had been routine.

I will refer to excerpts from NTSB's report #NTSB-AAR-73-14, dated 6/14/1973. The information was taken from the aircraft's flight recorder and Flight's 401 cockpit voice recorder, CVR.

When the landing gear was lowered, Stockstill noticed that the green lights for the landing gear that indicated the gear was down-and-locked were normal, except the nose landing gear was not illuminated.

Later during the investigation, NTSB inspectors found that the bulb had burnt out. The crew cycled the landing gear again, but there was still no nose wheel green light. At that point, the nose gear could be lowered manually if needed.

It was then that the captain told the tower they were abandoning their approach and requested to enter a holding pattern. Which was granted.

Flight 401 then climbed to 2,000 feet and had entered a holding pattern over the Everglades. Mind you, at that time of night, it was pitch-black, not much of a horizon, and the plane was still eighteen miles from the airport.

From that distance, it was only a speck of light, if that, as I have experienced many times while approaching Miami at night for runway 9L.

The L-1011, a wide-body aircraft, has a huge cockpit. It also has an access door to the avionics compartment below the crew's feet.

After removing the landing gear light assembly, Second Officer Repo let himself down into the pit, the avionics compartment.

He wanted to confirm via a small porthole, that the nose landing gear was down and locked. At that point, Donadeo had asked if he could be of help. Repo said yes, then Donadeo went down into the pit.

In the meantime, Captain Loft instructed Stockstill to put the L-1011 on autopilot, to maintain their altitude. Which Stockstill did.

One needs to fully understand the workings of the autopilot flight system of the L-1011 to fathom what happened next. It can become quite involved. To the layperson, it's meaningless. To us pilots who flew the L-1011, this system was critical.

For the next 80 seconds the aircraft-maintained level flight. Then it descended 100 feet, on its own. It flew level for another two minutes, then began another gradual descent on its own, which was never noticed by the crew.

When the plane lost another 250 feet, it triggered the altitude C-cord. A cockpit chime, located under the flight engineer's workstation lets the crew know that the altitude hold had disengaged.

Unfortunately, Repo was down in the avionics compartment and probably did not hear it. Nor was there any indication on the CVR that the C-cord chime was heard by the two pilots.

When I started flying the Tristar in December of 1976, one of the first things I noticed was the noise level of the aircraft's pack fans that were used for air-conditioning and heating the cockpit.

Occasionally it required you to raise your voice so the other pilot could hear you. I believe the fan noise drowned out the C-cord when it sounded.

50 seconds later, the aircraft was at half its assigned altitude.

The NTSB investigating team believed the autopilot switched modes when the captain accidentally brushed against it as he turned to speak to Repo who was still in the avionics compartment.

Modes refer to the control wheel steering of the control columns for each pilot. They also denote the pitch angle of the aircraft's nose. Making it appear to be in a slight nose-high attitude. Even though it may be descending.

Once the plane passed 250 feet, the altitude alert, designed to warn the pilots of an inadvertent deviation from the selected altitude, also went unnoticed.

Investigators believed this was due to the crew being distracted by the nose gear light and because the flight engineer was not in his seat. They concluded that the crew might have been frustrated and fatigued trying to determine if the nose gear was actually down and locked.

At the time, the autopilot was still engaged and in the correct mode that allowed the first officer to make turns. Unfortunately, the altitude hold of the autopilot was not.

While the jet was making a turn and still in the holding pattern, is when the first officer first noticed the altitude discrepancy. Ten seconds later it was too late for any correction.

The aircraft was traveling at 227 miles per hour when it crashed into the Everglades swamp. The left wingtip struck the ground first. Then the left engine and the left main landing gear hit. When the main fuselage hit the ground, it continued to move through the grass and water, breaking up as it went.

Of the 163 passengers on board, 101 died either from the impact, or after being rescued, from their wounds. Of the ten flight attendants, nine would survive. Unfortunately, Flight attendant Stephanie Stanich perished in the crash.

All three of the cockpit crew perished. Captain Loft died while trapped in the wreckage. First Officer Stockstill was killed on impact.

The second officer Repo, although rescued, succumbed to his injuries at the hospital. Technical officer Donadeo, although badly injured would recover from his injuries.

RESCUE, AFTERMATH, HERO'S

The moment of the crash was witnessed by two men. Robert Marquis and Ray Dickensin were out in their airboat frog-gigging. They responded immediately and sped to the crash site.

All night long, and the following day, they rescued people and brought them out of the crash site, and brought other rescuers to the site. It was not without their own injuries.

Marquis received burns to his face, arms, and legs from spilled jet fuel from the plane's ruptured fuel tanks. For his efforts, he would receive the Humanitarian Award from the National Air Disaster Alliance/Foundation and the Alumitec -Airboat Hero Award- from the American Airboat Search and Rescue Association.

The surviving flight attendants, despite their own injuries, were credited with their quick-thinking actions. Such as warning survivors of the danger of lighting matches, due to the jet fuel that lay on top of the swamp water. To help encourage them, they began singing Christmas carols to help keep up their spirits and to draw rescue teams to the crash site.

At home, and shortly after flight 401 disappeared off the radar came a telephone call to the then vice-president of operations, Frank Borman. Informing him that the flight had crashed in the Everglades.

Before the night ended, he was wading through the swamp, among the wreckage, in street shoes, helping rescue those who had survived into helicopters. What vice president of any company would do that?

Afterward, the NTSB'S final report, AAR-73-14, dated 6/14/1973, cited the crash as a pilot error. for the "failure of the flight crew to monitor the flight instruments during the final four minutes of the flight and to detect an unexpected descent soon enough to prevent impact with the ground. Their preoccupation with a malfunction of the nose landing gear distracted their attention from their instruments and allowed the descent to go unnoticed."

Then came one of the most controversial air crashes in the history of aviation. Ghosts!

THE GHOSTS OF FLIGHT 401

Flight 401's legacy did not end in the swamp. It wasn't long after the accident came mysterious reports of seeing the ghosts of two of the pilots who had died, on other Eastern L-1011 Tristars.

At first, those stories were shrugged aside. When more than twenty crew members swear they too, knew and had seen the dead pilots on their flight, people began to wonder.

Even several passengers also stated they had seen these apparitions when shown photographs of Captain Bob Loft, and Second Officer Don Repo.

As the stories began to spread, more questions were asked, books were written, and movies were made about the accident. The paranormal sightings, and apparitions, continue for many, many, years. To give you an idea, some of the testimonies of these sightings were as follows.

An Eastern vice-president, allegedly spoke with a captain he thought was in charge of his flight, only to realize he was the deceased, Captain Loft. Who quickly vanished.

A female passenger inquires a flight attendant about a quiet and unresponsive man in an Eastern Air Lines uniform, who is sitting in the seat next to her, then suddenly disappears in full view of them and other passengers.

The woman goes hysterical when shown a sheet of photographs of some of the Eastern flight engineers, and identifies Don Repo as the man that was sitting next to her.

There were similar reports time and time again. Most of the apparitions seen were of the second officer, Don Repo. Who was reported to have been seen in the galley of aircraft 318EA several times.

What caused the supposed hauntings, that's up for debate. There were many different opinions. There was one belief that stands out above the rest. Specifically, salvaged parts from Flight 401's wreckage.

These were used as replacement parts for our Eastern Tristars. Following their replacements, specifically on aircraft 318EA, came the first reports of those apparitions. The aircraft was eventually sold to Cathay Pacific Airways in February 1989.

One unique feature of the L-1011 was, the main galley was located below the main cabin floor. Access was by the use of two narrow elevators, which could accommodate one person each. It was also used for serving carts. Two flight attendants usually worked the galley during flight.

The galley itself contained ovens, a refrigerator for pre-packaged food, and a storage area for the serving carts. It also featured a small round window for those who worked in the galley to be able to look outside. Largely to prevent them from getting claustrophobic.

The one thing that always seemed to occur when flying at those high altitudes, the galley window would frost over. Since the outside air temperature could exceed -50 degrees below zero.

With that in mind, the window acted as a mirror, and you would see your reflection. Ergo, after many stories of ghosts in the galley, some flight attendants who were not familiar with it, and saw their reflection, thought it was Repo, and made a hasty exit.

According to a statement made by one flight attendant said. When she entered the galley from the elevator, she saw a man in an Eastern uniform fixing the galley oven, then disappeared. She later identified the man as Repo. The aircraft, 318EA.

One of the most ghostly encountered moments in the galley came with grave overtones.

Flight Attendant, Faye Merryweather said she saw Repo's face looking out at her from an oven on 318EA. Alarmed, she called two of her colleagues, one of whom was the flight engineer who had been a friend of Repo's, and recognized him instantly.

All three heard Repo warn them too, "Watch out for fire on this aircraft!"

The plane encountered serious engine trouble and the last leg of its flight was canceled.

There were other various reports of Repo's presence, some in the galley, some coming from the avionics compartment located below the floor in the cockpit. But the question was always, why so many references to the galley?

One possible answer came from the use of one of the parts from the destroyed aircraft 310EA. Its galley was used to replace the galley for aircraft 318EA. Although there were parts used from aircraft 310 on our other L-1011s, none had any reports of seeing ghosts.

Of course, all of these visions were poo-pooed by Eastern management. They were not about to boast of having ghosts on their aircraft.

As to Eastern pilots, many were very skeptical of these so-called sightings. Others, not so sure. For myself, years later when I flew the L-1011 as a first officer for two years (12/05/1976-10/13/1978) I never encountered any of the so-called apparitions, but there was one incident that did take place. More on that later.

There did come a time, years later, when 318EA was parked on an out-of-the-way ramp at San Juan's International Airport and a long way from prying eyes.

A group of pilots from Boston, who were involved with the paranormal, and exorcism, exorcised aircraft 318EA. After that, to my knowledge, the apparitions stopped.

BARBARA RIDES THE JUMP SEAT

I n May of 1973, I was flying the month with Captain Barney Hutain and Second Officer Jim Russell along with an extremely long layover in Fort Lauderdale. Think of warm weather, sandy beaches, bathing suits, and fine restaurant dining.

With that thought in mind, I decided to bring my wife Barbara along. Except, our sequence of flights would take us from Newark to San Juan carrying passengers. From San Juan to Miami, it would be a late-night freighter carrying cargo, and no passengers.

Eastern, at the time, had used its B-727'S QC'S, quick-change, for flying freight. Where it could be converted from a passenger service into a cargo-carrying aircraft in a short period.

It also meant she would have to pass-ride from Newark to Miami and meet me there. Unfortunately, there was no guarantee she could get on the flight because it was already booked in full.

When I mentioned the possibility of not having her come at all to Barney. He pointed out a clause in our pilot's contract where a family member could legally ride the jump seat.

That being, that our cargo flight operated under FAA Part 135, not FAA Part 121, passenger operation. Part 135 allows a broader definition of what you can, or cannot do.

Come May 9th we flew from EWR-SJU where Barb enjoyed the three hours and thirty minutes of Eastern first-class service. Later that night she was sitting on our jump seat in a chilly cockpit, where the outside air-temp was -50 degrees below zero, eating a cold box supper.

Three hours later we landed in Miami and parked on a ramp near one of our hangars where our cargo was then off-loaded. As we exited the airplane and made our way down our forward airstairs, waiting for us was another flight crew.

At first, I felt a little uneasy knowing we might be asked about my wife being on board, but nothing was said. When I called out her name to follow me, I heard one of the pilots who were taking over our aircraft say to another. "Hey. That's our new female pilot Eastern hired. She's good-looking."

It was obvious they were referring to Easterns first female pilot. Barbara Barret. Who at that time was being trained as a second officer on our B-727s. I wasn't about to disagree with them.

It was an extremely wonderful layover with my lovely wife. Palm trees, Sandy beaches, bathing suits, fine dining.

Barney Hutain, was another ex-Army Air Force pilot who flew B-24s during WW II. Probably one of the few who survived a mid-air collision with another B-24.

It happened, according to Barney, as they were practicing formation flying while in flight training. The left wing of the other aircraft struck his aircraft near its tail section. Although he was able to land safely, the other aircraft's crew wasn't so lucky. They were forced to bail out of an uncontrollable aircraft. Fortunately, all survived.

SWIM FOR YOUR LIFE

The following layover in Fort Lauderdale was completely different. Jim Russell and I had just finished lunch at Carlos and Pepe's a Mexican Restaurant located on S.E. 17th Street. Just a short distance from the hotel where we were staying.

As we were crossing over the S.E. 17th Street draw bridge that spans the Stranahan River, I noticed a 60-foot all-day drift-fishing boat.

It was about to dock at Pier 66's Hotel and Marina which sits right on the river and across the street from the hotel where we were staying.

The river is part of the Intra-Coastal Waterway that leads to the Atlantic Ocean just a mile or so away.

Seeing the boat aroused my curiosity and I told Jim I was going to see what kind of fish they had caught. He elected to go back to the hotel, reminding me that Barney wanted to leave for the airport within the hour.

I said okay and proceeded down the pier only to find the boat had docked to pick up six passengers who were waiting to board.

There were several other onlookers, who like me, were just as curious about the fishing boat. As we watched, the boat crew laid down a four-foot iron plank for those who were to board from the pier to the boat.

I started on my way back to our hotel, but for some reason, I hesitated and continued watching. The first three people boarded safely, the fourth, a woman, probably in her mid-fifties, stepped on the plank and took another step.

The Intra-Coastal Waterway is an extremely busy waterway. All sizes and types from row boats, to party boats, to yachts, make their way from the river to ocean, from ocean to river. When they do, they make wakes. Those wakes tend to push and pull against other boats, no matter what the size.

About that time another large fishing boat passed by, its wake pushed against the docked boat, then pulled it away from the pier. The plank, and the woman on it, fell into the river. Then disappeared beneath the waves.

Someone screamed. "She can't swim!" A man leaped from the pier, and he too disappeared. No one either on the pier or on the boat moved.

Without thinking, I took a huge breath and jumped off the pier. As I did the man had popped to the surface but he seemed disoriented.

I found the woman three feet below the surface. She was thrashing about, trying to come up. I got behind her so she couldn't grab me in her panic and take us both down.

I once found out how strong a person can be when they didn't know how to swim and thought they were drowning. He grabbed me from the front in a bear hug, pinning my arms to my side. After a short struggle, I managed to free myself and get him back to shore. He was only nine years old.

Luckily, the woman wasn't fighting me and seemed more relaxed once I had her in my grasp and brought her to the surface.

Another problem arose. All three of us were between the fishing boat and the pier. Due to the wake of passing boats the fishing boat was being pushed back toward the pier. With us three in between.

I yelled to the man to head for the openings between the pilings with me and the woman right behind him. Hoping not to be crushed by the fishing boat banging into them.

Just then the captain put his engines in full reverse. The sound of roaring engines and thrashing propeller blades filled the air. The good news, the stern of the boat was swinging away from us. The bad news. Those churning propellers created a suction, and with the river's strong current, we were being pulled toward them.

Only when the captain came out of reverse did the engine noise and trashing blades stop. As the three of us drifted, life rings were tossed down to us and we grabbed hold of them.

Still, there was this feeling of being pulled under, until I realized I had worn ankle boots on the trip. The only time I had ever done so. They had filled with water and were acting like miniature anchors. I managed to remove them and tossed them to the boat crew.

It took the boat crew several minutes before we were all hauled out of the water. I'm patted on the back, people wanted to shake my hand, and the captain couldn't thank me enough and offered me and my family free passage on his boat anytime. I thanked him for his fine offer.

My real concern was to get back to my hotel and get ready for my flight back to Newark. When I asked the captain to let me off the boat and back onto the pier, he told me that I'll have to wait. He had to get the man who was in the water with us to the hospital. With that, we began to motor to the other side of the river and dock.

While we motored, the captain filled me in about the people who ended up in the water. The guy who jumped in first was wearing very thick glasses. When he hit the water, they were knocked off, and he couldn't see very well. That was why he appeared to be disoriented.

Worst of all, he had scraped against the barnacles that were encrusted on the pilings causing deep lacerations on both his arms and legs and he was worried about him getting a serious infection. The man in the water was also the woman's brother. The woman who screamed. "She can't swim." Was her daughter. Who could not swim either.

As for me. I got a ride back to the hotel from the captain. The man who had cuts and scrapes was taken to the hospital by his family.

I stopped by Barney and Jim's rooms and told them what happened. At first, they thought I was kidding, until they realized how wet my clothes were. Then congratulated me on saving the woman's life.

Even with all that, I still had time to shower and rid myself of the brackish water I had been treading, for what seemed like a lifetime. We also made our departure to Newark on time.

En route to Newark, I took stock of what it had cost me. First, I was fortunate not to scrape against the pilings when I jumped into the water. Or get sucked into the boats thrashing propellers.

Clothes wise. It was the first time I had worn a new shirt, new pants, new ankle boots, and a new wristwatch. All ruined.

Then there was a $100, 1969 First Edition Commemorative President Eisenhower Pocket Watch Barbara had given me years before. Ruined by salt water.

It now lies stowed in my dresser drawer. A reminder, that I was glad I was able to help keep someone from drowning. Regardless of the cost.

CAPTAIN ON THE LOCKHEED ELECTRA

In August of 1973, came two great surprises. The first came on August 30, when I was fortunate to fly with a captain, I had met ten years previously but had never flown with him. The one I felt was responsible for my having had an interview with Eastern in December of 1963. Captain Pete Coxhead. Who by then, had become a check captain.

It was a wonderful day of flying and catching up on past years during that eight-hour turn-around, EWR-SJU-EWR.

The second, came a day later when the results of another section 28 bid were posted for December. I had applied for a captain's position on the Lockheed Electra, L-188, a four-engine turboprop. Much to my happy surprise, I was awarded a captain's position.

Flight training was to commence in Miami beginning in November. Flight training begins with the customary ground school covering all aircraft systems. Followed by those many four-plus hours in the flight simulator. You know. Engine/failures/fires, decompressions, hydraulic and electrical failures, instrument approaches, missed approaches, and simulating ditching the L-188.

Eastern first started its Electra service on January 12, 1959. Growing to almost 100 aircraft. Then slowly, as the newer B-727s, DC-9s, and other newer jet aircraft were purchased, the Electra that graced the skies for Eastern for nearly eleven years, we're beginning to be phased out.

By the time I was being trained on it, only a handful were left.

Those that were, were only used on the Eastern Shuttle. During our training, rumors abounded with talk that the company was going to park them all. As in, taking them out of service. That sort of put a damper on being upgraded to captain.

Of course, the Electra wasn't without a past history of mysterious and unforeseeable accidents. Namely, a Braniff Air Line Lockheed Electra in 1959 and a Northwest Air Line Lockheed Electra in 1960. Both disintegrated in mid-flight.

Those accidents, the cause, and the solution were well described in Robert Serling's book, The Electra Story, which was first published in August 1963 and one I had read at the time.

The cause was flaws in the wing structure. Due to harmonics, the twisting motions of the wing, and its engines, led to the failures. This also led to some redesign of the propellers and the wing.

It also caused in-flight airspeed restrictions. Initially, the aircraft was designed to fly at 400 mph cruising airspeed. Upon finding the cause of the accidents, in-flight airspeeds were reduced to 315 mph, and later 295 mph. After modifications had been made to the wing structure, all restrictions were removed at the end of 1960.

When being trained on any aircraft, there would usually be two or three pilots being trained at the same time. In this case, another first officer had joined me. Bill Cameron.

Bill Cameron always appeared, at least to me, as a happy-go-lucky individual. A little over six feet tall, stocky build, and a keen sense of humor, helped make our flight training seem to go quickly.

We would usually study, grab a beer, and eat dinner together during the training.

The hotel we stayed at was called, The Crossway Inn, and was located directly across the street from the training center.

It was a little past six p.m. on one evening. The sun had set and what few lights along 36th Street were dimly illuminated. I had just knocked on Bill's door for us to go to dinner. As he opened it, came the sound of screeching tires from the other side of the building, followed by a very loud whoomph.

I knew someone was hit by a car and ran to the other side of the building. Laying in the middle of the road, was a man curled in a fetal position groaning.

I ran to his side and knelt beside him. Just one look told me he was in pretty bad shape. I glanced toward the car that had hit him. It appeared to be at least forty-to-fifty feet away with no headlights on. Its driver was standing outside his car and just stood there.

Then another guy had come running from a pay telephone that was at a gas station next to our hotel and knelt beside me. He told me he was an off-duty policeman and had called for an ambulance.

I knew there wasn't much we could do for the injured man, except wait for the ambulance. The man took several more deep breaths, then no more. I thought he had died.

When that happened the cop began to retrieve the man's wallet. I stopped him and asked him what he was doing. He told me he was looking for the man's ID so he could contact the man's family. Just then a police car and ambulance arrived, and they took over.

The police seemed to know the guy who said he was a cop and were making notes from his statement. Another officer was measuring the length of the skid marks, and the distance from the front of the car to where the man lay in the street

I asked the police if they wanted any information from me. They just asked me one question. "Did I see the accident?"

"No."

"Okay. Thank you." That was all they had asked me.

A couple of things puzzled me about the accident. One was the quick arrival of the ambulance. The second one was a little more puzzling.

As I walked back to the sidewalk from the middle of the road and turned around. I could see the guy that was hit, in the same curled position on the stretcher as he was lying on the ground.

I would find out that the ambulance happened to be in the area when the cop called in the accident. The other. The paramedics had used a scoop. A scissor-type stretcher to pick him up, so as not to cause any more internal damage as they put him into the ambulance.

The following morning, while having breakfast at a local dinner, I read the newspaper's report on the accident. It said the man died en route to the hospital. I still believed he died while the two of us were kneeling by him.

Sitting at the counter next to me was a woman discussing the previous night's accident with a waitress. She was telling her that someone had robbed the man while he lay in the street.

I interrupted their conversation and told them I was one of the two guys trying to help the man who was hit. That the other guy was an off-duty policeman who was looking in the man's wallet for identification to help to notify the man's family. No one was robbing him.

They looked at me as though I wasn't there and went back to telling each other more lies about the man being robbed. I just shook my head, got up, and left the restaurant. No matter what, some people just don't want to hear the facts.

Weeks later, Bill and I had completed all the necessary ground school. The simulator training, check-rides, and the rest of the bundle that goes along with upgrading.

Then came the day we were to take our in-flight proficiency check-ride with an FAA inspector. As usual, it comes in two parts.

The first was a separate forty-five-minute session, oral, on my knowledge of Electra's systems. To be followed by two hours of flying the Electra and doing all the required maneuvers: engine failures, instrument approaches, missed approaches, and holding patterns. You get the idea.

Because I was senior to Bill, I got to go first. Forty-five minutes later, after passing the oral, I had to wait for Bill to complete his.

While waiting, I was told by one of our L-188 instructors, Eastern may well cancel our training now because they're having serious thoughts of parking all Electra's. As in, taking them out of service. This meant we would have to go back to our base without a type rating, or four stripes on our uniform.

In the meantime, Bill had passed his oral. Then it was out to the flight line. Seniority ruled and I was the first to fly. Two hours later, the required maneuvers and check-ride were over. But no word from the FAA inspector as to my status on becoming a captain.

For the next two hours, I sat in the passenger cabin waiting for Bill to complete his check ride.

After we landed we went through a 45-minute de-briefing. Whereupon, the inspector had congratulated both of us, signed the necessary papers, and presented us with a temporary type-rating on the Lockheed Electra. As we finished signing them, we get some unwanted news.

Two other pilots were taking their check rides after us and were also being upgraded to captain. They had taken our airplane but were called back while in flight. Check-ride canceled.

No captain upgrades for them. No more flight training on the L-188 until further notice. Boy was those two guys pissed. Especially after going through all the ground school, simulator, and pre-rating ride checks.

They were sent back to their base with no type rating, no captain slot, and back to being a first officer.

As it turned out, Bill and I were the last two pilots to get a type rating on the L-188.

Eastern would eventually park the Electrics, but not at that time.

A CHRISTMAS TO REMEMBER

December 20, 1973. My first flight as captain. With me is my mother-in-law. Not really. It was a name that was jokingly given to a check captain who was required to fly with a new captain for the first twenty-five flight hours. As per FAA regulations.

Technically, he was the pilot in command and would be the one to sign all the necessary flight papers. After the twenty-five hours were completed, the new captain would be responsible for the flight.

For the next three days, we made several round trips from LaGuardia to Montreal, and back to LaGuardia. That gave me the required twenty-five hours of flight time.

December 25, 1973. I received the best Christmas present anyone could ever ask for. After nine years, eleven months, and 28 days since my date of hire with Eastern, I got to fly my first flight as a captain. Some twenty years after my first solo on August 22, 1954.

It was something I had dreamt about ever since I first heard the Eastern Air Lines commercials on the radio in the 1940s.

It was a round-trip shuttle flight, EWR-BOS-EWR.

Afterward, a group of pilots I had known for over nine years at Eastern, were waiting for me. They congratulated me on my first flight as a captain. Then proceeded to rip the shirt off my back and autograph it.

This was common practice for a new captain. Of course, I had brought another one with me.

While I was changing shirts, Floyd Hall, the president of Eastern Air Lines at that time, walked into our crew lounge. Talk about a surprise.

He wished all of us a Merry Christmas, congratulated me on being a new captain, shook my hand, and then left to catch a flight to Miami.

The Electra was a superb aircraft to fly. Although it had a service ceiling of 32,000 feet, our shuttle flying was usually held to no more than 20,000 feet. It cruised at 320 mph. Had a fuel capacity of 5400 gallons, and a max range of 2500 miles. Power plants were 4 Allison 501-D-13 turboprops, that used Jet-A fuel.

Those engines had a sound of their very own. Every time I would hear or see one taxing, it sounded as though they were going 300 mph on the ground.

Alas, my time as a captain would be short-lived. I would fly the Electra two more times before it was taken out of service and parked.

On January 7th, 1974 I ferried an Electra to Fort Lauderdale, where it was then taken out of service. Other Electra's were flown to Miami for the same reason.

It was also fuel crunch time for America. The sale of gasoline, at that time, was a mere 53 cents per gallon and still rising. The cause was a fuel embargo.

I can remember seeing dozens of fuel tankers anchored miles offshore as we made our approach to land in FLL. They had sat there day after day while people waited in long lines to have their automobiles fueled. That was if the gas station was flying a green flag. Many a temper was tested.

A month later the Electra's got a reprieve and were put back into service. I was assigned to go to Miami and fly one back to Newark.

My crew and I had arrived late in the evening on March 22nd. The aircraft we were to fly was parked at the hangar and had undergone a final maintenance check.

I filled out the normal dispatch release and due to the embargo, fueled to the max, although the flight didn't require it.

As I arrived at the aircraft, our maintenance team had just completed replacing a leaking propeller seal in the number two engine. To assure all was well, had run the engine and shut it down.

As I stood and looked at the engine from the front, I had noticed fluid dripping off the back of the wing behind it. I mentioned it to one of the mechanics who said it was residue from the prop seal, which it was.

Then I noticed there was fluid dripping from inside the wheel well. When I realized it wasn't fluid from the prop seal, but kerosene, I pointed it out to them.

At first, they said it was prop seal oil that got sucked into the wheel well when they ran the engine. When I insisted it was kerosene, they examined it further. They then realized it was a fuel leak coming from a hairline crack inside the left main wheel well.

To repair the leakage, they began to put FAA-approved putty on it to seal the crack. I told them once I started the engines, and the vibrations from them, there was no way in hell that the putty was going to hold. If that happened, the fuel would be accumulating in the wheel well while in flight. Not a good idea.

The lead mechanic answered. "Captain. If you're worried about blowing up in flight. It won't happen. The slip-stream will siphon it away from the aircraft."

My response to that was. "How about coming along with us? Just in case." Even though I knew I was going to refuse to accept the aircraft under those conditions. He looked at me and said. "No thanks. I'm staying on the ground."

Late in the afternoon of the following day, my crew and I went to where we had left the aircraft parked. It was still there, but now the left wheel well was surrounded by a team of mechanics, and they didn't look happy.

I would quickly learn the cause of their discontent. Since I had fueled to the max, the heat of the day had expanded the fuel. This caused pressure to build inside the tank and it expanded the crack to where more fuel was leaking out.

The long and short of it. They had to de-fuel the aircraft, open the area of the wing near the wheel well and repair the crack from the inside. It took a month before that Electra was back on the line.

Eastern didn't officially retire its entire Electra fleet until late October 1977.

The oil embargo had a dire effect on the airline industry. It meant higher fuel costs per seat per mile and lost revenue because passenger boardings were on the way down. Money was tight.

Five months later come drastic changes within the pilot group. The ax Falls. Pay cuts and furloughs!

Junior pilots in the hundreds are let go. It would take nearly five years before any of them would be recalled.

I would fly the Electra as a captain for three months, logging some fifty hours of flight time in it. Then, I too get demoted back to being a first officer on the B-727.

I have to confess, after being in command for those several months, it was a blow to my ego, having to become a first officer again. The upside, I was not out on the street like hundreds of other pilots.

For the next six-and-a-half years, I would remain as a first officer.

The upside. During those years Eastern had expanded to the west coast, to me, it meant more new cities to fly to.

LET ME TELL YOU ABOUT BASEBALL

Q uite a few of my layovers were in St. Louis. Two events stand out. One was while having breakfast in the hotel where I was staying. The flight engineer and I were discussing the previous night's baseball game between the New York Mets, whom I rooted for, and the Philadelphia Phils, whom he rooted for.

Tom Seaver had pitched and had won the game for the Mets. I made a statement to the F/E in effect that Seaver would probably win twenty games that year.

Next to our table was an African-American gentleman who leaned over and said. "Seaver wins mostly night games, but has trouble winning during day games."

I was just about to answer his remark, with a, what do you know about baseball, I'm a little league manager. At that time, I had been coaching Scott and Keith's baseball teams for almost eight years. My teams won most of them.

Luckily for me, another African-American gentleman came over to his table and said. "Hey, Ernie. There are a couple of people who would like your autograph."

The guy I was going to ask what did he know about baseball, was future Hall-Of-Famer, Ernie Banks of the Chicago Cubs. The Cubs were in town to play the St. Louis Cardinals that night.

The other ballplayer was Billy Williams of the Chicago Cubs. Ernie laughed, shook my hand, and said. "Let's play two." Meaning, play a double-header baseball game. He then autographed a business card for me. Which I still have. What a guy.

The next incident happened when I decided to take a taxi and tour the Charles Lindbergh Aviation Museum which was located on the outskirts of St. Louis.

After visiting the museum, I had thought it would be a nice day to walk back to the hotel. It was a bad idea.

I ended up on some street corner that had a bus stop sign. Not knowing where I was, or if there would be any buses going in my direction I thought about a taxi.

Parked a half-block away was a police car with two officers in it. I had gone over to their car and told them that I was an airline pilot on a layover. Then asked them what bus I should take to get back to my hotel.

One of them asked if I had any money on me. I said yes, wondering why he would ask me that. "Get in the car!" said the driver. "This isn't the safest area to be in." En route to the hotel, they told me how bad the crime was in that area and that was why they drove me to my hotel.

As I got out of the police car, I thank them and shook their hands. When I did, the people who were standing there, looked at me as though I were a criminal just released from jail.

To top that off, the captain I was flying with had just come out of the hotel and saw me getting out of the police car with a very surprised look on his face. I just smiled and kept walking. He never did ask me why I was with the police.

COFFEE AND I DREAM OF GENIE, BARBARA EDEN

Being back as a first officer went rather smoothly once I put my ego on hold and I was enjoying it all. Especially on one layover in the summer of 1974.

The hotel we stayed at in Puerto Rico, was called the Condado Plaza Hotel. It was located on the north side of the island and overlooked the Atlantic Ocean.

The hotel would gather much fame on March 22, 1978. On that day Karl Wallenda, of the fame The Flying Wallenda's, a high-wire act, fell ten stories to his death when he attempted to walk a high wire during extremely gusty winds between the two towers of the hotel.

Of course, no matter what city I would layover in, be it Montreal in the middle of winter, or San Juan, I had always brought my bathing suit with me.

While I was relaxing poolside, a sudden hush fell over those who were there. All eyes had turned to look at this beautiful woman as she crossed the tiled deck. She was wearing a stunning two-piece bathing suit and a sheer see-through robe that was open and flowed with the warm breeze.

Trailing her was an entourage of photographers. The crowd and I watched as they went through a gate and down the steps that led to a small patch of beach. It was Barbara Eden, of, I Dream of Genie, fame.

Of course, several of us went to the gate and looked down. We watched as the photographers click away taking photos of her. With each click she would alter her pose with that, I Dream of Genie smile.

After they had left. The buzz around the pool seemed louder.

Jim Geraghty, our second officer, had an uncle who lived in San Juan and we had planned to go out to dinner that evening. As Jim and I were about to leave the hotel we passed by the ballroom.

Coming from inside, was the beautiful sound of a woman singing. Of course, we had to peek inside. The room was filled with guests.

On stage with a microphone in hand, was Barbara Eden. The audience was captivated by her performance, as we were. Had we not had the engagement with Jim's uncle, we certainly would have stayed.

Hours later, Jim and I returned to the hotel. As we were passing the dining room, I had noticed a man and a woman as the only two seated in the restaurant drinking coffee. Then I realized the woman was Barbara Eden. A quick thought had entered my mind and I said. "Jim. Let's go get a cup of coffee."

Of course, we sat down next to their table. When the coffee arrived, I opened up a conversation with her by saying how much we enjoyed her show. The one we missed out on. Surprisingly, she responded.

After fifteen minutes of wonderful conversation about her television show, I casually asked about her husband, Michael Ansara, and what movie he was appearing in. Ansara was Barbara Eden's husband and a well-known actor. That was when our conversation was politely terminated.

Weeks later, I found out they were going through a divorce, which few people knew about. Then I thought about my asking her about Ansara. Did she think I was putting her on the spot even though I knew nothing about it? That is something I will never know. Either way, it was a fine day and evening.

SERIOUS WEATHER-SERIOUS ACCIDENTS

Decomber 1, 1974. The captain was Roy Farra and I was his first officer and it was my leg to fly from Fort Lauderdale to La Guardia. As we were about to depart, ATC canceled all flights into the New York area due to high winds, and low ceilings.

Unbeknownst to us at the time, TWA flight 514 from Indianapolis to Washington National Airport had to divert to the Washington Dulles Airport due to high cross-winds at National. Which were recorded at 28 knots gusting to 49 knots.

At approximately 11:09 a. m., flight 514 had been making a non-precision approach, VOR/DME to runway 12 at Dulles due to stormy weather where it encountered severe downdrafts, snow showers, and limited visibility. It crashed near Mt. Weather, VA, some 25 miles west of Dulles. All 92 onboard died in the crash.

Oddly enough, after the NTSB investigated the crash. They realized a United Airlines flight had escaped a similar fate 6 weeks prior on the same type of approach. It landed safely.

Later that evening Northwest Flight 6231, a ferry flight, left JFK en route to Buffalo, New York to charter the Baltimore Colts football team after they played the Buffalo Bills.

The flight crew was then to fly them back to Baltimore. Unfortunately, flight 6231 crashed en route near Harriman State Park. Some fifty miles north of New York City. The three cockpit crew members were the only persons on board. Unfortunately, they all perished.

Upon NTSB'S investigation of the crash, it was determined the crew, although it was part of the checklist, did not turn on the heated pitot tubes.

While in flight, the NTSB believed atmospheric icing blocked the tubes which gives a readout of the aircraft's airspeed. Blocked tubes tend to indicate a higher airspeed than it is.

Since the readout was inaccurate, they continued to pull the nose of the aircraft upward to reduce the airspeed. Instead, they stalled out at approximately 24,000 feet and impacted the ground 83 seconds later.

It would be the worst day in aviation history to have two major airlines have fatal accidents on the same day.

In between those accidents, LaGuardia had reopened and we left FLL in clear blue skies and calm air. The flight was uneventful until passing Washington D.C.

As we began our descent into LGA we encountered instrument conditions and moderate turbulence. It became more severe as we made our ILS approach to runway 4.

At one point, so extreme, the instruments were nothing more than a blur. My hands and feet were full of aileron and rudder control due to the turbulence. As we were about to abandon the approach we broke out of the overcast and landed safely in strong-gusting conditions.

The lead-in ramp-service man was about to park us when a heavy gust of wind caught him. He slid three feet to his right, flat-footed. It was the severest weather I had ever encountered on a landing.

ANOTHER SHOOTING

Months pass and 1975 arrives. Flying goes on as usual, and as usual, I would fly with different captains and second officers. Notably one-second officer I'll only name Bill. Whom I had flown with many times before.

To me, he was one of those fellows who could be like a bull in a China shop. He stood about 5'10", had a stocky build, and was affable, but sometimes could be short of temper. Although I had no problems with him, and we got along just fine.

Bill was also one of the many pilots who lived in another state who would commute to and from their bases by riding the jump seat. Or by using employee airline passes.

On our first sequence of the month, he had told me he would be flying it all month. Which was usually the norm.

For some reason during our second sequence, he had confided to me about an eighteen-year-old girl he had taken in to help her kick a drug problem he thought she had.

As far as I knew, Bill was probably in his mid-thirties and not married. So, it was somewhat of a surprise when he did not fly the following sequence or any others for the rest of the month.

At first, I thought he was selecting other flights, as pilots often do to load up on a lot of flight time, thereby being able to string many days off in between flights and not have to commute so often.

But my inquisitive nature got the best of me and I had contacted a crew scheduler to see if he was perhaps, flying other trips. His answer. "He's dead!"

Of course, I bring it upon myself to inquire about his sudden demise.

It seemed the eighteen-year-old was really his girlfriend. Unfortunately, they got into an argument while driving down the main street of a town in central Florida.

Bill pulled out a gun and shot his girlfriend in the head killing her instantly. Then shot himself in the head. When he did, he lost control of the automobile and it crashed through a department store window in the center of town. Luckily no one else was injured. One never knows what goes through the mind of someone else.

EASTERN FLIGHT 66 WINDSHEAR AND MICROBURST

T he next several months passed and all was well. On June 24, 1975, Captain Len Finley was in command, and I was his first officer. We were on our way back to Newark from San Juan but had to make several stops along the way one being Baltimore. Then Baltimore to Newark.

While in Baltimore, we had to go through customs, as did our passengers. One of them had a small cardboard box labeled orange juice the custom agent started inspecting.

As I watched, the agent shook the carton several times. Instead of hearing a splash, splash, splash of O.J., it's clunk, clunk, clunk. When the agent opened the carton he began prying open the top of the cans. Inside, he found them loaded with bags of heroin. We were minus one passenger to EWR.

From BAL-EWR we were dodging heavy cells of thunderstorms, made our approach, and landed without incident. Inside flight operations, tragic news.

Eastern Flight 66 from MSY-JFK, the same flight I had been flying off and on over several months, had crashed while making its approach to a landing at JFK in severe weather.

It was the same line of thunderstorms we had been dodging when we made our approach to EWR. Unfortunately, 113 passengers and seven crew members died in the accident. Eleven survived.

In command of the flight was Captain John Kleven, whom I had flown with many times on the Connie, and the B-727. Assisting him was First Officer William Eberhart, and Second Officer Gary M. Ceurin.

Ceurin was being flight checked by one of our check/engineers, Peter J. McCullough. All perished, as did, two cabin flight attendants, Senior Flight Attendant Maureen Davis, and Flight Attendant Jackie Lindsay.

Miraculously, two flight attendants, Robert Hoefler, and Mary Ellen Moore, who were sitting on their jump seats in the aft cabin survived. I had flown with Moore quite often while flying the Eastern shuttle.

As the aircraft broke up on impact and caught fire, both were saved by the aft lavatories' blue chemical water that had been dumped over them which prevented them from being seriously burned.

The cause of the crash, and little known at that time, was the downward force of a micro-burst. It was later estimated to be approximately 60 mph when it drove the aircraft into the ground, and well short of the runway.

According, in part, to the NTSB-AAR-76-8 report dated March 12, 1976. "The probable cause of this accident was the aircraft's encounter with adverse winds associated with a very strong thunderstorm located astride the ILS localizer course. Which resulted in a high descent rate into non-frangible approach light towers."

At that time little was known about wind shears and micro-bursts.

The reality would strike home almost nine years later when on August 2, 1985, Delta Airlines Flight 191 encountered a severe wind shear and micro-burst and crashed while attempting to land at the Dallas/Fort Worth International Airport. 136 passengers and 8 of 11 crew members died in the crash. 27 survived.

Oddly enough, just before Flight 66's landing. Eastern Air Lines Flight 902, an L-1011 TriStar, had made their approach to runway 22L at JFK. They encountered the same wind shear and micro-burst as flight 66 who was making their approach behind them.

However, Flight 902 executed a missed approach, but, did not adhere to prescribed go-around procedures at that time. Normally, you would retract flaps to a go-around mode and then call for gear up.

Instead, the crew of Flight 902, as the aircraft was being pushed downward by the force of the wind-shear/micro-burst, did not retract flaps, nor did they call for gear up.

Seeing that they were about to crash, had put their feet on the instrument panel and pulled back on their control columns with all their strength, and on the verge of a stall, climbed out of the wind-shear/micro-burst. Saving themselves and their passengers from crashing. They had called and told the tower to close the runway. But it was too late for flight 66.

Years later Eastern implemented Flight 902's plan to escape wind-shear/micro-bursts. Which I would have to do while approaching a runway in Atlanta many years later.

A CAPTAIN'S SON MAKES A BAD DECISION

There were many captains who I enjoyed flying with. Some others, a flat no! One of the captains I liked working with was the same captain when our number one engine failed on take-off in Boston. Bill had a son who had all of the required flight ratings airlines wanted and was trying to get hired by Eastern as a pilot, or for that matter, by any airline, but had been rejected. I'm not sure if it was for not having many flying hours or for other reasons.

His son eventually became a flight attendant for Eastern. On occasion, when his son was part of our flight crew, he would come into the cockpit and watch. Then ask us questions about the flight. Which we would gladly answer.

He seemed to be well-mannered and always responded positively when we encouraged him not to give up trying for a pilot position with an airline. A week later, another unbelievable tragedy.

Bill's son had a long-time girlfriend, but for some reason, they broke up. From what was told, he tried desperately to get her back, but she refused to have anything to do with him. Heartbroken, he rented a four-place Cessna 172 from a nearby airport where she lived in southern New Jersey.

Knowing she and her mother were at home, started buzzing their house. First, diving the airplane at it and then pulling up over their roof.

This brought the ex-girlfriend and her mother out of the house. On the next pass, he dove the airplane into the house killing himself and destroying the home. Fortunately, both women were not injured. I know Bill was devastated, and he shortly retired.

FLYING THE L-1011

Over the next eighteen months, all was well. Another section 28 bid had come out in August of 1976 for December. I had bid to move up and fly the Lockheed L-1011 as a first officer. When the results were posted I was to begin training in November

November came and I was back to the Ramada Hotel on 36th Street to begin the three weeks of ground school. Followed by many hours of flight instruction in the L-1011 simulator. You know, instrument approaches, missed approaches, holding patterns, engine failures, and all the rest that went with it.

Then would come my first officer proficiency flight check with the FAA. Afterward, twenty-five hours of jump seat observation time.

Before that all happened, I would end up being trained with two different captains in the L-1011 simulator. The first was an Atlanta-based B-727 captain who was upgrading to the L-1011.

Our flight instructor had ingrained in us, to use the Avionic Flight Control System, AFCS, that I had mentioned previously about Flight 401's accident.

Every time we would make an instrument approach, he would turn off the AFCS, telling our instructor he could fly much better without it.

Our instructor then gave the ATL-based captain two choices. Use the AFCS or go home and think about it. He chose to go home.

The second was an MIA-based B-727 captain also upgrading to the L-1011. In his case, when he submitted his Section 28 bid, he accidentally, bid on JFK'S base. Which meant he would have to commute to JFK from MIA to fly his L-1011 trips. Which he did not want to do.

He flew the simulator very well throughout those many periods. Except for some of his ILS approaches. Which weren't the best.

At the time I thought his mind was more on not wanting to commute than on flying the sim. Long story short.

I had finished my first officer L-1011 training and had planned to return to New Jersey. This captain was supposed to have his check ride with the FAA in two days. I honestly thought he would fail it because of his weak ILS approaches.

Since I had been his first officer throughout our sim training our instructor had asked me if I would stay and be this captain's first officer during his upcoming flight check with the FAA. Of course, I said yes.

Two days later during his FAA check-ride, I did nothing except be the first officer. My first thought, when it began, was. Oh boy. Here we go.

Incredibly, he flew his check-ride perfectly, especially the ILS approaches. I had to look at him several times to make sure it was the same captain I had been training with. He passed.

Afterward, the captain thanked our instructor for the four hours of practicing nothing but ILS approaches the day before, but they never told me.

Another thing about flying a wide-body aircraft. The cockpit is higher from the ground than most aircraft, save for the B-747 at the time.

In a widebody, you make your approach with a nose-high attitude. Which challenges your depth perception on landing. Therefore, when we reached an altitude of 50 feet above the ground, callouts of 50, 40, 30, 20, and 10 until touchdown was required.

Like the Allison Engines on the L-188, those Rolls-Royce engines also had a sound of their own. You didn't have to look skyward as one passed overhead. You knew it was an Eastern TriStar just by that wonderful drone that came from them.

My first flight as a first officer on the L-1011 was from JFK to Mexico City, layover, and return to JFK the following day. Of all days it took place on December 5, 1976. My birthday.

Another oddity about that flight. It was the captain and second officer's first flight on the L-1011 without a check captain or check engineer. They too, had just completed their required twenty-five hours.

It was highly unusual having all three of us flying together after completing the requirement, although legal. To top that off, it's aircraft 318EA. The Ghost Ship. All went well in both directions.

I would fly the L-1011 from 12/05/1976 to 10/13/1978, before upgrading to captain on the B-727.

Many of my early flights on the TriStar were JFK-MEX-ACA, layover, and then fly back to JFK via MEX. Tex Maxwell was one of the captains whom I flew with on many of those flights. Very nice individual.

While on one of those Acapulco layovers, he and I were walking along the beach when we spotted people para-sailing right from the beach. I thought it was a good idea to try it. Tex said no way. I think I paid $120's ($5.00 USD) at that time, for the trip around the bay.

Once I had the harness on, followed by thirty seconds of instruction in broken English, came the sound of a motorboat engine at full power. I'm launched.

The first thing that catches my eye isn't what's surrounding Acapulco's beautiful bay. It's the 400-foot frayed rope that's pulling me around the bay. A couple of thoughts had raced through my mind. What if the rope breaks? Which has been known to happen. Are these waters full of sharks? What if, what if. After fifteen minutes of air time circling the bay, the landing back on the beach was a welcome return.

Several months later on the night of June 3, 1976, we were dodging thunderstorms on our way back to JFK after laying over in San Antonio.

The captain was one of those no-nonsense individuals who seemed to lack a sense of humor. So, for the most part very little conversation. Until the second officer brought up stories about ghosts on the aircraft we were flying, 318A. The ghost ship.

The conversation between the second officer and myself began when he mention the supposed sightings of Don Repo on this particular aircraft. After several minutes of discussion, the captain somewhat exasperated, pointed to his operating weather radar and said.

214

"There are no more ghosts on this airplane than this radar failing." The words weren't out of his mouth when his radar failed. Fortunately, we had two weather radars on our L-1011 and we had no problem dodging the storms ahead of us and landed safely at JFK.

Although there was no more talk about ghosts. I think all three of us secretly thought otherwise.

I must reference one item most crews did while laying over in San Antonio. The L-1011 had refrigerators in the lower galley. Some of our flight crews, namely the cockpit crew, would ask the van driver who drove us to the airport, to stop by a grocery store called, Piggly Wiggly's.

Off would come our uniform epaulets. The thought was, no one would recognize us as pilots, even though we were wearing black pants, black shoes, black socks, and a white shirt with epaulet straps.

We would then purchase cases of Coors Beer and stow them in the galley's refrigerators. At that time, Coors Beer was not being sold east of the Mississippi River. Of course, now it is.

DRUGS AND NUDITY

U nfortunately, some people make poor choices, such as making money the easy way. One was one of our boarding agents at EWR whom I knew and thought highly of. He, along with several Eastern baggage handlers in Miami, got caught dealing in drugs. Namely, heroin, and marijuana.

Those in MIA, would place the drugs in suitcases and then put them into an aircraft's baggage compartment. Then teletyped the agent in EWR the flight's number and its arrival time and the ticket number of the bag.

Police officers from the Drug and Enforcement Administration, DEA, Newark's office found out about one of their shipments and waited for the flight's arrival.

When the Newark agent grabbed the suitcases in the baggage pickup area, they arrested him. Unfortunately, the agent had a weak heart. The shock of being arrested sent him into cardiac arrest and he died on the spot.

Others also threw caution to the wind. Including streaking.

Like those who would run naked through their neighborhoods showing off all their talents.

Or, the sports fan that had too many beers, and suddenly decides to strip and run naked on the field of play. Only to be arrested by the police. Streaking on an airplane?

As I was boarding the crew bus to the employee parking lot in Newark, several giggling L-1011 flight attendants whom I knew had joined me.

They had just arrived from their Bermuda flight. As we rode to the parking lot they kept passing a photograph to one another, looked at it, and then giggled some more. Then they handed it to me. I think my eyes damn near popped out of my head.

The photograph had been taken during their flight from Bermuda. In the photograph were two women stark naked, as in, not a stitch of clothing on. They also looked rather voluptuous in all their departments.

The flight attendant who took the photo, while still giggling, told me how she managed to take their picture.

It seemed that the two passengers knew one another. They also had a few too many drinks on the flight back from Bermuda. Both had been sitting in the last row of the coach section when they asked the flight attendant if it would be okay for them to streak.

The attendant told me, she said it was up to them if they wanted to. The two ladies then took advantage of the lavatories in the back of the aircraft and disrobed.

In the meantime, the flight attendant said she always carried a Polaroid camera in her handbag. Took it out and waited.

The two women came out of the lavatories naked and raced up the right-side aisle. The L-1011 has two aisles throughout its length.

Then turned at the partition that separates the coach section from the business section and began racing down the left-side aisle to retrieve their clothing. By that time all the men were whistling and applauding their performance. The women passengers, not so.

When they began running down the aisle they suddenly realized all could see the front of them. Leaving nothing to the passenger's imagination.

That was when the flight attendant took the snapshot. Of course, they tried to cover themselves with their hands and arms, but it was too late.

There were complaints from some of the passengers in the coach section, but nothing ever came of it.

FIRE ON THE FLIGHT DECK

F lying the L-1011 was most enjoyable and it was that way throughout the year. That changed on December 30, 1977.

It was another day of very long flights. LGA-BDL-EWR-SJU-MIA. Layover in Fort Lauderdale. Then do the reverse the following day.

It was probably one of the few times I had flown with a slight head cold. Nothing serious, just a few sniffles. It became more apparent as we began our descent into SJU when I began to feel a slight pain in my left ear that was increasing. It sometimes happens due to the changing of cabin pressure during the descent.

To relieve it, the general rule was to clear the pressure by closing your mouth and pinching your nose, and exhaling hard into it. When I did, I felt a sudden pop in my left eardrum.

The pain subsided and there was no more pressure. When I stuck my finger into my left ear. Blood. Not much, but I knew I had a pin-hole rupture. I wasn't worried about it because the bleeding had stopped. I felt it wouldn't happen again.

The three-and-a-half-hour flight from SJU-MIA was another story. All had gone well throughout the flight until we started our descent into Miami.

Aside from our cockpit crew, there was a jump-seat rider. A Peoria International Airport control tower operator.

Although Eastern did not have service to that city, it wasn't uncommon to have FAA personnel ride our jump seat. Such as those FAA safety inspectors.

The kind that shows up unannounced and informs the captain that he will be riding his jump seat to monitor the cockpit crew's performance.

Including looking over your shoulder to make sure you comply with the government's FAR'S. If not. Flight violations on the cockpit crew where their pilot's certificates could be suspended. To my knowledge, no other profession is more sunnitized than an airline pilot.

During those three-plus hours, the four of us managed to down several paper-lined cups of coffee. All of which were stuffed into an eighteen-by-twelve-inch paper trash bag.

The bag was lined to prevent any leakage from leftover coffee and other liquids. Added to the now over-flowing bag, were tissues, scraps of paper, an empty cigarette package, the captain was a chain-smoker, and finally, the sticky back of a maintenance worksheet. Its front, with a list of maintenance write-ups, stuck into our maintenance log book.

As we descended through 17,000 feet, the captain lit up another cigarette. As I watched, he shook the match to put out the flame, turned to his left to put it in his ashtray, then suddenly turned back to his right and dropped the match into the trash bag.

In an instant, a still-lit ember of his match ignited the glue on the back of the worksheet. Flames shot out of that trash bag as high as two feet.

The captain leaned as far as he could to his left to get away from the fire. I leaned as far as I could to my right and at the same time reached up to don my oxygen mask. Then realized there was no smoke, only fire. Oxygen and fire, are a dangerous combination. I hung it back up.

The jump-seat rider leaped on top of his seat to escape the flames. The second officer, who was right next to the trash bag jumped out of his seat, but not before the flames began to melt his double-knit trousers.

Instead of grabbing the cockpit fire extinguisher, he kneeled and began beating the fire down with his bare hands.

As he did, the bag began disintegrating, and portions of the burning trash were being pushed under both the captain's and my seat. After several frantic minutes, he beat the fire out with his bare hands.

Coincidentally, neither of our seats had caught fire due to being comprised of fireproof material.

As to the second officer, although the fire melted a small portion of his double-knit trouser pant leg to his skin, he only suffered a slight burn. Nor were his hands burned. Incredibly lucky.

After all the hullabaloo we landed safely in MIA. When I asked the captain if he was going to write a report on what had happened. His answer. "No way. I'm retiring in three months and I'm not about to rock the boat."

I reminded him that we had a jump-seat rider and he might mention what had taken place to others. I also told him that if I'm ever asked about what happened, I won't lie. I will tell them exactly what took place. Nothing ever came of it. If anything, I thought the second officer should have been highly commended for his quick action.

REPELLING THE SIDE OF A HOTEL IN ACAPULCO

During those two years of flying the TriStar, I would make many trips to Acapulco and would often fly with the same crews. Some flights were rather memorial. One flight engineer I flew with was a nice guy but had some rather strange and quirky ideas.

One of the hotels we stayed at was called the Americana. One I did not like at all. The hotel people were very nice and its location was in the heart of the city.

For some reason, an idiot in Miami who made hotel arrangements for crew members decided to use this particular hotel's suites. Which meant the cockpit crew all stayed in the same hotel room.

When you spend most of the day sitting next to one another in a cockpit, you wanted your own space when the flight was over.

This particular suite had one large living area and three separate bedrooms. It went as follows. The captain had a king-size bed, the first officer had a queen-size bed, and the second officer's bed was no bigger than a cot.

The living area led to a balcony through glass sliding doors.

Cockpit crew members usually stayed on the eighteenth floor, the flight attendants, four floors below ours. They also had to share suites.

This particular incident happened when I decided to fly another sequence of flights to different cities.

As was told to me, the captain whom I'll refer to as J.B. had been resting poolside with other guests. As he looked up toward the room where he and his cockpit crew were staying, he damn near had a heart attack. As did other guests who were looking upward.

The outside of the hotel was being painted and at the end of the day, the painter's scaffolding was raised to the top of the roof leaving its long ropes dangling near the side of the outside elevator.

Larry, the flight engineer, had decided to drop in on the flight attendants. He walked out on the balcony of the suite, grabbed a dangling rope, and went over the balcony.

Then gingerly lowered himself down four floors to their balcony, climbed over the railing, and calmly knocked on their sliding glass doors. They almost fainted when they found out how he got there.

The hotel wasn't impressed. They canceled the Eastern contract. As in, being kicked out of the hotel. We ended up laying over at another hotel called the Hotel Fiesta Tortuga. Directly across the street from the Americana.

On my next trip to ACA, with J. B. and Larry. I asked Larry why he didn't take the outside elevator down to the flight attendants' room.

He said the rope was quicker. He also said that he didn't know what the fuss was all about. He was an ex-paratrooper and used to doing that sort of thing. The good news. We all had our own room in the other hotel. The bad news came months later.

The rooms in the Fiesta Tortuga also had balconies. Except, they were very small. Approximately five feet in length and three feet wide. With very low railings. Below, a concrete-covered alley.

Several flight attendants had got together one evening and decided to see who could do the best cartwheel in one of their rooms.

Several had taken turns cartwheeling, and all was well. The last was one of our male flight attendants, whom I knew.

Unfortunately, he accidentally went by the open French doors as he was doing his cart-wheel and went over its low railing. He was killed instantly when he hit the concrete alley several stories below.

I had flown with many of them but I was not on that particular layover.

Although I was told about it.

ST ELMO'S FIRE

M y time flying the L-1011 was nearing its end. On the horizon. Captain on the B-727. Before that was to happen, I'm confronted by a great ball of fire on another L-1011 flight. August 6, 1978. The captain was Bill McLawhorn a likeable individual. It was to be another long day of flying that began at Newark. Which was nearly the same sequence of flights when the fire in the cockpit occurred.

On our climb, we leveled off at 9,000 and entered a heavy cloud layer with some misting. Instrument flying conditions.

Suddenly, from outside my front window came the first traces of swirling St. Elmo's Fire. It kept growing and growing until it filled the entire window. That is approximately 17X15 inches.

If you have ever seen the movie, The Ten Commandments, with Charlton Heston as Moses, and remember what the Pillar-of-Fire scene looked like. This was it.

That tornado of churning flame stayed there for nearly thirty seconds before it slowly swirled off to my right. All during that time, I had hoped it wasn't going to come through the window and hit me in the face. It kept swirling until it disappeared down the right side of the fuselage.

Seconds later, our senior flight attendant came into the cockpit in a panic telling the captain the right side of the airplane was on fire. Bill gave him a quick explanation of what it was. Then announced to our passengers what took place.

After we arrived at our destination, some of our passengers who were sitting on the right side of the aircraft said. The swirling mass of fire went all away down the right side of the aircraft before it dissipated near the tail.

My last flight on the TriStar as a first officer was on October 13, 1978. The aircraft. 318EA.

There was one other memorial flight that I had on the L-1011 that would take place years later in the 1980s.

At the time I was a captain on the B-727 and on this particular day, I was to deadhead from Newark to Miami.

Before the passengers had boarded, I had taken my assigned seat in the first-class section. The first row left side aisle seat and struck up a conversation with the senior flight attendant whom I knew. Then came the passengers.

The first was a woman whom I had seen many times on television. Eartha Kitt. The celebrity took the window seat next to mine. I said "Good morning." She said. Nothing.

For the next two-and-one-half hours we sat side-by-side in silence. After we ate, she curled up in her seat and napped for the remainder of the flight.

Upon our arrival at the gate, I happened to look out the first-class left-side window while the passengers were deplaning. I noticed a white limousine pulling up to the stairs of the jetway. Two gentlemen exited. One of them promptly rolled out a red carpet that went from the limo to the jetway stairs.

The other was carrying a huge Boquete of red roses. Coming down the stairs was my seatmate, and seemed very happy when she received the roses. Then gave a quick wave to the few ground crew who had gathered entered the limo and left.

Oddly enough, for security reasons, no one was supposed to be allowed on the ramp who were not employees. I often wondered who permitted that to happen.

After all the ado, the senior flight attendant, who witnessed the non-conversation between my seatmate and me, asked if I might have said something that might have offended the woman. I said yes. "I said good morning."

After giving it some more thought, I decided what lay ahead was going to be much better.

CAPTAIN ON THE B-727 REMOVING A SEVEN-YEAR-OLD BOY FROM MY FLIGHT

A ugust 1978. Our section 28 bid sheet had come out for December and with it came great news.

"Hallelujah!" I'm being upgraded to captain on the B-727. Ground school and sim training are to commence in the middle of October. The next several months seem to crawl at a snail's pace.

Come October it was down to Miami. Then for the next six weeks, it would be days of ground school and simulator training on an aircraft that I had been flying since 1966. This time as a captain.

All went well, including the proficiency flight check as a captain with the FAA. What was left was that good-old-fashion-mother-in-law-flight-check by one of Easterns check captains. Lo-and-behold it was with Captain Bob Wilbur Jr.

That Captain Wilbur, whose co-pilot, First Officer James Hartley, was mortally wounded on Eastern Shuttle Flight 1320.

We flew together for three straight days. November 19, 20, 21. Those were three days of enjoyable flying. When they ended, I was officially qualified as a captain on the B-727.

My first flight as a captain came on November 26, 1978. A round trip shuttle flight. La Guarida, Boston, La Guarida..

I would fly the B-727 for thirty years. Those being 1966 thru 1996. Except for the short durations on the L-188/L-1011 aircraft. All I can add is, that the B-727 was one fantastic aircraft.

The following night, November 27, 1978, we were following a Southern Airways DC-9 into Mobile, Alabama. During their approach, they reported having multiple bird strikes.

After we landed, I went over to where their aircraft was parked and looked at the damage.

The Radom that houses the aircraft's radar antenna, was streaked with blood. Protruding from it, were the remains of one of the birds that appeared to be a large geese that had crashed through it.

The cowlings on both engines were heavily damaged, as were the front wing roots, and leading edges. Must add, the crew did a marvelous bit of flying to bring their flight to a safe landing. I was glad that we were not in front of them.

The first several months of 1978 went well. Then not so well. On April 23rd our flight was to leave the warm weather of Sarasota for the cold and freezing weather in Detroit.

Just before closing out our flight, as in buttoning up the aircraft, the senior flight attendant entered the cockpit. In tow, was a young boy who appeared to be about seven years old. He was dressed in short pants, and a short-sleeved shirt, and wore no shoes.

The flight attendant told me he was going to Detroit alone. Where his grandparents were to meet him. Then she told me she does not want him on the airplane without shoes. In case of an emergency evacuation.

From that point, I contacted our gate agent. He told me that the boy's father had put him on the airplane and left. Go find him.

The dad came back, took off his size 10 flip-flops, stuck them on his son's feet, and left.

Of course, the child's feet are too small for them, and now he's in pain and crying. Another call for the dad. Except he was no longer in the terminal, and paging him didn't help.

A couple of our agents had gone out of the terminal and had located him in the parking lot walking bare-footed across the hot tarmac.

He was using the shadows of parked cars so he wouldn't burn the bottom of his feet. He told the agents that he didn't have shoes for his son to wear.

The flight attendant still refused to accept the child without them. That left me no alternative but to have this innocent seven-year-old removed from the aircraft and left in the care of the father.

Several possibilities had entered my mind at the time. Was the child kidnapped? Why wasn't the child dressed properly for the cold weather in Detroit?

On top of that, there was no local telephone number to contact the dad once he left the area. The only telephone number was the grandparents in Detroit. It was fortunate our agents had caught up with the father.

When we arrived in Detroit the grandparents were there waiting. I explained to them what had taken place. Long story short. They told me that the boy's parents were separated and neither wanted to take care of the child. That was why they were sending him to live with the grandparents. Nice parents.

Unfortunately having to remove someone from your flight is usually the fault of the passenger. Having had to remove a seven-year-old has stayed with me for a long time.

A week later, I have to have another passenger removed from my flight.

A HALF-NAKED PASSENGER GETS REMOVED

Atlanta International Airport, Friday evening May 1, and long before jet-ways were being used. At that time all boarding for the B-727 was through the use of the electric forward airstairs of the airplane, which was just behind the cockpit.

Our flight that evening would take us from Atlanta to San Antonio, with one stop in Houston. Then layover.

While our passengers were boarding, I noticed a young couple making their way from the gate to the aircraft. The young woman appeared to be in her early twenties.

She was wearing a beautiful Gardenia on her white dress and held a hand-carried travel case in her right hand. The gentleman wore a suit and tie with a red flower on his left lapel. In the back of my mind. newlyweds.

As they looked up toward me, I waved. He waved back. The woman reached down and grabbed the hem of her dress and pulled it up to her chin exposing what she was wearing. White panties with red polka dots. Smiled, then let go, her dress covering the panties. I thought that was impressive. They board. My attention was then focused on getting ready to start the engines.

Ten minutes hadn't passed when the senior flight attendant entered the cockpit and made a complaint.

She told me that there was a young lady in the first-class section sitting next to a young boy. Then added, according to his parents, who were sitting across from them, she was being overly friendly.

My first thought it was the woman wearing the Gardenia.

Then I asked about the guy who had boarded with the woman, and where he was sitting. She said that he just escorted her on board and left. I told the attendant to move the kid to another seat. She leaves.

Less than a minute later she's back in the cockpit, stating. "The woman came out of the lavatory and exposed herself to the first-class passengers."

"What do you mean exposed herself?"

"She showed everything!"

"Everything!" Just to clarify that she meant naked.

"She pulled her dress up and wasn't wearing any panties."

Not good. I called for the gate agent to have her removed.

When he came on board, the woman told him she won't leave and entered the cockpit with her handbag. Then defyingly, told me she wasn't going to leave.

I had expressed to her that we could do it the easy way, or we could do it the hard way, and pointed out the window to the gate entrance.

Standing there were two very big airport policemen in case she didn't want to leave voluntarily. She left in a huff.

The following morning when I entered flight operations in San Antonio, I was handed a note from the girl's parents. Who were to meet her the night before. In short.

The parents had thanked me for putting their daughter off the airplane and for causing such an embarrassing incident. I thought it was rather nice of them to do that.

PANIC IN THE AIR

When it rains, it pours, as the saying goes. May 24, 1979, was one of those days when thunderstorms were surrounding Washington D.C., and raining heavily. It also meant having had to delay our southbound flight to Raleigh until the storms passed.

An hour later they had subsided enough to be able to deviate around them with the use of our Doppler Weather Radar. I was expecting some bumpiness on our climb-out and had made that announcement to our passengers.

One thing about flying out of Reagan International Airport, and others like it. Was the so-called noise-abatement procedure.

Once the wheels were in the well, it was designed to have you reduce power on the engines, at the most critical phase of flight, so as not to disturb those who lived near the airports. Of course, with the type of weather that lay ahead of us, I was not about to reduce power.

After taking off we started to get some pretty good chop, turbulence, during our climb. No sooner had the landing gear been in their wheel wells, when I received a call through our aircraft's intercom system.

It was the senior flight attendant who was sitting on her jump seat, just behind the cockpit door. Then another from the other flight attendants who were sitting on their jump seats in the coach section, saying.

"There's a woman in the coach section who just jumped out of her seat and is running up and down the aisle screaming we're going to crash." If you don't think that didn't catch the passenger's attention.

Several passengers began to panic and were un-fastening their seatbelts.

Fortunately, the flight attendants got up and corralled the woman and put her back in her seat, and tried to calm her down.

Unbelievably, the woman's phycologist was also on the flight, although sitting in another section. He had recognized his patient as she was running up and down the aisle. He identified himself to the flight attendants and took over to reassure the woman that everything was okay.

It's at these moments when you have to make a decision. To return and land over-weight back at DCA. Or, continue to Raleigh.

Through the use of our intercom, I talked to the phycologist and he assured me that he would sit next to her for the remainder of the flight.

The person who was sitting next to her volunteered to sit in the phycologist's seat.

We continued to Raleigh without further incident. Followed by another letter to the chief pilot's office.

CRASH LANDING THE SIMULATOR

Mid-June, 1979. At the time all captains were required to do a six-month proficiency flight check in the simulator of the aircraft they flew.

First and second officers had a one-year grace period before they had to do their proficiency flight checks.

As usual, it would be four hours of hydraulic failures, instrument approaches, and engine-out procedures. Or anything else that the check captain could conjure up.

On that day Captain, Larry DuPre was the check captain. Along with us was First Officer Bud O'Toole, who was getting his yearly flight check. Acting as our second officer was Bob Wilkinson, a check engineer.

As usual, the captain goes first. After two hours, all was well, and I had completed my portion of the sim check. Followed by a quick break before O'Toole had to do his.

All of our instrument approaches were based upon landing on Miami's 9L runway. As usual, the weather was below landing minimums and Bud had to make a missed approach.

Before passing the outer marker, which was usually ten miles out, from landing, I had decided to snap my shoulder harnesses to my seatbelt. Something I had never done while flying in the simulator.

While executing the missed approach, Bud banked to the right to enter the prescribed holding pattern according to the missed approach instructions on the chart.

Without warning, the simulator snapped violently to the left at a 45-

degree downward angle and came to a jarring halt. All electrical power in the simulator went out and the cockpit emergency lights had come on. Bud looked over at me and kiddingly said. "You've got it, captain!"

Then the simulator began to fill at what we all first thought was smoke and that the simulator had caught fire, and we quickly abandon it.

What we thought was smoke, turned out to be dust particles and debris that had been accumulating on the floor of the simulator over time. The impact from the simulator crashing had thrown the particles into the air throughout the simulator.

Larry made a quick call to our maintenance department and told them of our dilemma. During their inspection of the sim, they realized the night maintenance crew had lubricated the hydraulic lift that allows the simulator to rise and fall as though it were in flight.

A cotter pin that should have been inserted through a bolt of the lift was missing. While we were doing our flight maneuvers, it unscrewed and fell off. When that happened, the simulator separated from the hydraulic jack falling violently to the left.

The only reason it didn't roll over on its roof, it had come in contact with the steps and the railing leading to the simulator's entrance and had stopped.

As to the loss of electrical power. When we crashed, Wilkinson punched the electrical shut-off switches so hard to kill all electrical power, that he virtually drove them through the side of the simulator. Two bulges in its fiberglass siding could be seen quite clearly.

While all this was being hashed out, I had felt burning sensations coming from both of my shoulders. I told Larry that I was going to the men's restroom while he and Bud went to the debriefing room.

After I removed my shirt, I could see two very large red welts where my shoulder harnesses had been. They had saved me from having my head bashed against the glare shield. Why did I put those harnesses on? I could only surmise that someone was looking out for me.

As I leaned against the sink to get closer to the mirror, I hadn't realized someone had been there before me and had splattered water all over it. The water soaked the crotch of my pants.

Back in the debriefing room, I told Larry and Bud, pointing to my crotch, it was not from the simulator crashing. Both laughed and said. "Yeah right." I did learn one thing. Seatbelt and shoulder harnesses do work!

Larry concluded that I had completed my flight check before the accident. Whereas Bud had to return another day to complete his.

THE SHOT HEARD AROUND THE WORLD

T he rest of the year had gone quite smoothly. Enter 1980. On February 22, 1980, the shot around the world was heard!

Actually, it was a slap-shot off the hockey stick of the United States Olympic Hockey Team's captain. Mike Eruzione.

It had come during the final ten minutes of the third period against the Russian Hockey Team during the 1980 Lake Placid Olympic Winter Games in Lake Placid, New York.

The Americans led the game 4 to 3. The arena rocked with anticipation as to its outcome. Those who were there, or had watched the tape delay of the game, had heard those now-famous words said by announcer Al Michaels.

"Do you believe in miracles!"

After America's victory over the Russians, they had to play Finland. Two days later, and again coming from behind, the Americans beat Finland to capture the Gold Medal.

What followed could be considered akin to the end of World War Two. There was total exhilaration throughout the United States and the hockey world.

Automobile horns were blaring, and people waved American flags, banners, signs, and posters. People shook hands with people they didn't even know. America was caught up in a frenzy of patriotism.

Then-President Carter sent Air Force One to bring Captain Mike

Eruzione and 150 Olympians to the White House to celebrate their victory in winning the Gold Medal.

On February 25, 1980, Mike was asked by NBC to appear on their Today Show the following morning. Although exhausted from all the preceding events he had been asked to appear at, boarded an Eastern Air Lines flight that evening to New York. My flight.

When the senior flight attendant told me that he was on board, and having watched the event on television I invited him into the cockpit.

After an exchange of greetings, we, the cockpit crew congratulated Mike and his team for winning the Gold Medal.

Then came a moment of patriotic sentiment. Knowing President Carter had sent Air Force One to shuttle the Olympic team to Washington, I asked Mike if he ever had seen a cockpit crew start engines. He said no.

Shortly afterward the engines were started, our flight was cleared to taxi for take-off. While taxing I allowed him to sit on the jump seat to witness what it was like.

As we approached the runway, ground control told us to switch to the tower frequency for immediate take-off. Mike got a quick briefing on how to use the oxygen mask that hangs near the jump seat and was told to strap himself in. Seconds later we were airborne.

During the flight, the senior flight attendant entered the cockpit and asked Mike if he would mind signing autographs for passengers who knew he was on board.

He asked me if it was okay. I agreed, and told him, that if he wanted, he could see what it was like on a landing.

He accepted the invitation and watch our landing. After the flight was over, we, the cockpit crew, were still caught up in all the hoopla.

We autographed the flight's take-off and landing data card and gave it to him. A memento of the flight.

On my drive home, it suddenly dawned on me I never asked for Mike Eruzione's autograph. For the next thirty-nine years, each time the anniversary of 1980 America's win over the Russians and their Gold Medal were celebrated, I would think about that night and how I wished I had asked for his autograph.

Enter a Quantum Leap thirty-nine years later after that flight.

On February 24, 2019. I had been reading, an article called, on this day in history in our local newspaper, The Daily Sun. The Villages, Florida. It referred to the thirty-ninth anniversary of the United States Olympic Hockey Team winning the Gold Medal on February 24, 1980.

A wild thought had raced through my mind with an urge so strong I couldn't resist it. I went on the internet to see if, by some chance, I could find Mike's email address. Incredibly I found it.

I then sent him an email asking him if he remembered that flight thirty-nine years previous from Boston to New York that both of us were on.

I also told him that all five of my grandkids were hockey players, including our two granddaughters. In all honesty, I did not expect an answer.

Lo-and-behold I did get a response. It was an email from Mike Eruzione stating that he had never forgotten that flight and happily remembers it very well.

Then came another email. It was not from Mike. It was from Neal E. Boudette who was co-writing a book with Mike to be called. The Making of a Miracle.

It was scheduled to be released in February 2020 celebrating the Miracle's Fortieth Anniversary. It also included Neal's telephone number asking me to call him.

The telephone conversation with Neil lasted nearly forty-five minutes. Neil had asked me many questions about that flight thirty-nine years previous. Afterward, he told me he had planned to use some of that information in the book, provided his editor will allow it.

Before ending the phone call, I mentioned to Neil that during all those past years how I regretted not asking Mike for his autograph.

The following evening, while at home, a FedEx package arrived at our front door. I had thought Barb had ordered something and handed the package to her without looking to see who it was addressed.

That was until she told me it was for me. It was from Mike Eruzione. Inside the package.

A 1980 official USA Winter Olympic Hockey Jersey. With the captain's "C" and the number 21 on it. Mike's number. It was autographed by Mike and the words. Miracle on Ice was written on it.

Each of my five grandkids and I also received autographed photos of Mike in his #21 USA Olympic Hockey uniform. I just could not believe it and e-mailed him and Neil, a very profound thank-you.

His book, Making of A Miracle, came out in February 2020, forty years after the Miracle. True to their words, they had mentioned my name on two different pages of their book.

It was an incredible honor to be mentioned with all those wonderful, great hockey players that played for the United States in the 1980 Lake Placid Winter Olympic Games. Something I will never forget. Thanks Mike Eruzione and Neil Boudette.

CONTROVERSY OVER AN EASTERN PILOT

April 1980. Another controversy descends on Eastern Air Lines about one of its pilots. It makes national and international headlines.

It revolved around having a second female pilot on the pilot's seniority list. One was Barbara Barrett, who was the first female pilot Eastern hired on May 14, 1973. Then came the second female pilot who was already on the pilot list and she was senior to Barrett. How can that be?

On September 23, 1968, Eastern Air Lines hired Kenneth Ulane as one of its newest pilots. Before Eastern, Ulane had joined the United States Army and flew many combat missions in the Vietnam War from 1964 to 1968.

Following his employment with Eastern, Ulane transitioned from Kenneth to Karen Frances Ulane in April 1980. Then came the controversy.

Management said they had hired a pilot named Kenneth Ulane, not Karen Francis Ulane. One year later, after many different opinions within the pilot group and the management group as to Miss Ulane's mental stability. T.R. Button, then the Senior Vice President of Flight Operations presented her with a letter of termination on April 24, 1981.

It read. "It is our belief that the controversial nature of the operation you have undergone will distract from and prevent any flight crew of which you are a part of from operating in the integrated, coordinated fashion that is necessary to attain the highest degree of safety." The letter also noted that other Eastern pilots had refused to fly with her.

Ulane then filed a discrimination charge with the Equal Employment Opportunity Commission which resulted in the civil case, *Ulane vs Eastern Airlines*.

In her case, she reported coping with gender dysphoria from the age of 5 or 6. Although she won the case against Eastern in December 1983, it was overturned on appeal in the U.S. Court of Appeals for the Seventh Circuit many years later.

It should also be noted that the case *"Ulane vs Eastern Airlines,"* became the federal legal precedent for transsexual legal status under the Civil Rights Act of 1964.

Unfortunately, Ulane died in the crash of a chartered DC-3 she was piloting on a training flight on May 22, 1989. Two others also died in the crash.

Her name, along with well over 7,000 other names of pilots living and dead who flew for Eastern Air Lines are enshrined on a bronze plaque that graces the walls at the Atlanta-Hartsfield-Jackson International Airport, Atlanta, Georgia for all to see.

During those intermediate years from April 1980 thru 1983, there were other headlines about Eastern when a few Eastern stewardesses posed nude in the men's magazines Playboy and Penthouse.

Of course, there are additional ways to have an income besides posing nude. Many of our pilots and flight attendants were more than just your flight crew.

Outside of flying, they were very successful in other vocations. Such as writing cookbooks, becoming lawyers, artists, actors, land developers, real estate agents, and so on.

Fail a flight physical, or any other unseen circumstance and you might be out of a job. So, you better have a backup plan.

MAYDAY! MAYDAY! MAYDAY!

On January 23, 1981, what was to be a routine flight from New Orleans to Cancun, Mexico became a rescue flight for a downed Aero-Commander that had to ditch in the Gulf of Mexico. Whenever you have a flight that will be extended over water, such as the Gulf of Mexico, the Atlanta Ocean, or the Caribbean Sea, you are required to monitor the guarded emergency frequency 121.5 in the event someone declares an in-flight emergency.

Our flight had reached the midway point between New Orleans and Cancun when we heard a "Mayday! Mayday!, Mayday!," call coming from an Aero-Commander. A twin-engine aircraft.

We asked what his emergency was and his position. In short. One engine had failed, the other was overheating and he couldn't maintain his altitude. At the same time, a coast guard aircraft picked up our conversation with the aircraft in distress and took over.

As we were relaying its position, his other engine failed. The aircraft ditched, and both men on board the flight we able to get out of it before it sank. They were eventually rescued by the coast guard.

Fortunately, that was a successful rescue. There are times, when an engine fails, or the pilot gets lost over those great expanses of water and they're never heard from again.

LET'S GRAB LUNCH AT A MEXICAN RESTAURANT

May 2, 1981. It was to be simple, two days of flying. The first night we laid over in Philadelphia. The following day we flew to Houston. Where we had a three-hour and thirty-minute layover before flying back to Newark.

My first officer, Tony Bartolo, had suggested offsetting the lengthy layover by going to a Mexican restaurant he knew for lunch. That was barely a mile away from the airport.

It sounded good to our second officer and me. With a three-hour layover, there should be plenty of time for us to eat and return to the airport for an on-time departure back to Newark.

When we first arrived in Houston, the weather report indicated the possibility of thunderstorms developing later that afternoon.

The good news, we were to fly the same aircraft back to Newark. If there were to be any weather delays for inbound flights it wouldn't affect us as having to wait for another aircraft.

We gave the taxi driver a hefty tip for the short ride from the airport terminal to the restaurant with his promise he would pick us up after we had eaten. Just call the telephone number he gave us. What can go wrong?

Before entering the restaurant, we removed our uniform pilot epilates and entered wearing our white shirts, black pants, black socks, and black shoes.

All through lunch, we began hearing the booming of thunderclaps, and heavy rain falling on the restaurant's roof. It all subsided as we finished lunch.

I made a telephone call to the number the cab driver had given us. A dispatcher told me a cab was on the way. Outside the restaurant, it was clear skies, the stormy weather had passed.

A half-hour passed, no taxi, another phone call. I'm told a cab is on the way. Again, no cab. The three-hour lunch was now down to thirty-five minutes before departure.

Another phone call, but this time it was to Houston's flight operations. It was my request asking for the type of weather we could expect en route to Newark and the amount of fuel I would need for the flight.

Then, more bad news. While we were at lunch, unbeknownst to us, the heavy rain caused road flooding around the airport.

Underpasses were flooded out and the roads were grid-lock to the airport's terminal.

We had to make a quick decision. We decided to put our epilates back on and began to hitchhike to the airport. Surely, some motorist will see that we were pilots and pick us up.

As we started hitchhiking we thought that the roads must be starting to open. Automobile after automobile passed us by but they weren't stopping and the clock was still ticking down for our departure to Newark. Finally, one did and we piled in.

I thanked the driver and told him our plight. That we were supposed to fly back to Newark and the reason why we were hitchhiking.

He then told me that he was from Morristown, New Jersey but he now lived in Houston. I mention my uncle who owned a flower shop in Morristown. He said he knew him. I couldn't believe that we were picked up by someone from New Jersey and that he knew my uncle.

He turned off the main highway onto a service road that paralleled the airport. Thinking he could bypass the traffic. Only to find, it too was gridlocked. The clock kept winding down.

Off to our right was the Dobbs House catering building that supplied the airlines with food. A thought entered my mind. Climb the fence and get to the Dobbs House.

I thanked the driver, then the three of us raced for the chain-link fence that guarded the airport property. At the top barbed wire.

That didn't stop us. We climbed the fence, carefully made our way atop the barbed wire, jumped down on the tarmac and sprinted for the building, and dashed inside.

Inside, were a dozen workers preparing meal trays. When they saw us, they threw up their hands. White shirt, gold epilates, black pants, black socks, black shoes.

I thought they must think we were cops doing a drug bust. Tony must have the same thought. He told them we were not cops, but Eastern Air Line pilots, and we needed to get back to our flight operations immediately.

Parked outside, next to the loading dock, was an empty catering truck. Its driver told us to hop in the back of the truck. We hung on for dear life as he sped along the tarmac, weaving his way around parked aircraft, and stopped next to the aircraft we had arrived in.

By that time we were down to fifteen minutes before departure.

Tony boarded the aircraft and got our flight clearance to Newark, while the second officer did a quick pre-flight.

In the meantime, as our passengers were being hurriedly boarded, I signed all the necessary dispatch papers. Made a final check of the weather en route, jumped back on board the aircraft, started engines, and we taxied out for take-off for an on-time departure.

On the way to Newark, Tony and I laughed our heads off that we were able to get the flight out on time and not have to write a letter to the chief pilot.

SENIOR FLIGHT ATTENDANT SAVES A LIFE

On June 30th we lifted off from JFK for a two-and-half-hour flight to Fort Lauderdale. Our flight had been smooth until we crossed over Wilmington, North Carolina on AR-7.

Then out over the Atlantic Ocean and 200 miles offshore. Forty-five minutes later we entered an area of moderate turbulence during meal service and I announced to the passengers to have all their seatbelts fastened.

In the first class section, Senior Flight Attendant Carol Chapman was checking her passenger's seatbelts when she saw one of them in distress. She asked him if he was okay. He couldn't answer. A piece of food had lodged in his throat and he was choking to death.

Chapman got behind his seat reached over and began the Heimlich Maneuver and the food was dislodged. Her quick thinking saved the man's life. Oddly enough, the person sitting next to him wasn't aware of the man's dilemma. Another report to the chief pilot's office. Followed by some good news.

Due to my report, Chapman and I were asked to come to Miami where she received Eastern Air Lines's highest award. The Five-Star Award.

Photos were taken, and her act of heroism was published in our company's magazine, the Falcon.

When it came to training flight attendants, Eastern's training department was the best.

L-1011 ENGINE EXPLODES IN FLIGHT

September 22, 1981. Although it didn't gather a lot of media attention. Eastern Air Lines flight 935, a Lockheed L-1011 TriStar had departed Newark International Airport for San Juan, Puerto Rico.

Captain Adam C. Kagel was in command. Assisting him were First Officer Richard B. Donica, and Second Officer John L. Barrett Jr.

As they were climbing through 10,000 feet, came a sudden and severe explosion of the number two engine.

A section of the fan module, slammed into the fuselage, slicing into one of the lavatories. Flying debris punctured the stabilizer. Outboard ailerons were lost, as were the rudder control pedals.

The National Transportation Safety Board's Aircraft Accident Report: NTSB-AAP-82-5 explains the accident in its Synopsis dated June 2, 1982. The probable cause.

"The displacement of the fan module in the course of the engine failure sequence caused loss of hydraulic systems A, B, and D and jammed the captain's and first officer's rudder pedals in a neutral position. Meaning they had no input in directional control.

Only the skill of the pilots performing appropriate emergency procedures, which was not covered in any of their flight training manuals, requested an immediate landing at John F. Kennedy International Airport. Dumping about 48,000 pounds of fuel out over the Atlantic Ocean as they do. The aircraft with 11 crew members and 190 passengers aboard landed safely. No one was injured on board or the ground."

Years prior, I had flown with Captain Kagel as a first officer. He was another one of those B-17 pilots who flew bombing missions over Germany during WWII. One who seldom talked about his experiences during that time. Very laid back and cool under a lot of pressure.

WINTERTIME BRINGS SNOW, ICE, A CRASH

J anuary 13, 1982. Wintertime. Snow and icy conditions prevailed at Washington National Airport.

After a prolonged ground delay due to the weather, Air Florida Flight 90, a Boeing 737, began its take-off roll. Its destination was Fort Lauderdale, Florida.

Shortly after lifting off runway 36 it failed to maintain altitude and slammed into the 14th Street Bridge and the depths of the Potomac River.

Of the 79 people on board only six survive. One survivor, Arland Williams, in an act of heroism, drowned as he passed the rope from a rescue helicopter to others. The bridge was renamed Arland Williams Bridge in 1985.

According to NTSB Report: AAR-8208 dated August 10, 1982.

"The probable cause of the accident was the flight crew's failure to use engine anti-icing during ground operation and takeoff. Their decision to take off with snow and ice on the airfoil surfaces of the aircraft, and the captain's failure to reject the takeoff during the early stage when his attention was called to anomalous engine instrument readings."

In addition to the NTSB report: "Contributing to the accident was the prolonged ground delay between deicing and the receipt of ATC clearance during which the airplane was exposed to continual precipitation, the known inherent pitch-up characteristics of the B-737 when the leading edge is contaminated with even small amounts of snow or ice and the

limited experience of the flight crew in jet transport winter operations."
Unfortunately, accidents due happened. From them. We as airline pilots,
learn and continue to learn, as to the best way we can to avoid them.

THE LONGEST DAY, THE LONGEST DAY

F ebruary 26, 1982, twenty days after the Air Florida accident. A day that remains in my mind that would become a classic event.

Following a layover in Atlanta, our proposed day of flying consisted of going from Atlanta to Denver, returning to Atlanta, and then flying to LaGuardia.

We were already looking at our schedule on-duty time being pushed to the max of ten hours when we checked in at flight operations that morning.

What my flight crew and I hadn't expected was to be in the cockpit for over twenty hours.

The flight to Denver was normal. The flight back to Atlanta was not so. We had encountered in-flight holding delays due to rainy cold weather in Atlanta. By the time we had landed, and refueled for the flight to LaGuardia temperatures in Atlanta had fallen to freezing levels.

As a precautionary measure and with Air Florida in mind, and knowing we would be flying into icing conditions, I had chosen to have our aircraft coated with Glycol to prevent any ice buildup on the wings, fuselage, the vertical and horizontal stabilizers.

By then it was nearing 9 p.m. and we were approaching our maximum on-duty time. Once I started the engines and taxied away from the gate, we could continue the flight even though we would exceed our on-duty time. One of those hazy FAR rules.

At that time in Atlanta, all Glycol procedures were not done at the gate, but in an area away from the terminal. As we taxied, we fell in line behind twenty other aircraft that were going to be Glycoled.

I did a mental calculation on how long it takes to Glycol an aircraft and multiplied it by twenty. It could take a couple of hours before our aircraft could be sprayed. It also meant that by the time we would arrive at LaGuardia, we would be on duty for nearly sixteen hours.

When we were ten slots from the spray area they ran out of Glycol and more delay.

I contacted Atlanta's flight operations with the thought of returning to the gate. By then, we were way beyond our maximum time on duty.

Then more bad news. One of our B-727 flight crews had reached their maximum on-duty time before they started engines and told their passengers they couldn't legally continue the flight. Additionally, there were no other flight crews to relieve them.

That was when all hell broke loose on their aircraft. Passengers began rioting. Baggage bins were broken, seats were ripped apart and broken, and the police were called. Arrests were made. Luckily none of the crew were injured.

When I heard that, several thoughts had run through my mind. Since we had already started engines and were away from the gate, we could remain on duty for as long as we were able to.

Secondly, at that time of night, our 106 passengers would find it nearly impossible to find a hotel room. I thought it best for them to remain on board, and us with them. I didn't want a riot on my aircraft.

As far as my crew and I, had we returned to the terminal and no hotel rooms were available, we could sleep on the aircraft.

I took a vote from my first and second officers and my flight attendants. They all agreed. Stay with the aircraft. There was a bigger problem. LaGuardia.

LaGuardia's Airport had a curfew. No arrivals or departures between the hour of midnight thru 6 a.m.

All the while, I kept my passengers informed of what my intentions were and what they could expect by going back to the terminal.

I also told them to expect to be on the taxiway for some time because of the Glycol delays. I did not mention the rioting or LaGuardia Airport's closure.

It was somewhat comforting to know all of my passengers agreed with me. Except for one, who wanted off the airplane and wanted his luggage. In other words, taxi back to the gate. Which I was not going to do. Had I done so? I would have to cancel our flight due to on-duty restrictions.

I gave him two choices, stay with the rest of the passengers. If he still wanted off. I would have a vehicle sent out to bring him to the terminal. I will not have any baggage handler offloading bags on a taxiway searching for his baggage! I had to repeat that twice before he got the message. He relented and stayed on board.

Timing it with LaGuardia's opening at 6 a.m. we were airborne at 4 a.m. When we shut down engines at LGA, our on-duty time was twenty hours and thirteen minutes. Our actual flight time for the day was thirteen hours and two minutes.

Would I ever do that again under the same circumstances? Probably?

MUSEUM OF NATURAL HISTORY

D uring the spring of 1982 Barb and I had decided to take a trip to New York City. Namely the American Museum of Natural History. Then take in the city's sights.

While in the museum and admiring its main feature, the Tyrannosaurs, I overheard two young boys talking. One asked the other.

"What would you do if it came alive and bit you on the neck?" The other said. "I'd run away." Of course, I laughed.

While viewing the other exhibits, their remarks kept haunting me. What would happen if, by some unexplained chance, these exhibits did come back to life?

For the next three months, with pencil, paper, typewriter, and creative thoughts racing through my mind, I sat down and began writing about how I could bring the exhibits back to life.

I even took a nighttime creative writing class at the local high school while doing so. Showing my work to those in the class and to our creative writing instructor.

I titled my book, Eclipse. The idea was based on an extraordinary event that took place. I used Professor Albert Einstein's Theory of Relativity. "...That for each event in this universe takes place; not only at a particular spot.... but also, at a definite time...."

I had the book Copyrighted in the summer of 1982 and marketed through Vantage Press in New York City. It had some success.

Years later in June of 1993 came, Jurassic Park. I even saw an attorney for copyright infringements. My book was similar, but not enough to warrant any compensation.

In December 2006 came Night at the Museum. It too takes place in the American Museum of Natural History in New York. In the movie, the T. Rex, and other exhibits come to life. As in my book when I had it copyrighted in 1982.

When that movie came out, I was asked by those who knew of my book and had purchased it, if I had received any royalties from the movie. Thinking the movie was based on my book.

No. Because I did not follow up by contacting an attorney after the movie came out. I had thought I had waited too long afterward to do so.

I did learn that Milan Trenc, a Croatian Illustrator wrote and illustrated a children's book in 1993 called, The Night at The Museum" after visiting the museum eleven years after my book was first published. Hmm.

PAN AMERICAN FLIGHT 759

O n July 9, 1982, nasty weather tragically raised its ugly head once again. Pan American World Airways Flight 759, a B-727, had lifted off from New Orleans International Airport. Years later it was changed to Louis Armstrong International Airport in 2001 in honor of his 100th birthday.

To the east of its departure path, were rain showers, with gusting and swirling winds. The aircraft had climbed to a height of between 95 to 150 feet above the ground. Then it suddenly plunged to the ground killing all on board.

The NTSB accident report AAR-83-02 dated March 21, 1983. "Determined that the probable cause of the accident was the airplane's encounter during the liftoff with a microburst-induced wind shear which imposed a downdraft and a decreasing headwind. The effects of which the pilot would have had difficulty recognizing and reacting to it in time, for the airplane's descent to be arrested before its impact with trees.

Contributing to the accident was the limited capability of then-current ground-based low-level wind shear detection technology that would have provided definitive guidance for controllers and pilots for use in avoiding low-level wind shear encounters."

Unfortunately, at the time of Eastern Air Lines flight 66's accident on June 24, 1975, seven years before, it had no technology for micro-burst and wind shears.

After the Pan-Am NTSB report came out in 1983, our flight training department in Miami on several occasions, integrated the same weather scenario for some of our B-727 crews. This was only done after normal simulator flight checks were completed and with the flight crew's permission. Most did.

After completing one of my simulator flight checks, our instructor asked my crew and me if we would be willing to take off under the same conditions as Pan-Am Flight 759. Of course, we said yes.

When we reached the height of 100 feet all hell broke loose! The aircraft, simulator, reacted so violently, it was as if it were in a micro-burst and wind-shear. We lost control of it and slammed into the ground. All in a matter of seconds. The good news, I had both my seatbelt and shoulder harness on. It's incredible what you can do in a simulator.

Of those crews who were asked to do the same scenario. All, to my knowledge, had crashed.

LOW FUEL ON BOARD, AND PAY CUTS

1983. Another year of turmoil within Eastern Air Line unions. Both the International Machinist, (IAM) and the flight attendants union, Transport Workers Union (TWU) threaten to strike. Under the same issues. Money and working conditions.

At that time Eastern was still losing money, even with all the agreed givebacks to Eastern from its employees. Givebacks were pay cuts and working conditions.

After nearly eighteen months of failed negotiations, strike votes were taken. In the meantime, a poll had been taken within the Eastern pilot group. In the event of a strike would we be willing to load passenger baggage into cargo compartments? The result was most pilots would.

In early March of 1983, I had been on my way to JFK for a flight to MIA. From where I lived in New Jersey it was usually a 1:45-minute drive to the airport.

On that morning as I was about to crossover the George Washington Bridge traffic had come to a standstill. It appeared that I was going to be late for my flight. At that time there were no cell phones.

Luckily there was a payphone available just before the toll booths. I made a quick telephone call to crew schedule and told them about my dilemma. They in turn had called out a reserve captain who lived near the airport to take my flight.

Shortly afterward, the traffic began moving again. By the time I arrived at the airport, I had less than twenty minutes before departure.

As I stepped into the elevator to crew schedule I bumped into the captain who was to take my flight. After a quick change of conversation, we both agreed that I should fly my trip.

He had assured me that he had checked the weather en route and at Miami and it should not be a problem. He had also requested minimum fuel for the flight. Which I did not think unusual.

Stormy weather has a bad habit of showing up when you're not expecting it. While en route my senior flight attendant had asked me if it would be okay for Frank Borman, the president of Eastern Air Lines, to enter the cockpit. Of course, I said yes.

Then came those unexpected weather conditions. Thunderstorms in Miami. Airport closed. Followed by having to enter a holding pattern on AR-7 some 150 miles north of the airport.

While we were holding, I had asked Mr. Borman how management's negotiations with Charlie Bryant, who headed the IAM, were going. At the same time, I kept an eye on our fuel gauges because of the minimum fuel load the other captain had ordered.

I still remember his reply. The company wasn't going to give in to their demands and most likely the IAM would strike. After a few more comments, he realized that I was paying more attention to the flight, than to him and he went back into the cabin.

After another 35 minutes of holding, we were close to eating into our fuel reserve. Once that happened I would have to go to my alternate airport which was Fort Lauderdale. Just minutes away from Miami. Thankfully, the airport had reopened and we were cleared to continue to Miami.

Then it closed again due to a change in wind direction. Instead of landing to the east on runway 9L. We would have to land west on runway 27R.

That meant having to go into another holding pattern at the MIA-VORTAC located several miles north of the airport.

After several turns in the holding pattern, and the airport still not open I decided to go to my alternate airport.

When I told ATC of my intentions, they told me Fort Lauderdale Airport had just closed because of the thunderstorms.

My only other choice was West Palm Beach Airport (PBI) seventy miles north. As I was about to depart for PBI, the Miami Airport reopened.

I then requested a priority landing at MIA due to having low fuel on board. They immediately gave me a radar vector to runway 27R and to be the first to land. Once we were parked at the gate, I took a good look at our fuel gauges. Let me just say. It was close.

Why did I not declare a fuel emergency vs requesting a low fuel priority? You have to write letters to the FAA explaining why the emergency. Whereas requesting a fuel priority, you don't.

The proposed strike by the IAM and the TWU had been set for March 24, 1983. Before that happened, Eastern management reached an agreement with both of them. That included pay raises and better working conditions.

As to getting the pilots and non-union workers to take over the loading of baggage, and cleaning aircraft? It had all been a bluff by the company to get the IAM to sign management's proposed contract.

Employee managers and non-managers, along with we pilots were stunned and angry at this betrayal. That Eastern management would pit one union against another and employees against employees.

I can still remember seeing Frank Borman staring daggers at the back of Charlie Bryant's head as he stood behind him during a news conference on television, announcing they had reached an agreement.

Even with the new contracts, the company was still bleeding cash. Then came new agreements in 1984 and more givebacks.

We Eastern pilots took a 22% pay cut and our flying hours increased from 80 hours per month to 85 hours per month.

The IAM, the TWU, and non-union workers took an 18% pay cut.

Of course, while all of this was going on, you tried to keep the politics of the airline business out of the cockpit.

That's not to say it didn't rise on occasion. Especially when the talk turned to your job and livelihood. A lot of the animosity was directed at our IAM with the thought of them striking again.

During those cost-cutting years, our aircraft were gathering more problems as to maintenance items not being completed. Enter the Minimum Equipment List (MEL). Under the MEL list, the aircraft could be dispatched with a part missing. Providing it was not an interictal component to the safety of the aircraft,

There were occasional clashes between flight crews and mechanics of work not being done. "We don't have the parts." That would be their answer, and I believed it to be true most of the time. One reason was some of our replacement parts had to be borrowed from other airlines. If they had them available.

Pressure to fly, pressure to repair. Man's attentions tend to drift under such circumstances.

MULTIPLE ENGINE FAILURES IN FLIGHT

On May 4, 1983, Eastern Air Lines flight 885, a Lockheed L-1011, aircraft number N334EA, lifted off from Miami International Airport bound for Nassau International Airport. A flight of less than an hour.

The preceding night the aircraft had undergone an overnight maintenance check. It included inspections of magnetic chip detectors inside the Rolls-Royce-powered RB-211 turbofan jet engines.

In command of the flight were Captain Richard Boddy, Captain Steve Thompson who was serving as a supervisory check airman, and Flight Engineer Dudley Barnes.

As they began their descent into Nassau, which was less than 50 miles from landing, the low oil pressure light on the #2 engine illuminated. The captain ordered a pre-cautionary shut-down of the engine. Since there was no maintenance available at Nassau he elected to return to Miami.

En route to Miami, low oil pressure lights for the #1 and #3 engines illuminated, and the oil quantity gauges for all three engines read zero. The possibility of having zero oil pressure and zero quantity on all three engines were practically nil.

They believed the gauges were faulty. Five minutes later the #3 engine failed. Shortly afterward their #1 engine had flamed out while they were attempting to restart the #2 engine.

With no power on any of the engines, the cabin lights went out and flight deck instruments stopped working. The aircraft began a descend from 13,000 feet to 4,000 feet at a rate of approximately 1,600 feet per minute.

With a catastrophe starting them in the face, they successfully restarted the #2 engine and executed a one-engine landing. One of the most difficult landings to be made.

After the landing, power from the #2 engine was so insufficient for the aircraft to taxi, a tug had to be used to tow them to the airport terminal. None of the 172 passengers and crew aboard were injured during the incident. If there were any heroes that day, it was the flight crew of flight EA855.

The NTSB AAR-84-04 dated March 9, 1984, found that the probable cause of this incident was. "The omission of all the O-ring seals on the master chip detector assemblies led to the loss of lubrication and damage to the airplane's three engines as a result of the failure of mechanics to follow the established and proper procedures for the installation of master chip detectors in the engine lubrication system. The repeated failure of supervisory personnel to require mechanics to comply strictly with the prescribed installation procedures, and the failure of Eastern Air Lines management to assess adequately the significance of similar previous occurrences and to act effectively to institute corrective action.

Contributing to the cause of the accident was the failure of Federal Aviation Administration maintenance inspectors to assess the significance of the incidents involving master chip detectors and to take effective surveillance and enforcement measures to prevent the recurrence of the incidents."

In addition, let us not forget the cabin flight attendant's role. After the captain informed the senior flight attendant of the possibility of an imminent water landing, the flight attendants immediately began to prepare the passengers for ditching.

As a result, some cabin preparations were rushed because of time. In general, the NTSB found the preparation of the cabin and passengers for ditching adequate. Nevertheless, there were problems, not with the flight attendants, but with some passengers. In their highly emotional and anxious state, there were difficulties in retrieving and donning the life vests. The investigation indicated that at least eight persons inflated their life vests in the aircraft. They also found that the most serious problem in donning a life vest was restricting the passenger's vision downward and to the front. Another reason not to inflate the life vest inside the aircraft, it made movement more difficult and they were more easily punctured.

During the flight attendant's briefing on how to launch and inflate a life raft, they called on able-bodied men to do so. Some passengers felt neglected in favor of them and were concerned that they would be left on board. All in all, the flight attendants were praised for handling and responding immediately to the emergency.

Although the aircraft did not ditch into the ocean, the U.S. Coast Guard had responded to the emergency and was prepared to conduct an extensive rescue operation. As did other surface vessels who were alerted to the possibility of the aircraft having to ditch.

HYDRAULIC FAILURE ON TAKE-OFF

On December 29, 1983, I would have a maintenance-related inspection failure incident. Our flight from Tampa to JFK was scheduled for two hours and thirty minutes. With me doing the flying.

Accompanying me were First Officer, Joe Holub Jr., and Second Officer Roger M. Ouellette. My cabin flight attendants were Senior Flight Attendant Judith M. Martinelli, along with flight attendants, Linda M. James, Carolyn B. Queen, and Carol A. Sonstrom Brown. Onboard were eighty-two passengers, cargo, and 36,000 pounds of fuel.

To our north, a strong line of thunderstorms was aligned west to east across the center of the state. One we had already planned on circumventing.

As we lifted off from runway 18L and had a positive rate-of-climb, I called for gear up. At the same time, we entered a 400-foot overcast. Instrument conditions.

When Joe put the landing gear handle in the up position I felt a sharp shudder in the aircraft. At the same time, Roger had called out. "We've lost system A hydraulics, both quantity and pressure."

System A operates the landing gear, a portion of the flaps, rudder control, and numerous other systems. The right main and nose gear retracted normally, and the left landing gear remained down and locked. It was obvious we would have to return and land.

Once we told ATC we had a problem with our landing gear they directed us to a holding area away from the airport. That put us out over the Gulf

266

of Mexico twenty miles from the airport and near thunderstorm activity. I turned the controls over to Joe while Roger and I began turning our attention to the problem. One man flies, and the others focus on the failure. After completing the appropriate checklists, we were able to extend the right main landing gear manually by the use of a hand crank. Then attempted to crank down the nose wheel landing gear but was unable to do so.

Because the left main landing gear and our take-off flaps couldn't be retracted it created a lot of drag. Drag means increasing the power on the engines to maintain flying airspeed. It also means eating up more fuel.

On the B-727 when you use take-off thrust it usually requires 12,000 pounds of fuel flow per hour, for a short period. We were carrying 36,000 pounds. So, in essence, if we had to maintain that, we would only have one hour of flight time before we had to land. Three engines times 12,000 equals 36,000. Of course, we were in level flight as we went through our procedures, but still burned 6,000 pounds per hour per engine because of the drag.

All of our attempts to lower the nose landing gear had failed. Even after consulting our maintenance department using SELCAL.

In between, I asked Judith to come to the cockpit and explained what had happened, and to move all of our first-class passengers to the back cabin.

One hour later, after several more unsuccessful attempts, I decided to land with the nose gear in the up position. I announced to our passengers what they might expect to happen. Regarding the nose of the aircraft scrapping the runway and the possibility of seeing smoke coming from it.

Factoring in my decision was the stormy weather, how far ATC had us holding from the airport, and most importantly, not running out of fuel in the event we had to make a go-around.

On my mind was, during one of my yearly recurrent ground schools, our instructor brought up United Airlines Flight 173.

Almost five years to the day, on December 28, 1978, flight 173 a DC-8 ran out of fuel while troubleshooting a landing gear malfunction.

The crew was so absorbed in the problem, they failed to realize their remaining fuel onboard and the distance to the airport from where they were. They crashed six miles from the airport when all four engines began flaming out. Of the 179 passengers and crew on board, ten died.

As I had begun our return to Tampa, maintenance made one more suggestion that was not covered in our B-727 manual. They had suggested putting the gear handle in the down position and turning the A hydraulic pumps back on. Hoping for any cavitating of any fluid left in the return lines might drop the nose gear.

As we passed the outer marker on our approach to runway 18L. Nothing. At 500 feet and two miles from touchdown, the nose gear came out, went down, and locked into position just before we touched down. Along with three beautiful green lights on the instrument panel and we landed normally.

With what little nose wheel steering we had, we managed to clear the runway and were eventually towed to the terminal.

We heard a lot of happy shouts and applause from our passengers when we parked at the gate.

Upon maintenance investigation, it was determined the left main gear-up line had ruptured preventing retraction, and the nose gear cable drum bearing had frozen due to corrosion. Something maintenance had missed on their inspections. Thereby preventing manual cranking down the nose gear.

We also learned in our attempt to get as much pressure using the hand crank, we had stretched the cables to the landing gear and popped some rivets.

After that fiasco inspection of all of Eastern's B-727s was required to help prevent it from happening again.

I cannot say enough about my flight crew Joe, Roger, Judith, Linda, Carolyn, and Carol. They did an exemplary job in the cockpit and the cabin.

A MENTALLY DISTURBED PASSENGER

For the next couple of months, it's. All Quiet on the Western Front. Calm throughout, and no problems.

Our flight from LGA-TPA had gone smoothly until we were about one hour from landing. My senior flight attendant informed me that a male passenger was making unwanted advances toward a young girl in the coach section.

It was one of the few times that I, as a captain, had to go back into the cabin to address a situation while in flight. A very long story short. I took one look at the guy and realized there might be something mentally wrong with him.

His eyes had the wildest look I have ever seen on someone. I never talked to him, with the thought in mind that doing so could make matters worse. At that point I had the flight attendant move the girl to the first-class section. Once I was back in the cockpit I radioed ahead to have the police meet the aircraft.

According to them and the flight attendant, the girl was traveling alone to Tampa to meet her godparents for the first time. En route, the man, who was sitting next to her in the coach section had struck up a conversation with her.

During the conversation, he asked her how old she was. She told him she was seventeen when she was only thirteen. He then asked her to come to the apartment he had in Tampa and began fondling her thighs. That was when the girl became frightened and rang for the flight attendant.

The police told me the girl would have to be the one to file charges against him. Not I, nor her godparents when they came on board to meet her.

In the meantime, the police told me they would take him into custody under the Baker Act. A law that allows someone to be held for psychiatric evaluation for 72 hours.

They also said, that before this incident, he had been ordered not to leave the state of Florida. It made me wonder if he may have committed a crime while there in New York.

On my next flight to Tampa, I found out the girl did file charges against him.

AN AIRLINE SOAP OPERA?

S oap operas are well-known on television. An airline soap opera? Here within the hollow halls of our JFK base, two pilots and one well-known stewardess, with the company, had all the ramifications of being one.

Accusations abounded. Each accused one other of being harassed. One pilot even wrote a letter to our chief pilot about being threatened by his ex-wife and of her trying to shoot him on two separate occasions.

The other pilot in question was also the stewardess's ex-husband declaring that he too was being harassed by her. In either case, no action was taken against the stewardess.

Copies of letters to the chief pilot's office were often posted on the shuttles bulletin board in our LGA's flight operations. Namely to let other pilots and flight attendants know the type of person this stewardess was. Although most of us who were flying the shuttle knew.

Enter the stewardess and husband number ten. According to the letter given to me by one of her pilot exes.

I had met husband number ten on a flight from LGA-MIA. He was a passenger sitting in first class and she was the senior flight attendant working the first-class section.

As the captain of the flight, she told me her husband would like to talk to me before we land in Miami. Knowing her, I reluctantly went into the cabin to meet her new husband. The Reverend Austin Miles.

Reverend Miles was formerly a well-known celebrity, both on television for many years as a Ringmaster, and later with the Pentecostal Church.

After a short introduction and conversation with his wife, he proceeded to open a briefcase and took out numerous letters that were written between his wife and said, pilots. He also told me one of her ex-pilot husbands was to meet the aircraft in Miami, and he may cause trouble when we land.

Then he went on to say, if he does, he will contact the news media, and sue Eastern.

I read two pages of one letter and handed them back. I told him that this was between, him, his wife, and her exes, and not Eastern Air Lines, and returned to the flight deck.

We land, no ex-pilot husband. No media was being called. I did make a phone call to the chief pilot in New York and let him know what took place.

He told me he was well aware of the pilots and the stewardess and their contempt for one another. End of the telephone call.

It wasn't long after that fiasco, the stewardess began making accusations against the reverend. Followed by Reverend Miles divorcing the stewardess.

He even wrote a letter to one of the pilots in question and apologized. Blaming her for creating so many lies that pitted him against them. That letter was posted on the bulletin board in LGA's flight operations for all to see.

For the rest of 1984, things go smoothly. Enter 1985.

THE LOSS OF EASTERN FLIGHT 980

South America beckons. With the demise of Braniff International Airline, its South American routes had become available.

President Ronald Reagan, not wanting to allow Pan American Airways to have a monopoly in South America, approved the C.A.B. decision to give the routes to Eastern Air Lines. On May 14, 1982, Eastern began air service to Latin countries.

Flying into, what you might call, third-world-countries, in regards to updated navigation aids, were very limited. Language problems sometimes plagued communications between flight crews and air traffic controllers.

When Eastern purchased those routes to South America, it issued a memo warning all pilots to exercise a "dose of pilot-type skepticism" when in contact with them.

For the next three years, all flights into South America operate safely in its rugged and dangerous Andes mountainous areas.

At 5:57 p. m. on January 1, 1985, Eastern Air Lines flight 980 had lifted off from Asuncion, Paraguay bound for La Paz, Bolivia.

It was to be the first stop of two stops on its way to its final destination Miami, Florida. The other was Guayaquil, Ecuador. In command of the flight was Captain Larry Campbell, whom I had flown with many times while he was based in JFK. He was the first officer and I was a second officer.

It was Larry's first time flying into La Paz. Assisting him were First Officer Kenneth Rhodes and Flight Engineer Mark Bird and five acting Chilean flight attendants who were based in Santiago. Paul Adler, Pablo Letelier, Marilyn MacQueen, Robert O'Brie, and Paula Valenzuela.

273

Onboard were 19 passengers, and two airline pilot supervisors. Captain J. B. Loseth Jr. and Second Officer Haywood H. Hargrove Jr. Both rode as passengers.

At approximately 7:47 p. m. flight 980 was cleared by Bolivian ATC to descend from 25,000 feet to 18,000 feet. From that point, the aircraft navigated off the airway for some unknown reason. There would be speculations later, that their departure from the airway was due to weather and to their onboard navigation system called Omega.

25 miles from runway 9R at El Alto Airport, flight 980 struck Mt. Illimani at its 19,600 point. Some 1,500 feet below its summit. Most likely at over 300 miles per hour. The aircraft disintegrated on impact. All on board perished.

Rescue attempts had begun immediately, but due to weather, the altitude at the site of the crash, and the fact that even helicopters could not operate at such an altitude, were forced to delay any rescue.

In October 1985 the United States NTSB and with the cooperation of the Bolivian government lead a team of U.S. investigators to the crash site in hopes of finding both the Flight Data Recorder (FDR) and the Cockpit Voice Recorder (CVR.) However, because the wreckage was spread over a vast area and covered by 6 to 9 meters of snow (20 to 30 feet) it was impossible for them to locate either one.

ALPA's accident investigation board noted that on flights between Paraguay and Bolivia, it found that the Omega system steered aircraft four miles off course in the direction of Mt. Illimani.

There were other attempts contemplated to make recoveries by a few Eastern Air Line pilots, but those were abandoned as being too risky.

What followed next was much conjecture as to what caused Flight 980's fate, including a bomb going off in-flight when no bodies or blood was found at the crash site. Speculation that proved wrong some thirty years later.

As to the approach to La Paz's El Alto International Airport. The airport sits at an elevation of 13,325 feet above sea level the highest international airport of any airport in the world. The air is so thin that planes land at

200 miles per hour because they would probably stall out at their normal landing airspeeds of 140 miles per hour.

As to the pilot's preparation for the approach and the operation of the B-727 Captain Campbell was flying, other factors might have come into play. One was the airport's altitude.

The pilots were required to don their oxygen masks all through their approach, and landing. Per FAA regulations.

Unfortunately, because there was no voice recorder recovery, no one was sure what was taking place in the cockpit. Questions arose.

Had they delayed putting on their oxygen masks in preparation for the drop-down descent at night, in bad weather to land, at an airport they were unfamiliar with?

If so, were they experiencing stages of Hypoxia and its effect on the body? Confused thoughts as to where they were? No one knows.

On June 4, 2016, the cockpit voice recorder and many smashed parts of the plane's Black Box, were recovered by a team of two in the Andes mountains. Unfortunately, the box was in several pieces and would prove useless in determining what took place in the cockpit.

Years previous parts of the aircraft had been recovered as were body parts. There were no indications that a bomb brought the aircraft down.

To date, no probable cause of the accident has been determined. The U. S. NTSB-public document information on this accident is stored on NTSB microfiche number 29062. With still no determination of what caused the accident.

A VERY, VERY, VIOLENT LIGHTNING STRIKE

On April 6, 1985, flying gets a little hairy. Literally. Flying for the day was supposed to be rather simple. Newark to Bermuda. From Bermuda to Baltimore Washington International Airport then on to Philadelphia and layover.

From EWR to BDA the flight had gone quite smoothly even though we were skirting thunderstorms. From BDA to BWI the thunderstorms were building to a much higher intensity.

We had passed over the Maryland shoreline at 17,000 feet skimming through the tops of some scattered clouds at 350 knots, and in between two large building Nympho-Cumulonimbus clouds. My first officer was doing the flying.

Knowing there was always the possibility of moderate turbulence associated with them, I told him to reduce our flying airspeed to 280 knots. I also mentioned the possibility of being struck by lightning.

Remembering that day when we were approaching West Palm Beach years ago, and of the lighting strike while landing in Pittsburg.

The words hadn't come out of my mouth when I felt the heated shock wave of a lightning bolt coming our way on the right side of my face.

Its electrified air made the hair on my head and arms rise. Followed by what felt as though the aircraft was struck with a mighty blow from a gigantic sledgehammer. So violent, it seemingly staggered from the strike.

The bolt had struck several feet below the right-forward galley door that is located just several feet behind and below the cockpit.

An instant later our compasses began oscillating and became unreliable. Fortunately, we had broke out into a clear sky and were able to land at BWI without having to rely on them.

In the interim, I announced to our passengers what had happened. After we landed and were parked at the gate, I had an opportunity to talk to some of them. Many thought we had collided with another aircraft.

We then made a full inspection of the aircraft with our maintenance team. What we found was quite shocking. No pun intended.

A huge silver/chrome/gold weld spot of approximately twelve inches in diameter could be seen below the right forward galley door where it had struck.

All of our static wicks that are on the trailing edges of the wings for static discharges, were blown off. Two light dome covers in the cockpit were missing, except for what looked like microplastic dust on the cockpit floor. We thought they had disintegrated when the bolt struck.

The flight attendants who were in the first-class section and had been standing near the cockpit when it struck, thought it had been blown off. They were afraid to open the door for fear it was missing. It was that violent. The aircraft was taken out of service and de-magnetized.

Had the bolt struck the wing where it joins the fuselage and where the fuel is stored in the wings, it might have been a different story.

Many other aircraft have been known to be struck violently in flight and crashed while making their approach to landings. One was Pan American's Flight 214, a B-707 as it passed over Elkton, Maryland in 1963, killing all on board. The site was not far from where we were when we got hit. Must admit. The whole crew went to the bar that night.

All through the years, since aviation first took to the skies, there have been numerous reports of aircraft being struck by lightning while flying. Fortunately, the majority land safely. Especially after being struck by a bolt that travels through the air at approximately 200,000 miles per hour. As to the claps of thunder you hear, approximately 750 miles per hour.

From lightning strikes to the birds and the bees. May 22, 1985.

While descending through 500 hundred feet on our final approach to land at Albuquerque, New Mexico, we flew through a swarm of bees that had to be in the tens of thousands.

So many, their remains covered all of our front cockpit's windows and we were unable to see through them because of the goo they had left.

To see the runway and make a safe landing, I had to side-slipped the B-727 to touchdown. One of the few times I ever had to do so. Getting that glop off the windows, the Radom, and the leading edge of the wings was something else.

FROM FLIGHT ATTENDANT TO HOLLYWOOD

I had mentioned that quite a few Eastern employees looked to other possible careers other than flying. Several come to mind.

Martha Braverman was one of our stewardesses who was based in New York and was also a part-time actress having appeared on several well-known soap operas during the 1980s playing a nurse.

Another was Eastern Flight Attendant Tom Moore. He became well known for his 1986 role in a very popular wartime movie. Who?

Although Tom and I had only flown several trips together, there was one layover in Sarasota that still comes to mind. It was the following morning in September 1985.

I had come down to breakfast at the hotel where my crew and I were staying. Martha saw me as I entered the restaurant and invited me to join her and another stewardess.

I looked to my left and Tom was sitting next to a window by himself reading. I asked Martha if Tom could join us thinking he wasn't asked. She told me he was studying a script for a movie he was to try out for. At the time I did not know Tom had acted in a few movies prior.

She also said he had become a flight attendant so he could use employee pass privileges to fly to other cities when acting opportunities presented themselves.

After that particular flight, we never flew together again. Whether the script he had been reading that morning had anything to do with what would become one of the most-seen war movie at the time. Or, make him a screen idol? I don't know.

Oh. Tom Moore's stage name. Tom Berenger. He played Staff Sargent Barnes in the movie. Platoon!

One of the most realistic war-movie that was ever brought to the screen. It was nominated for 8 Academy Awards in 1986.

INFLIGHT ENGINE FAILURES

O ctober 29, 1985, and it's still hurricane season. Hurricane Juan was fast approaching the Louisiana coastline. The winds at New Orleans International Airport on that day had reached gale force as we began our take-off roll for LGA.

As we lifted off from runway 10 our number 2 engine began compressor stalling. Which makes a sound as though the jet engine was loudly backfiring. This sometimes happens when taking off in a heavy crosswind.

Especially when it concerns the number two engine on a B-727 inlet duct. That is called an s-duct. Without going through its whole aerodynamics, the inlet duct is located at the top of the fuselage of the number 2 engine.

The air intake is then directed downward through the curvature of the duct that allows airflow through the engine. When the flow of air is disrupted, the blades of the jet engine can be badly damaged.

When that began to happen, I throttled the number two engine to idle, just long enough to allow normal airflow to continue through it. As we built up our flying airspeed the stalling stopped and I increased the throttle to our climb power.

After we leveled off at our cruising altitude of 33,000 feet, the number 2 engine began compressor stalling again. Before I could shut it down, the number 1 engine began compressor stalling. It was highly unusual to have two engine's compressor stalling at the same time.

I decided to throttle the number 2 engine to idle. Thinking, if number 1 failed, I still would have number 2 available as a backup.

I informed ATC that I would have to make an emergency landing in

Atlanta and the reason why.

Fortunately, neither engine failed. If both had, I would have had to make a single-engine landing, using the number 3 engine for power. That is the worst-case scenario you can have on the B-727. Once you commit to land, there is no going around for another attempt.

During our maintenance team's inspection of the engines, they found that the inlet blades on both engines were bent and badly damaged. Both engines had to be replaced.

BEGINNING OF THE END FOR EASTERN?

Bad news arrives. On February 24, 1986, Texas Air Corporation agreed to buy Eastern Air Lines for $600 million. Eight months later, the Department of Transportation approved the acquisition, but not for $600 million, but $676 million.

Shocked employees can't believe what was happening. The dark side of the universe's aviation world takes control.

Frank Lorenzo the Chairman and C.E.O. of Continental Airlines, of which Texas Air was the parent corporation, succeeded Frank Borman to take charge of Eastern Air Lines on October 1, 1986.

Mr. Borman's reign which began on December 16, 1974, and lasted for nearly twelve years was now over.

In the interim, the airline seemed to be always in debt. Even with all the give back the employees had given in wages and benefits, which was some $836 million that allowed it to keep flexing its wings. Barely.

At the time, I think all of us employees felt it was directed at ridding Eastern of its three unions. ALPA, the TWU, and the IAM, and, to break them if he could. We all knew there was no love lost between Eastern management and Charlie Bryan, who was the leader of the machinist union in Miami.

It wasn't long before the rape of Eastern Air Lines began. Lorenzo deposed the famous Eastern Shuttle that serviced, New York, Newark, Washington, and Boston.

In May of 1986, slots and gates at the airports were sold to Pan American for $65 million. They would be later sold to Donald Trump in 1988 for $365 million. Talk about distraction while flying.

The biggest conversation of worry. Rumors of us Eastern pilots being merged into the Continental Airlines pilot's list. It was something that required a lot of willpower to not bring up the subject in the cockpit while flying.

There was mention of making a national seniority list for all airline pilots, regardless of what airline they had flown for.

The idea, if your airline went belly-up, you would be able to have a pilot position on another airline based on your date of hire with what was your original airline.

Of course, those pilots who were looking at their airline going out of business were all for it. The pilots whose airlines were still operating successfully laughed in their faces. In the end. No national pilot seniority list ever happened.

Life in the sky still went on. Sunrises, sunsets. Exit 1986. Enter 1987. Anything out of the ordinary is bound to happen no matter where you are. In the skies, it gets a little more complicated.

The flight from Fort Lauderdale to La Guardia had gone fairly smoothly. As we crossed northbound over Wilmington, North Carolina my senior stewardess had come into the cockpit and told me one of the passengers in the coach section was in severe pain.

I told her to make an announcement to see if there was a doctor on board and to let me know what was happening.

Ten minutes passed when she re-entered the cockpit and said that a doctor did look at the man and he thought he should be okay.

She insisted the man's pain was getting worse. I asked her what kind of doctor he was. Her answer. A physiatrist. That was when I took it upon myself to go back into the cabin and look at the man.

I could see tears beginning to well in the man's eyes and asked him what he thought was causing the pain.

He said he had been in a Fort Lauderdale hospital for a prostate problem and that he couldn't urinate. Then stated the doctor wanted to perform a Transurethral resection of the prostate (TURP.) In the meantime, the doctor had him use a catheter.

Instead, he decided to go back to New York where he lived and have the procedure done there. He had the catheter removed and left the hospital. In the interim, he had drank coffee, water, and more coffee on the airplane.

He told me while we were en route to LGA, he had gone to the lavatory and tried to urinate, but couldn't. My concern was his bladder might rupture.

Thinking of my passenger's well-being, I decided to make an emergency landing in Richmond, Virginia. I radioed ahead to have an emergency medical service (EMS) ambulance meet the airplane when we landed. Which they did.

After arriving at LGA, I contacted flight operations in Richmond to see about our passenger's condition.

According to them, had I not made that stop in Richmond, the EMS team told them, they felt it was a matter of minutes before his bladder would have burst.

They also added the EMS team had to use a straw, to void his bladder. What? Then added, it was a sterile ureteral stent.

MORE MAINTENANCE PROBLEMS

Although we Eastern employees were doing our best to help the airline, more trouble within our maintenance department. In February the FAA cites Eastern for infringements in its maintenance department.

During the month, the company leased six Airbuses to Continental for $225,000 per aircraft per month. Even that didn't help our cash flow.

In November 1987 came another bitter pill to swallow. With the airline losing millions of dollars a day arises the possibility of laying off 3,500 personnel due to Lorenzo's mismanagement.

At the end of December 1987, Eastern's contract with the IAM expired. Negotiations began, then ceased.

The IAM wanted a wage increase of more than 6% even though the airline was losing millions. Management decides to downsize by 12%. The selling of Eastern Air Lines begin.

Our Kansas City hub was eliminated. That didn't help.

October 1988, the whirlwind of elimination was spinning faster.

Donald Trump took control of the Eastern Shuttle from Pan American Airways. With it, he received 17 Boeing 727-200's and 90 landing slots.

Those of us often flew the shuttle, which included flight crews from three major cities, Boston, Newark, La Guardia, and Washington. Felt if any portion of our airline was making money it was the shuttle.

The one good inclusion with the sale of the shuttle also included 200 Eastern pilots and other Eastern employees. In seniority.

Those that went with Trump could see the handwriting on the wall as to what was lay ahead for Eastern.

I had the opportunity to go with Trump, but I declined. I still had hope that Eastern would survive.

In the meantime, I again tried my hand at writing. In February 1989 I sat down and wrote an article about black jockeys of the nineteen hundred's. I had titled it, Black Winners of the Kentucky Derby.

The idea had come from my father who enjoyed betting on horses. He had once told me a story about several of those jockey's winning the Kentucky Derby numerous times. Which I had never forgotten.

I submitted the article to Ebony Magazine in February. Much to my surprise, I received a telephone call from one of its senior editors, Charles Sanders.

He told me the article would be in their May 1989 issue. Along with a check for $600 when the article was published. On the cover of the magazine. Bill and Camille Cosby

Then I had to put my writing on the back burner.

In February 1989 Eastern announced it had lost $718 million in 1988. That same month negotiations between Lorenzo and the IAM collapsed when Lorenzo refused binding arbitration.

The head of the Mediation Board had asked then-President George H. Bush, for a Presidential Emergency Board (PEB) to help resolve the impasse. He refused. His close ties with Lorenzo were quickly questioned. Did President Bush want to see labor unions busted?

Since 1928 the NMB had asked for a PEB 211 times, with no refusals from any sitting president of the White House. President George Bush broke the pattern.

On March 1, 1989, the FAA gave Donald Trump to go-ahead to begin the new, Trump Shuttle. Unfortunately, it lost money for several years before it was acquired by U.S. Airways in 1992.

In the meantime, Easterns Master Executive Board (MEC) presented four demands on Lorenzo. A business plan that would work. Stop looting Eastern assets and giving them to Continental. They wanted Eastern operations merged into Continental's which might bring the combined operation back into ALPA.

The fourth demand. A contract with Lorenzo's holding company, Texas Air Corporation, and not with Eastern.

They knew that any bankruptcy court could invalidate any promise Lorenzo made to them in Eastern's name. If he and the MEC couldn't come to turns, the Eastern pilots would walk. On March 2, Lorenzo rejected ALPA's ultimatum.

Three days later on March 4, 1989, Eastern's IAM went on strike.

WALKING THE PICKET LINE

That same day we Eastern pilots, not all, and our Eastern flight attendants, not all, honored the IAM picket lines. Our groups called our attempt at supporting it, a sympathy strike. From that day forward, and for the next two years, the roller-coaster ride of would Eastern Air Lines survive. Had begun.

At every city Eastern Air Lines served, picket lines began to form at airport terminals. Every crew base had already prepared for the possibility of a strike happening and had plans implemented.

Our strike headquarters was located at the Electrical Unions headquarters in Iselin, New Jersey. A short distance from Newark International Airport where we would be picketing.

Of the 3,600 Eastern pilots, approximately 120 pilots crossed the picket line during the first week of the strike. Many flight attendants and mechanics also crossed picket lines. They would forevermore be known as, Scabs!

For the next nine months, we striking pilots and flight attendants carried signs at the entrance of the Eastern Air Lines Newark terminal. Denouncing Frank Lorenzo and the reasons why.

Joining our sympathy strike were members of the police, fireman, and electrical worker's unions.

It also became apparent as though it were the Civil War. The North against the South. Brother against brother. Father against son. Except it was Eastern.

Eastern had quite a few pilots who had sons, brothers, and daughters who flew for Eastern at that time. Some family members walked the picket line, while others chose to cross the picket line. I can't imagine how difficult it must have been for the same family member to have had to make those choices.

As the strike wore on, a large amount of duress came with it.

There were pilots whom I walked the picket line with who had thoughts of crossing the picket line. Not to support Frank Lorenzo nor any flight crew member who had already crossed. But to preserve one's love of flying and for its benefits. Even if it meant being merged into Continental Airlines.

It was a known fact if the airline you had flown for folded, and you were fortunate to latch on to another airline you would go to the bottom of their pilot's seniority list. At their minimum wage pay scale, and on probation. Regardless of how experienced you were. Either way, it was a grim outlook.

What was hard for me to take, were the many pilots, flight attendants, and flight operation personnel I had known for over twenty-five years who crossed the picket line.

On one occasion while picketing, I asked one of the pilots I had often flown with why he crossed. His answer was the middle finger of his right hand.

When we struck, there were no paychecks to pay your bills. Not only that, there were no unemployment benefits in New Jersey at that time for people who went on strike. Enter ALPA.

The Airline Pilots Association at that time was headed by a Delta Airlines captain. Hank Duffy. Quite honestly, there was no love lost between Delta's pilots and Eastern Air Line pilots, strictly from a professional point of view as to who were the better pilots. Eastern pilots.

If I were to try to explain all that took place from March 4, 1989, to the shutdown of Eastern Air Lines on January 18, 1991, I would have to add another 1,000 pages. So, I will give you what I believe were the highlights of those very, very emotional, stressful, and tumultuous two years, and the enormous effect it would have on family members and friendships.

DAMAGED LIVES, LOST
FRIENDSHIPS, SUICIDES

E astern had at that time 28,000 plus employees. Add spouses and children. Another 66,000. Let us not forget the suppliers who serviced the airline. Add thousands more. Then add what it really costs! Divorces, bankruptcy, suicides. All because of one man. Frank Lorenzo!

Nine days after the strike began ALPA responded. The Master Executive Board (MEC) chairman voted for strike benefits of $2,400 per month, per pilot, plus a package of loans if needed.

The money came from a percentage of income from pilots of other airlines that belong to ALPA. Even the American Airlines pilots union, The Allied Pilots Association" contributed $100,000 to the fund.

Furthermore, Duffy announced that the entire $37 million in ALPA's Major Contingency Fund would be available to beat Lorenzo.

With the support from ALPA, new players to beat Lorenzo were called upon. The first was Farrell Kupersmith, an analyst from Touche Ross who had conducted an extensive analysis on Lorenzo.

He convinced ALPA that if Lorenzo didn't agree to a four-point plan, they could find the financial pressure to gain control of the airline.

Lorenzo parried by declaring bankruptcy on March 9, 1989. In New York, and not Miami where Eastern's headquarter was.

Another player was Judge Burton R. Lifland. He was not one for favoring labor. Nor was he in favor of pension obligations, unpaid salaries, and creditors who were owed millions.

A small ray of hope during that time had come from Judge Lifland's bankruptcy court. He appointed Washington lawyer David Shapiro, examiner, to facilitate a search for a buyer for Eastern. Even Lorenzo had said he favored it.

Then enter Peter Ueberroth, who was a former commissioner of baseball. He had solid financial backing and suggested a season airline manager to run Eastern which the union had backed. Marty Shugrue.

Shugrue was a former executive with Texas Air Corporation Lorenzo had once owned, and who Lorenzo fired. That was the good news that brought the roller-coaster ride to the top of its apex.

Then came Lorenzo's negotiating. Every time a deal had been thought done, Lorenzo wanted changes. In the meantime Lorenzo sold off more of Eastern's assets, making the airline more worthless. The crowning blow was when Donald Trump purchased the shuttle in May of 1989. Exit Peter Ueberroth. The rollercoaster is beginning another deeper plunge.

During the summer of 1989, a group of us New York pilots had taken it upon ourselves to sit in on one of Judge Lifland's bankruptcy court sessions in New York City. In uniform.

As we marched toward 1 Bowling Green in Manhattan, we were surrounded by reporters and news cameramen, and a large throng of people. We then had to push our way into the courthouse.

Inside, and having had to watch and listened to the proceedings for several hours, I had come to one conclusion. This was after Judge Lifland told our attorney to shut up and sit down when he objected to a point being made by Lorenzo's attorney. That this was a no-win deal for anyone, except Lorenzo.

What had first become a solidarity commitment by striking pilots, began to crack. In July, the heads of the pilot's Local Executive Committee (LEC) met in an Alexandria, Virginia hotel.

At issue. A strike vote. Whether to continue striking or go back to work unconditionally. The worry. Some 700 scab pilots had completed their initial operating experience (IOE).

That meant that for those of us pilots who were still striking, only 1,300 to 1,700 would be recalled. Inside Lorenzo's headquarters, the rumor was only 950 pilots would be recalled. The rest going to new hire scabs.

What followed cast more doubt on our successful attempt to beat Lorenzo. After five months of solidarity, an additional 500 pilots cross the picket line. Still, many of us vowed to stay the course and our picketing continued.

GOOD MORNING AMERICA WITH JOAN LUNDEN

I n New York, we Eastern pilots who were still walking the picket line were invited to appear on Good Morning America with Host Joan Lunden.

Thanks to her, we were able to voice our opinion to the millions of her viewers as to what was really taking place at Eastern Air Lines with Frank Lorenzo at the helm. I can't be sure, but after that show that millions of people must have watched, Eastern's passenger boardings went down.

Six months into the strike it was apparent loyal passengers who preferred to fly Eastern, were now switching to other airlines. There were a dozen or more reasons why. Depending on who you talked to.

Most did not want to cross a picket line and were concerned about the safety of flying an airline with a history of maintenance problems.

Then too, was the media's attention in support of the strikers. Whatever the reason, passenger loads kept falling, and the airline was nose-diving into deeper debt.

In October another issue arose within the rank and file. It was obvious the bankruptcy court was in Lorenzo's favor. Suitors to buy Eastern from Lorenzo came and went.

The strike was weakening. A vote was taken on whether or not to continue strike assessments to still pay us striking pilots. It passed, by a very narrow margin.

In Eastern's training center in Miami, rumors had abounded that approximately 40% of the 700 new hire scabs fail to complete their training. In other words, bust their check rides and were let go. When the word was leaked to the media, passenger loads fell dramatically.

Nine months into the strike, we Eastern pilots who were still on strike lobbied Congress to impose a back door PEB, which would force President Bush to rethink his position and to use his power to intervene on behalf of the pilots. With his ties to Lorenzo, there was no way in hell he was going to do that.

On November 23, 1989, although we Eastern pilots valiantly fought to preserve an airline that was literally being torn apart by Lorenzo, realized the battle was lost and called an end to our strike. A very bitter pill to swallow.

From start to finish, March 4, 1989, to November 23, 1989, and 272 days of striking, we pilots had persevered against all odds. We became known as the 272-pilot group that fought Lorenzo. Ahead, another fight for the pilots to be recalled to get our flying careers back.

FRAGMENTATION AND THE RIGHT TO BE RECALLED

In the summer of 1989, Hank Duffy, the head of ALPA believed with Lorenzo's mismanagement, Eastern would not have survived, regardless of whether the Eastern pilots called off their sympathy strike.

That there was nothing ALPA could do could to save it. The question, then, if Eastern did fold, what could he do to salvage our careers?

In the July 1989 issue of the Air Line Pilot Magazine, its union magazine, had done an editorial on the moral obligations of all pilots to persuade their airlines to hire us Eastern strikers.

"A willingness to share seniority is not only the moral way to operate –even though it may impinge upon one's own advancement- it is also an important check of our Association's character." Duffy wrote.

"Conversely, a move that results from Eastern equipment sales to "our" company is a move up off the backs of striking pilots. To profit thusly is a serious breach of faith."

He had suggested a form of fragmentation, even if it meant Eastern's striking pilots going to the bottom of Delta's seniority list. His approach to the CEO of Delta, Ron Allen, at the time, was met with sarcasm.

According to Duffy. Allen's answer. "Why should I hire trouble? I can hire all the 28-year-old ex-military pilots I need."

Delta did get some of Eastern's equipment, in a round-about way. Eastern spun off some of its aircraft to then Pan Am, without any Eastern pilots.

When Pan Am folded, some aircraft and Pan Am pilots went to Delta. Fragmentation of sorts.

Midway Airline pilot's leadership tried to honor Duffy's encouragement. When some of Eastern equipment and routes went to Midway, they tried to get some 400 of Eastern's striking pilots hired, in seniority. Management refused.

United, became a bright spot for Eastern pilots. Its pilots demanded that Eastern's strikers be given first-right-of-hire, or something approaching it. Eventually, 600 Eastern pilots would end up in United cockpits. Some 300 would become instructors in United's training center.

In June 1989, Judge Lifland rejected ALPA's petition to have a trustee installed to run Eastern in Lorenzo's place.

Creditors were still asking Lorenzo for the money owed to them. He had promised that he would pay them At 100 cents on the dollar, through the sale of more assets and downsizing the airline. Lifland had gone along with his plan.

By December 1989 nothing Lorenzo did, would generate more passengers or profit.

In January 1990 Lorenzo reneged on his promise to pay back creditors fully and offered instead only 50 cents on the dollar. Most of the money was to be paid to them by the sale of Eastern's South American routes to American Airlines.

In March 1990, Examiner Shapiro found that Lorenzo had indeed cherry-picked Eastern's assets and had not paid a fair price for them. He also found that Lorenzo had cheated Eastern and, by inference, its creditors. Lorenzo settled out of court, in effect pleading guilty to looting.

ALPA then asked Lifland to appoint a trustee to run Eastern, but he stayed the motion. In the interim Phil Bakes had become the President of Eastern. Still, the losses kept mounting. It was ascertained that between March 1989 to April 1990, Lorenzo had lost $1.2 billion.

At the beginning of April Lorenzo reneged again on his promise to the creditors. Instead of 50 cents on the dollar, it would be 25 cents on the dollar, of which 5 cents was cash. The remainder would be in junk bonds.

By then, the creditors had enough and echoed their thoughts to Lifland. He finally agreed. On April 18, 1990, Lifland named Martin Shugrue as trustee. Lorenzo, humiliated and publicly revealed as incompetent, was out.

With Shugrue as trustee, Bakes resigned as Eastern's president.

Next up recall. The battle for fragmentation began.

From the moment Lorenzo was out, ALPA began mounting the process of having us striking pilots recalled. Five more months of court proceedings were on the agenda. The roller-coaster ride didn't stop.

The pilot recall list dwindled. Some pilots retired early, some with disabilities, and some through suicide. All of which had a dire effect on our retirement funds. Although at the time I did not realize it.

Eastern pilots had two retirement funds called an A-Fund and a B-fund. The A-fund was an annuity. The other is invested in real estate, stock, etc. Those who could, when they retired, could choose a lump-sum payment from the B-Fund. They would also receive their A-Fund.

At the time, I had no intention of retiring. I wanted my flying job back! So, I wasn't aware of those who were retiring or what they were receiving.

By then, the panic was gripping the scabs, with them knowing two things. Shugrue was not Lorenzo and he owed them nothing. Once we striking pilots were recalled and back in our seniority, and back in the cockpit with them. It wasn't going to be a very pleasant atmosphere.

In May 1990, they tried to form their own union, calling it the Eastern Pilots Association, and petitioning the National Mediation Board. It went nowhere. All the while ALPA lawyers were fighting the court to have us strikers recalled.

By that time, it had been more than a year since I had last flown an aircraft. How I yearned to get back into a cockpit.

During the summer of 1990, our son Scott, an Air Force pilot at the time, was based at Offutt Air Force Base in Omaha, Nebraska flying the RC-135.

The RC-135, a Boeing 707, was an electronic intelligence-designed aircraft. Later used extensively during Operation Desert Storm, in which our son would fly combat missions during it.

As the months rolled by, Barb and I drove from New Jersey to visit Scott and his wife Suzanne. While there Scott had made arrangements with the base commander's permission, to allow me to fly the RC-135 simulator.

A SHOT OF ADRENALINE AS I PUSHED THE THROTTLES

As I pushed those four throttles forward to begin our take-off roll. It was as though I had got shot with a dose of Adrenaline. How I wanted to be back in the air again and be in command.

At altitude, they had set up the simulator for me to do air-refueling.

With us receiving fuel from a KC-135. It was something that I had never done. I couldn't believe all the turbulence that came from the jet wash of that KC-135.

I then did an instrument approach to a landing at Kadena Air Base, Okinawa. A couple of more take-offs and landings. Then it was over.

Now I really wanted to get back into an Eastern B-727 and be in command. Scott would fly for the Air Force for nine more years before becoming an airline pilot.

That time in the simulator with Scott brought back the memory of when I had flown the air force's T-38 simulator.

Keith was also an air force pilot, and at the time was based at Columbus Air Force Base, Mississippi during the mid-1980s.

Following his instructions, doing climbs, turns, and rolls, I felt very comfortable flying the T-38. Then he asked me if I wanted to try to fly through a hangar. Sure!

Simulators are probably the best investment any airline or military branch could make. Very realistic visual aids. I had descended from altitude and saw the hangar. Then descended lower skimming the ground as I aimed at the center of the hangar door opening.

The opening allowed enough space for the wings and the top of the T-38's tail to fit through. I flew through the hangar with the greatest of ease and pulled up to do a victory roll. The simulator stopped. I had crashed doing my victory roll.

We decided to try it once again under the same scenario. I started at altitude, drop down, aimed at the hangar opening, flew through, pulled up, and began my victory roll just as our time in the simulator ended.

Our son Keith spent 20 years in the Air Force flying the Hercules C-130. He Had flown combat missions during Bosnia, Iraqi Freedom, and Afghanistan.

Today, both sons are captains with major airlines. Scott's a captain with United Airlines, and Keith is a captain for Southwest Airlines.

SELLING REAL ESTATE

While waiting to be recalled, it was back to the unemployment office.

By then, ALPA had stopped our strike benefits and I needed an income. No matter the amount. I hated having to go to the unemployment office.

Fortunately, another option had presented itself. Our good friends Gerry and Linda Hunnewell owned their own construction company called Kendall Homes.

They were well established in northern New Jersey and had a marvelous reputation for building quality homes and communities.

Upon their advice, I attended several weeks of night school to obtain a realtor license. Afterward, I had gone to work for them. Not in an office where listings of homes were for sale, but in a construction trailer located out in the country on acres of newly purchased land.

They had built one model home on one of the acres, that sold in the hundreds of thousands. During the first week there, a couple had stopped by. As we toured the home, I pointed out all its quality features and the local history that surrounded the area. To my amazement, they offered to purchase a plot of land and have a home built on it.

Contracts were to be made and to be signed at the trailer, with the Hunnewells tending the contract. In the back of my mind, I would be receiving a substantial commission.

After the contract to be signed was handed to the buyers, came a pause. The husband then excused himself to smoke a cigarette outside the trailer.

Five minutes passed before he returned. He then announced he would have to think about it. The couple left and never came back. No sale. No commission.

As the weeks passed, there had been others who had stopped by and inquired about the homes. None bought.

All during those weeks, when I was alone, thoughts of having had to wait to be recalled haunted me throughout the day. I must have paced back and forth in that trailer for hundreds and hundreds and hundreds and hundreds of miles.

Eventually, the Hunnewells shut the site down. I was then assigned to another building location they had. The site was within walking distance of New Jersey's largest lake. Lake Hopatcong. A most beautiful lake.

Another sale had loomed at the new site. It too fell through. Shortly after, came great news. I was to be recalled in September 1990.

HALLELUJAH! I'M RECALLED!

On September 1st, I, along with several other recalled striking pilots arrived in Miami for flight training. Only to find that Eastern's management had asked the courts to put an injunction against our return. We were sent home. The fight to be recalled would continue for several more months.

At the beginning of December 1990, the court had cleared us striking pilots the right to be recalled. Another trip back to Miami.

Approximately forty of us recalled pilots were required to do two things. One had us taking what we believed was a written psychological evaluation/personality test. We all believed it was nothing more than a mental and emotional stress test to see if we were still fit to fly.

The results were then charted and given to each pilot. According to my evaluation, I was considered to be very methodical. I didn't need a test to know that. I already knew it.

The second was a meeting with Trustee Marty Shugrue.

I found him to be very honest as he could be with us recalled pilots. Especially when one of our captains had asked him.

"If all of us pilots refused to accept any income, would it save the airline?" After a pause. "No." Deep down, I think we all knew it would be just a very short time before Eastern would fold.

The following day was not very pleasant either. My simulator training was slated to start late in the afternoon.

As I was about to enter a gate that guards the simulator building, I heard the word, scab, called out. To my right at another gate further down the

304

block were several still striking members of the IAM. Then came another scab remark aimed at me.

I wasn't about to let it pass again and went to confront the three of them. In short, I told them that we striking pilots had honored their picket line for nine months until our union, ALPA, called an end to it.

That it had been more than a year-and-a-half for us striking pilots to get back into the cockpits that we have been denied. They backed off and wished me luck.

The training center was a den full of pilots and instructors who had crossed the picket line. Though there was only one instance that I had about striking.

That was from someone whom I had known for over twenty years and who had crossed the picket line. He was about to explain to me why he did. I cut him short, telling him I didn't want to hear it.

The group of simulator instructors that I had, were very helpful in getting me requalified, and very courteous doing it. Although we recalled striking pilots were under a lot of duress during it. As in, don't fail the check rides.

Then came the flight check-in the simulator with the FAA. Must say that went smoothly. Even though I was keyed up doing it.

On December 20, 1990, came the last part of being requalified. A day of flying with my mother-in-law, the check captain. That being, the required three landings to a full stop. Per the FARs.

On December 21, 1990, I'm back in the cockpit of an Eastern B-727 as a captain. It became three days of high tension in the cockpit.

My first officer, of all people, was the same one who had given me the middle finger of his right hand while walking the picket line.

I informed him, not about the finger, but he was not going to do any flying for those three days. I was about to start catching up for that year-and-a-half I had not flown.

January 17, 1991, less than a month later, I had my last flight as a captain for Eastern Air Lines. At 12:01 a.m. on January 18, 1991, Eastern Air Lines ceased operating. It broke my heart.

Beginning January 27, 1964, I had flown for Eastern for twenty-seven years. Now it was over. Not quite?

SALVAGING PENSION FUNDS

S hortly after Eastern shut down I made applications to receive my pension from both of our pilot's pension funds. The A-Fund & the B-fund.

In short, the A-Fund was an annuity, I began to receive several months after the shutdown.

The B-Fund was a fund that invested, in real estate, stocks, etcetera.

While I was striking, there were a thousand or more pilots who had retired early. When they did, they were allowed to take their B-fund in a lump sum. Each time that happened it depleted the pilot's B-Fund by 100's of millions of dollars.

Since I was still striking and receiving income from ALPA, I hadn't paid attention to my B-Fund. When I did, my Fund had been reduced by a very substantial amount, well over $100,000.

I took the remainder in a lump sum and went with an investment firm. Still. That wasn't the end of it.

The A-Fund, we Eastern pilots would find out many years later, had not been fully funded by Lorenzo and was woefully short.

Initially, we were led to believe it had been funded up to 94% but were later told it had been funded to approximately 74%.

Several years after the shutdown, thousands of us Eastern pilots were receiving income from the A-Fund. Once Eastern was out of business it was turned over to the Pension Benefit Guaranty Corporation. (PBGC.)

Since the A-Fund had been underfunded, the PBGC began reducing the amount of our income from it. Some as much as $1,000 per month.

Then came another blow from the PBGC. Payback!

It was based on the number of years you had been receiving money from the A-Fund. Because of the difference of 94% vs 74%, it had to be paid back.

My required payback was well over $27,000. Others more. They gave us seventeen years to pay for it. This was done by reducing the amount of the monthly benefit we were receiving from the PBGC.

Mine was $350 per month. The good news. If you died before it was paid off. Your family was not responsible for the remainder. Nor would your family receive any more payments from them. Thank you, Frank Lorenzo.

Still, it was not the end of the fallout from Lorenzo.

When ALPA and we striking pilots were fighting Lorenzo, many of Eastern's upper management was taking what we pilots called, Golden Parachutes.

They must have seen the writing on the wall, for many of them requested, and received severance packages, that were estimated to be in the hundreds of millions.

Before April 16, 1993, ALPA on behalf of Eastern pilots filed a claim against Continental Airlines Inc.

In turn, Continental eventually filed Chapter 11. On that day quote. "The Computer Trust Company of New York is acting as the distribution agent for cash distributed pursuant to the Revised Second Amended Joint Plan of Reorganization under Chapter 11 of the United States Bankruptcy Code (the "Plan") of Continental Airlines, Inc., et al. The Plan was confirmed by the United States Bankruptcy Court for the District of Delaware on April 1993. It is anticipated that this will be the final distribution of cash to you pursuant to the Plan and represents your pro-rata portion of the distribution on account of your allowed claim under the Plan." Un-Quote. The Plan had been a Continental Stock Plan.

I had two claims allowed. The first was for $65,616.80. Because of the bankruptcy. I received a distribution of $10.50. Approximately $.09 on the dollar.

The second allowed had been for $32,808.40. I received a distribution of $2.00. Or, approximately $.04 on the dollar. Of the total $98,425.30 that was due. I received $12.50.

The difference is still being written off as a tax loss. I was not the only pilot who had suffered Lorenzo's debacle. There were more than 2,000 other Eastern pilots who received the same tidings.

Of course, by that time the airline was out of business. Nor was there an ALPA union or its lawyers to back us to fight the injustice.

It had left us with just one choice. Hire a lawyer and pay them out of pocket, which I was not going to do.

BECOMING A FREIGHT DOG

Heartbroken at the demise of Eastern, I had thought no airline would hire a 54-year-old captain. All I could see was more gloom on the horizon. Until the telephone rang a few weeks later with an offer to fly.

During the summer months of 1990, while I was trying to sell real estate, the Gulf War, initially called, Operation Desert Shield, from August 2, 1990, to February 28, 1991, had broken out.

Then on January 17, 1991, the day before Eastern shut down, Desert Shield had become Operation Desert Storm. It was the same day our son Scott began flying combat missions in the RC-135 during Desert Storm. Along with a parent's worry.

Enter Ryan International Airlines. A freight-hauling airline that operated out of Indianapolis, Indiana, and Dayton, Ohio.

The telephone call had been from someone who had worked with ALPA. They were contacting non-scab Eastern recalled pilots who were currently requalified on the B-727 and the DC-9. Ryan needed pilots and they needed them now. Would I be interested? "Hell yes!"

They also asked me if I knew of any other recalled pilots who might be interested. My first thought was my classmate and friend, Captain Tom Schineller, who also had been recalled.

The only drawback. We had to make our way to the different cities where Ryan's flights would originate. Which could be anywhere. It was called, out-sourcing. Your crew base was your own home.

I contacted Tom and gave him all the information that was given to me and a telephone number. Without hesitation, he had said yes.

Then came the day of having to ask the captain of the different ALPA airlines who had supported us, permission to ride their jump seats to get to those cities. Otherwise, it would be out-of-pocket expenses to get there.

The only ALPA airline, to my knowledge, who refused their jump seats were Delta's pilots. I have to admit, I never bothered asking them, knowing what the answer probably would have been.

Initially, we B-727 crews thought we would be flying out of Indianapolis. Not so. Our days of ground school would be held there. After that, all B-727 crews would be flying freight out of Dayton.

Then came another training session in the B-727 simulator. Followed by another proficiency flight check in an airplane that I had been flying for twenty-five years.

The DC-9 crews who were under contract with Ryan were to fly the mail for the U.S. Postal Service, flying out of Indianapolis.

By the way. When it came to seniority with Ryan, they had used Eastern's date of hire. Tom was again, one number senior to me.

HERE TODAY, GONE TODAY, ANOTHER CRASH!

L ate in the evening on February 16, 1991, there was a group of us pilots hanging out in our Indianapolis flight operations.

A DC-9 crew, a captain and a first officer, had just finished filing their flight papers for their flight to Cleveland and had stopped to chat with us before leaving on their flight. Three hours later at 00:19 Sunday the 17, 1991, they were both dead.

According to the NTSB/AAR-91-09 report dated November 16, 1991, the probable cause of the Ryan International Airlines Flight 590 accident was: "The failure of the flight crew to detect and remove ice contamination on the airplane's wings, which was largely a result of appropriate response by the Federal Aviation Administration, Douglas Aircraft Company, and Ryan International Airlines to the known effect that a minute amount of contamination has on the stall characteristics of the DC-9 series 10 airplanes. The ice contamination led to wing stall and loss of control during the attempted takeoff."

Before the accident, there had been pilot reports of moderate turbulence and rime icing from 7,000 feet to the ground. After flight 590 had landed de-icing service by the crew had not been asked for.

The aircraft stalled during takeoff and rolled 90 degrees to the right at 50-100 feet. The aircraft then suffered compressor stalls, and rolled further to the right with an increase in pitch, followed by a severe pitch to the left before impact.

Fortunately, they were not Eastern pilots. That's not to say they weren't good pilots. Just unfortunate.

So began my very short flying career with Ryan International Airlines. Along with the humbling experience of having had to ask permission to ride the jump seat of another airline.

I must say, that most of my jump seat riding had been on USAIR Airlines. Their pilots were very accommodating.

Then came my welcome to Dayton International Airport, the Bat Cave, and flying freight all night long.

Late in the evening on February 25, 1991, and shortly before my first flight for Ryan, I got to rest and take a short nap in the Bat Cave.

The Cave was merely a hole-in-the-wall room, but large enough to house several tiers of bunk beds. You know the type. Squeaky springs, thin mattresses, snoring pilots. It reminded me of when I was back in the Navy's boot camp.

My first flight, February 26, 1991, started at midnight. Then after flying to several different cities, it ended back in Dayton. I then rode a jump seat back to Newark, New Jersey, and home.

To give you an idea of what the freight ramp was like at night. Think of being on a dimly lit interstate roadway at night, with dozens of semi's speeding past you. It was a bustling beehive of activity.

The one rule Ryan was very adamant about was wandering away from your aircraft. We were always told to stay close to it as possible.

Our black uniforms became nearly invisible to those truckers who were either loading or unloading our QC-727 aircraft. Who had a habit of driving as quickly as they could to complete their job and go on to another.

I had been told a couple of pilots had been struck before, and that was why Ryan was adamant about that rule.

For the next four weeks, I was riding a jump seat from Newark to Dayton, Milwaukee, Toronto, and a dozen other cities. Then ride another to get back home. Then a ray of hope appeared on the horizon.

During the strike, many of us striking pilots would get together and exchange information about the possibility of a flying position somewhere.

Usually, those meetings were held at a restaurant.

Where I lived in New Jersey, the meetings were held at the Rockaway Townsquare Dinner, in Wharton, New Jersey. Another group held theirs at the Flemington Dinner, in Flemington, New Jersey that I would occasionally attend.

While at the diner in Flemington, another Eastern Captain, Bill Machauer, had mentioned that a group of Eastern pilots who lived in Connecticut, had been gathering to fly for Air Aruba Airlines.

Bill had mentioned the name of the retired captain who was behind it. Captain Helmut Hetz. Whom I knew and had flown with many times while at Eastern.

The chief pilot would be Captain Ernie Trowbridge, whom I also knew and had flown with at Eastern. That was all Bill said he knew.

At home, I made a quick call to Ernie and asked him if he could use another pilot. Me.

He had told me that all his pilot slots were filled. But he would keep me in mind in the event things change.

I thanked him, thinking that I would be doing many more all-night freight flights. After that telephone call, those all-night freighters seem to be a lot longer.

Ten days later another telephone call. It's Ernie. Was I still interested in the job? " Hell yes!" Followed by a trip to Connecticut to meet with Captain Hetz and the rest of the pilots who had been picked. Most of whom I knew. It was certainly great to see Ernie and Helmut again.

Helmut had been in contact with Hapag Lloyd, a German airline that operated out of Hanover, Germany, and who had a B-727-100 series for lease. As I mentioned before, Helmut had once flown for the German Luftwaffe during WWII and still had ties there.

The question was. Why would a German company be interested in a group of American pilots who were out of a flying job?

The island of Aruba, a Dutch island, had been using Air Holland as their main airline passenger service to Newark, and the Dutch Islands of Curacao, and Bonaire. Air Holland had to suspend all of its air services at the end of

1990 due to financial difficulties. Sound familiar.

By the end of December 1991, it would resume operating again. In the interim, Aruba still needed flight service to the United States. Ere-go, enter Hapag Lloyd and nine out-of-work Eastern pilots.

Thanks to Helmut, an agreement had been reached between, Aruba, Hapag Lloyd, and we nine Eastern pilots. Service was to be started between Aruba and Newark, New Jersey in the middle of April 1991.

Then came the rundown of the events to follow. Beginning with the where and when for ground school, the simulator, and the flight training. The tail number of the B-727-100, we would be flying was, AHLM.

Helmut also told us. "We won't be flying under FAA's Part 121 rules. Instead, we will be operating as a foreign carrier, and will come under FAR Part 129."

In brief, any foreign air carrier must have a permit issued by the Department of Transportation, (DOT) plus other requirements, if it's to be allowed to operate from a foreign country into the United States. Aruba is a foreign country.

MY LAST DAYS AS A FREIGHT DOG

O n my next flight out of Dayton I had given my notice to Ryan's chief pilot that I would be leaving, and the reason why. He was very nice about it. He even told me that if I, and all of the Eastern pilots who were then flying for Ryan, ever left, they would always have a job waiting for them if needed.

Several days later on March 17th, I jumped-seated into Toronto, Canada, to begin my last group of four days of all-night flying for Ryan.

I spent a restless evening in one of the airport's hotels trying to get some sack time before my flight left on the 18th at 03:40 a.m. bound for Dayton. Then flew back to Toronto and spent another night there.

Left again on the 19th at 03:05 a.m. bound for Atlanta and spent an evening there. Then on the 20th, left Atlanta at 04:48 a.m. to return to Toronto to spend another night there. Life's good. What could go wrong?

On the morning of the 21st, our flight schedule was a lot heavier than normal. It would be an all-night and all-morning sequence of flights to five different cities before returning to Toronto. Where I had planned to catch a jump-seat ride back to Newark and home.

We left Toronto at 03:13 a .m. and flew to Dayton arriving at 04:27 a. m. and our inbound freight was off-loaded.

As the ground crew began loading our outbound freight, a severe thunderstorm hit the area. Tons and tons of water came cascading down from the heavens.

As this deluge fell, the cargo door had been left wide open as the freight was being loaded. Areas of pooling water lay on the floor of the cabin, then

316

swept out after the loading was completed.

As we taxied out for takeoff for Atlanta, our Doppler Colored Radar had been sweeping the skies above and in front of us. It showed numerous cells along our intended flight path.

I elected to delay our takeoff and let the squall line move away. Forty-five minutes later we were cleared for takeoff. As I pushed the power levers to max power. The radar glowed a very bright red and quit. Followed by an aborted takeoff.

Back at the ramp, maintenance opened both hatches called the lower 41 and 43, to inspect the electrical units, they were drenched by gallons of water.

Somehow the water had found its way from the cabin floor and leaked into the electrical compartments during the storm. I'm not sure what would have happened while in flight, but I was glad that I aborted the take-off when I did.

In any event, we arrived in Atlanta three hours behind schedule. By the time my crew and I were tired and hungry after being up all night with little sleep and no food on the airplane. Not even a box lunch.

The agent who met the airplane told me that we had to make a quick turn because we were way behind schedule.

I told him my crew and I were going to get something to eat. He pointed to a food and beverage vending machine inside the hangar. I told him there was no way my crew and I are going to do that.

I knew of a place just down the road from where we were, called the Barbeque Restaurant. This after spending many a night in a hotel next to it when flying for Eastern.

I called our dispatcher and told him of my plans to go eat, and why. He had no objection.

An hour later we were back in the air on our way to Baltimore. Then had to enter a holding pattern for an hour due to a line of thunderstorms that closed the airport.

It was the same weather front that was over Dayton. More delays meant more time on duty and we still had to fly back to Atlanta, Dayton, and

Toronto.

By the time we returned to Atlanta, we were on duty for nearly fourteen hours. Not counting our checking in one hour before departure in Dayton, and, we still had two more cities to fly to.

I decided I wasn't about to do another one of those twenty hours on duty like the one I did with Eastern.

I called our dispatcher and told him we were fatigued and to get us a hotel for that evening because I'm parking the airplane. Which I did.

Another crew flew the last leg two of the legs that we were supposed to fly. Surprisingly, the chief pilot didn't call me for doing it.

At 05:30 on March 22nd, we left Atlanta, for Dayton, and Toronto. Which was my last flight for Ryan International Airlines. Then rode a Midway Airlines jump seat back to Newark and home.

I was no longer a Freight Dog.

As I look back at being a Freight Dog, I fondly think about those all-nighters. Just us three pilots together in a chilly cockpit. No stewardess. No passengers. Only cold lifeless freight.

Then I think about all those other Freight Dogs who fly all night long, regardless of what airline they fly for. They have little recognition of what transpires while they are doing it. Flying freight all around the world, in all types of weather, into third-world countries that have antiquated navigation aids.

No smiling stewardess to serve them hot coffee and a hot meal. No conversation with them. Having to eat cold box lunches,

and drink warm coffee in a chilly cockpit. There are no passengers in the cabin. No movies, no interaction like regular passenger-carrying service. Just cold lifeless freight.

There is no parking for the aircraft at the main terminal and mingling with the hubbub of passengers. No one to tell you how much they enjoyed their flight with you.

Just a freight loading ramp, a long way from the main terminal, and a long way from having that dream of one day, flying for a major passenger-carrying airline.

AIR ARUBA AIRLINES

I ncredibly, Air Aruba Airlines would be the third airline I would fly
for. All in less than five months after being recalled to Eastern and
it's shut down.

As usual, it began with B-727 ground school in Indianapolis followed by
simulator training in Miami. One that I was very familiar with. It was the
same simulator Eastern Air Lines had used.

Once all requirements were accomplished, came route qualifications for
foreign operations. This was to the same country I had often flown to while
with Eastern.

In this case, our route would be Newark-Aruba-Newark. Enter Fritz
Kepler.

Kepler was a German check captain who was a qualified inspector
working with Germany's Luftant-Bundesamt. Their equivalent to our FAA
for civil aviation. Before we were to begin our actual route qualification,
we would have to have those required three bounces to a full stop.

Instead of using Newark International Airport, we had flown to Bradley
International Airport, located at Windsor Locks, Connecticut.

Did the required three bounces to a full stop then came our next stop.
Aruba.

As to the responsibility of keeping AHLM air-worthy, were two very
nice Dutch aircraft mechanics. They were very thorough in caring for that
B-727. I had never seen a cleaner cockpit or passenger cabin with them in
charge.

During those many months with Air Aruba, our two mechanics lived in a motel near Newark airport and away from their native country.

When I told them my mother was part Dutch, they could not do enough for our whole crew. On several occasions, Barb and I invited them to spend a few nights with us.

One huge difference in flying AHLM was having to use liters of fuel burn-off instead of pounds of fuel burn-off for flight planning.

Max fuel for the 100 series was approximately 50,00 pounds vs 29,000 liters. When I first began looking at those fuel gauges, my first thought was. Do we have the right amount of fuel onboard because comparably speaking, they appeared to show only half of what was required? Took a few flights to get used to it.

Another difference. Flying under Part 129, foreign operations, they used a figure of 5% fuel contingency, or, extra reserve fuel to be carried. Whereas domestic flight operations used 10% under Part 121.

The other oddity. Air Aruba was considered a major airline. Normally, most airlines have pilots totaling in the thousands. Plus, thousands of stewardesses. Our group consisted of a total of nine ex-Eastern pilots and twelve stewardesses from Aruba.

Our Chief Pilot was Ernie Trowbridge. The rest of our group was Dave Ellis, Doug Moses, Bill Faircloth, John Curtain, Chris Larvick, Gary Fruchter, Karen Smith, and myself.

Of the nine, three of us flew as captains, Ernie, Doug, and myself. Three as first officers, Dave, Bill, and John. As second officers, Chris, Gary, and Karen.

Flight operations had begun on April 20th, 1991. On that day Doug had acted as my first officer, and Chris was my second. Qualifying us was Fritz Kepler the acting check captain. Chris was being checked by Gus Musfeld, their flight-check engineer.

The approximate distance in air mileage from EWR-ABA is 2,100 miles. Flight time is approximately 4:30, which is just about the max range of the 100 series.

We taxied out at 13:35 p. m. and landed in Aruba at 18:35 local time. Some 4:50 minutes later. Nearly 25 minutes longer than our flight plan called for due to a weather delay at Newark

It became quite apparent fuel monitoring was going to be of the utmost importance.

Our contract called for us to fly for only four days. Every Thursday, Friday, Saturday, and Sunday.

What also became quite apparent, was the flight crew could not do a round trip EWR-ABA-EWR on the same day due to duty time limitations.

Furthermore, we did not have enough pilots to cover other requirements. Enter North American Airlines.

We would end up flying the Thursday, Friday, and Sunday flights. While North American Airlines flew the Saturday flights to and from Newark.

The best news was, the crew that ended up in Aruba on Friday night didn't have to leave until Sunday. This gave us an extra day laying over in Aruba.

For the next seven months, it became as though we were on an extended vacation.

All of us, at one time, brought family members along. Especially when we didn't have to fly the Saturday flight.

The hotel we stayed at was called the Renaissance Aruba Resorts. It had a private island and a launch that would bring you there. Great fun for the flight crews and fun for family members.

The Renaissance was also a layover hotel for other foreign flight crews. Who also took advantage of Renaissance's private island.

The island had two distinct swimming areas. The family area. For those who were so inclined, the nude beach area.

More than once I had noticed stewardesses from those other airlines swimming topless in the family area. Though it never created a problem. From what I understood Europeans were used to that type of atmosphere. How nice!

On several occasions, family members would come with us by using our airline pass privileges. That was the upside.

The downside. Some of our flights would be completely booked back to Newark. That meant no pass-riding back to Newark.

The answer to that. Stay another night in Aruba and hope there was space available the following day. If not. Buy a ticket on another airline that flew to Newark.

The third choice was Part 129. Foreign operation. The one that gave you more leeway. The one that we would always choose. Where the family member would ride our cockpit jump-seat back to Newark.

During those seven months, no flight inspector from the FAA or inspectors from Germany's Luftant-Bunesamt ever gave us an in-flight check. It seemed the FAA thought the Germans were doing it, and the Germans thought the FAA was doing it.

AN EASTERN PILOT LOSES HIS LIFE FLYING FOR A FOREIGN AIRLINE

A month into our contract. Tragedy struck. Not with us, but with Lauda Air. On May 26, 1991, Lauda Air Flight 004, a Boeing 767-3Z9ER was en route from Kai Tak Airport, Hong Kong, to Vienna International Airport, with a stop-over in Bangkok, Thailand. Lauda Air was founded by world motor racing champion Niki Lauda.

In command of the flight was Captain Thomas J. Welch. Assisting him was Austrian First Officer Josef Thurner.

Before flying for Lauda, Tom had been a captain for Eastern Air Lines. Another one of those decent pilots who had to look for a flying position elsewhere after Eastern shutdown. In Tom's situation, it meant having to fly for a foreign air carrier.

Tom lived in Connecticut and all of us Eastern pilots who flew for Air Aruba knew him. As did most pilots who were based in New York while with Eastern. He was a very likable person, and whose path I would come across occasionally while laying over in some city while with Eastern. As we ate dinner, he would tell a funny joke or two that kept me in stitches.

On the night of the accident, Tom and his first officer received a cockpit visual warning indicating that a possible system failure would cause the thrust reverser on the number one engine to deploy in flight.

After having consulted the aircraft's quick reference handbook, they determined that it was, just an advisory thing, and took no action. This was according to the cockpit voice recorder.

Shortly thereafter, the number one engine went into reversed thrust while the plane was over mountainous jungle terrain. It was also determined thru the CVR of Thurner's last recorded words. "Oh, reverser's deployed" and a shuddering sound, followed by a metallic snap.

The aircraft began a diving left turn, an increase in background noise, and a second snapping sound, followed by several loud bangs, then stopped recording.

The aircraft went to a diving airspeed of Mach 0.99 and may have broken the sound barrier. The aircraft broke up mid-air at 4,000 feet and crashed in what is now Phu Toei National Park, Suphan Buri. All 223 passengers and crew died.

One of the saddest things about this accident, along with the loss of lives, volunteer rescue teams and local villagers looted the wreckage, taking electronics and jewelry, so the relatives aboard the flight were unable to recover any of their possessions.

An official investigation, led by Thailand's Aircraft Accident Investigation Committee stated: "The Accident Investigation Committee of the Government of Thailand determines the probable cause of this accident to be an un-commanded in-flight deployment of the left engine thrust reverser, which resulted in the loss of flight path control.

The specific cause of the thrust reverser deployment has not been positively identified. Different possibilities were investigated, including a short circuit in the system. Due in part to the destruction of much of the wiring, no definitive reason for the activation of the thrust reverser could be found."

Many pros and cons followed as to what caused the accident. Both by Boeing and by Niki Lauda.

To me, Captain Welch was another victim of Frank Lorenzo. Had Eastern survived and remained in business. Tom would not have been flying for a foreign air carrier.

FLYING OVER OPEN WATER

F lying to and from Newark to the islands, meant you were out over the big ponds, called the Atlanta Ocean and the Caribbean Sea. Sometimes all goes well and sometimes it doesn't.

On June 28, 1991, our flight 724 from Bonaire to Newark brought us over to Bimini. With me, that day was First Officer John Curtain and Second Officer Chris Larvick.

Fifty miles north of Bimini we heard. "Mayday, Mayday, Mayday" and it's not on 121.5mg the one we monitored. Instead, it's on the normal ATC frequency.

The pilot who was in trouble was broadcasting in the blind. Hoping someone will hear him. We responded to his radio call and asked him for his position and the reason for his Mayday broadcast.

According to the pilot, his VORDME showed he was thirty miles east of West Palm Beach. Followed by. "My engine just quit and I'm going to have to ditch." That was the end of our contact with him.

We relayed his last reported position to ATC. At the time I had thought the ocean had swallowed another aviator.

Several months later while reading a nationwide magazine there was an article about a pilot having to ditch into the Atlanta Ocean east of West Palm Beach.

It said that he had floated for three days in the Atlantic Ocean before being rescued. I was sure it was the same pilot we had talked to before he had to ditch.

All good things must come to an end. As was our contract with Air Aruba and Hapag Lloyd. We had hoped it could have been extended.

Unfortunately, on one of our maintenance team's inspections of AHLM, it was found to have corrosion in its belly just below the aft cargo compartment. They had thought it too expensive to repair and took it out of service.

There were other negotiations ongoing at the time. We all thought we might be trained to fly the Douglas MD-80, a twin-engine jet, with a two-man crew. That didn't happen. Instead, Air Aruba had chosen the MD-80 for its passenger service and had used Midway Airlines flight crews to fly it.

My last flight with Air Aruba ended on October 4, 1991. Thirty-four years earlier. Sputnik. Another memorial day. With me on that day were Dave Ellis and Gary Fruchter. It was also their last flight with Air Aruba.

Flying for Air Aruba had been one of the highlights of my flying career thanks to Captain Ernie Trowbridge. He had allowed me to fly with a group of wonderful Eastern pilots for those seven months. Another highlight of a long flying career.

Then. Do I one to become a flight simulator instructor?

FLIGHT SAFETY & BALTIA AIRLINES

W hen our contract ran out with Air Aruba, it was back to looking for another flying position. Before that, the New Jersey unemployment office beckoned.

One thing I learned about the unemployment office looking to find a job for an out-of-work airline pilot. It's impossible. Enter Flight Safety International.

I first learned about FSI while at one of those pilot breakfasts. Their aviation training programs offered a multitude of courses where one could obtain a certificate on almost anything in the world of aviation. They had several headquarters throughout the United States.

This particular FSI was located at the Teterboro Airport, Moonachie, N.J. From what I was told, they were looking for simulator instructors. With no flying job on the horizon down to FSI, I went. Along with my flight logbooks.

Introductions went well and they offered me a position as a simulator instructor. Once I went through their simulator training program, for the Dassault (French-made) Falcon 900.

To me, the Falcon looked very similar to a B-727, although it was much smaller. It was a sleek-looking three-engine aircraft that boasted Allied-Signal TFE-Turbofans, that produced 4,750 pounds of thrust per engine. It flew at Mach .84, the same as the B-727, and cruised at 590 mph. The service ceiling was 50,900 vs 42,000 for the Boeing and had a range of over 4,000 miles. Passenger-wise, it could hold up to nineteen. There was one catch. No pay.

In return, I was offered a type rating on the Falcon 900. No charge. That kind of rating would have cost me tens of thousands of dollars. After I completed that program, I would begin training as a simulator instructor for the Falcon 900. No pay! Until I completed my training and began working there.

After I had agreed to all their requirements training began on the Falcon. A month later came the flight check, and a type rating for the Falcon 900, which also applied to the Falcon 50.

It was also my fourth flight check within one year. Have to explain one thing about flight checks. Screw them up, and you may not have a pilot certificate of any kind.

Then came the delays. Simulator training would begin on this date. Came to the date, sim training was postponed. This went on for several weeks. In the meantime, another flying position became possible.

This time though one of our Eastern pilots who flew for a corporation. He told me an aircraft leasing company, that was also located at Teterboro Airport, had been looking for pilots who had a Falcon 900 type rating.

Another interview, another promise of a flying job. The only thing I had to do was wait to be called by them to go to Philadelphia for a physical. A week later. No phone call. Ten days pass. Nothing. So, I called them.

The conversation was brief. Plans have changed. The corporation that had planned to lease the Falcon 900 was no longer interested in using it. Another setback. Then came another opportunity.

Another start-up airline called Baltia Airlines had been looking for pilots to fly their B-767. Namely Eastern pilots who did not cross the picket line.

Baltia had planned to operate flights out of JFK to Moscow, Russia, and have enough pilots to fly x-number of flights per week.

This meant the same old, same old, in regards to on-duty flight time, rest, and the number of flying hours allowed per month, per year. Pay-wise, captains were to receive some $6,000 per month. First officers somewhat less.

After all the pilot interviews were completed, those that had been chosen, myself included, began weeks of ground school out on Long Island.

After we had completed that, it was out to Saint Louis to practice ditching, aircraft evacuation, and B-767 simulator training. Followed by those required three bounces. All training would be done by Trans World Airlines.

That had worked well for me. My brother Glenn had been a captain for TWA and lived in St. Louis and had flown the B-767.

While flying the B-767, he had an engine explode on take-off. Then had to make a single-engine approach. Only having to abandon it due to another aircraft still on the runway. Then made another single-engine approach to a safe landing. Incredible airmanship.

After several four-hour periods in the 767 simulator came another pre-rating flight check. This was number 5 in just a little over one year.

After that flight check ended successfully I had been scheduled to do my final flight check with the FAA two days later. It had to be postponed due to the unexpected passing of my mom on June 2, 1992.

After the services, I intended to return to St. Louis for the FAA check ride. Then came a telephone call from Baltia.

They had filed for bankruptcy and had shut down all flight operations. It would be the fourth airline that I had flown for that went out of business.

On top of that, I was out the $6,000 they had promised me. Other Eastern pilots were also stiffed because of their bankruptcy. None of us were ever paid during our time with Baltia. Although there had been a lot of promises made. Sound familiar.

All of us pilots were pretty pissed, and once again, we were without a job and income.

All I could do was add that to the two hundred thousand or more that I had lost with Easterns B-Fund and the Continental Airlines stock loss. Hello, unemployment office.

Just when things couldn't get any darker, A bright ray of hope shines thru.

KIWI INTERNATIONAL AIR LINES

Another pilot breakfast at the Townsquare Dinner brought with it a spark of life to get back into the air again. A new start-up airline to be formed was to be called Kiwi International Air Lines.

The entrepreneur behind it all. Captain Bob Iverson.

Captain Iverson had been another Eastern Air Line captain whose airline career had been cut short. His vision was one of many who often dream about doing. But don't.

In his case. Build and start your own airline. I had known Bob while at Eastern, but never had the opportunity to fly with him. Other pilots that I talked to who knew him, and had flown with him, offered nothing but praise.

Bob would eventually write a book detailing how, and how long it had taken him to achieve its success.

Allow me to take a passage from the introduction of his book "When Kiwi's Flew a Diary of a Mad Airline Entrepreneur." I believe it spoke for all of us Eastern employees who suffered hardships during those final years of a once-great airline.

To quote Bob. "FUELED BY ANGER and obsessed with justice, I went from an unemployed Eastern Air Lines pilot to founder and CEO of the "Best Airline in America" in less than two years. Without a penny or a clue. I started Kiwi International Air Lines from scratch by tapping into the deepest needs of my battered and bruised, out-of-work fellow aviation professionals.

In March 1989, the pilots, mechanics, and flight attendants of Eastern

Air Lines walked out on strike. The company eventually failed, and some 27,000 workers lost many of the best jobs in America. Some built new lives, some muddled through, and some never recovered. But several hundred invested their money and talents with me to create an exciting new career opportunity. In 1993, Conde Nast Traveler named KIWI "Best Airline in America."

By combining our financial, professional, and personal resources we reclaimed a measure of dignity from an industry that had done its best to destroy us. Instead of lashing out or curling up, we rallied, believed in each other, and overcame every obstacle in our path. The risky journey began in early 1990. When I left in 1995, KIWI was a $120,000,000 airline employing 1,200 workers, with 15 Boeing 727s carrying 1,000,000 passengers a year, and poised for an IPO." Un-quote.

His book should be read by everyone who has ever flown as a passenger, flight crew member, or aviation worker, and, especially for those who may think about starting their corporation no matter what type.

I won't profess that I know all the ends and outs of starting an airline or for that matter any corporation. I do know when you put your mind to a project you truly believe in, it can succeed. Just do it.

First. Why would you name an airline after a bird that has wings but cannot fly?

In a sense, Bob used the Kiwi, who had wings but could not fly as a symbol for us pilots who once had wings but for most, no longer flew. With the name Kiwi, he was giving us back our wings to fly once again. The Kiwi also symbolized, family and loyalty. That Kiwi International Air Lines had when it began first operating. Our motto at the time. Whatever it takes!

At breakfast that morning, several of us Eastern captains and first officers who had been coming to them since March 1989, when the IAM strike began, became involved in the startup of Kiwi.

Those pilots who were working with Bob at the time had mentioned to us during breakfast, that Kiwi management was having roadshows for pilots who were interested in being part of its start-up.

Of course, I didn't hesitate to let them know that I was interested, and was invited to attend their next roadshow. It was held at the Ramada Inn and right next door to Kiwi's new headquarters. The sixth floor of the Hemisphere Building. Just opposite Newark Airport.

Barb and I listened intently as Bob and his staff laid out the plans for launching Kiwi. Including an up-front $50,000 per pilot, and $5,000 per flight attendant if you wanted to help start and be a part-owner of an airline.

The startup monies would also give you a higher seniority number. Here came that number again. In other words. The sooner the investment, the higher would be your flying position. It also considered whether you would be a captain, a first officer, or a second officer.

Then there was that other carrot. According to their financial advisers, a fantastic return on your dollar when they issued their (IPO) Initial Public Offering. It all sounded so good.

Another perk Kiwi offered also caught my attention. Kiwi pilots who had sons or daughters and who were qualified could also fly for Kiwi. For them, their fee would be $10,000, and employed as second officers. With the possibility of becoming a first officer, then as a captain.

That intrigued me more. At the time both my sons were military pilots. Kiwi's route structure was nearly the same when I flew for Eastern. Atlanta, Orlando, Chicago-Midway (new), Newark, Tampa, and San Juan.

Then came the next questions. When will Kiwi begin operating? When do we start training and where? When will the IPO be issued? Will we unionize and be part of ALPA?

The last question was easily answered. "Hell no!"

That evening, Barb and I discussed Kiwi's possibilities. Age had become a factor for me. No other airline would hire someone who was in his mid-fifties, regardless of how much flying experience they had. If, by some quirk they did. It would be at the bottom of their seniority list and a lower pay scale than what Kiwi was offering.

Kiwi's beginning pay scale was $48,000 per year for pilots. $30,000 per year for the flight attendants. $14.00 an hour for mechanics. $12.00 per hour for agents, and ground handlers. All of which were within the 35% to 50% of the industry range at the time.

There too, was the thought that if both my sons flew for Kiwi it would be a wonderful chance for us to fly together.

Once Barb and I had gone over all the pros and cons, we took out an equity load against our home to give us the cash to proceed.

After they had accepted it, I was officially on the Kiwi International Air Lines pilot list. My fifth airline in less than two years. Then the waiting began for a training date.

THE FLIGHTLESS BIRD BECOMES AIRBORNE

On September 21, 1992, Kiwi launched its first flight from Newark to Atlanta and back. Captain Ed. Gilsky had been in command. Ed was one of that down-to-earth gentleman who you enjoyed having breakfast with every Monday when we first began to meet in March of 1989.

When he was asked about that first flight, his reply had been. "It was just like flying for Eastern. But better." He also said. "The only problem was we kept using the Eastern call sign every time we talked to air traffic control." I too, managed to do that quite often when I began flying for Kiwi. A hard habit to break after flying for Eastern for twenty-seven years. They were that similar.

Finally, after many months of waiting, I was sent to Miami for flight training. As Yogi Bera the fame catcher for the New York Yankee's once said. "It's deja vue all over again." Same ground school, the same simulator, the same training sessions, and the same check-rides. That was my sixth check ride for another airline in less than two years. Plus another three bounces in the aircraft.

As to the three required bounces. Several of us who would be captains with Kiwi had flown to Stewart International Airport, Newburg, New York with our flight instructor, Captain Bill Machauer. The same captain who had told me about Air Aruba. Now he was a check captain with Kiwi.

It had become somewhat of a circus atmosphere doing those three bounces. It went like this.

The first captain to be, slid into the left seat with Machauer in the right seat. Did his three bounces each to a full stop. He slid out, and the next captain slid into the left seat and did his, and slid out. I slide in and do my three, slide-out, followed by the next captain-to-be. So it went. Although we were all now qualified, it still required a flight-line check.

My first flight as a captain for Kiwi came on February 25, 1993. Newark to Chicago-Midway Airport. Captain Doug Stratton was my mother-in-law. Bill Turberville, had been my second officer. All went rather well and I'm back in command.

Interestingly, Chicago-Midway Airport (MDW) was once called Chicago Air Park. Then in July 1949, it had been changed to Chicago-Midway Airport in honor of those that had fought in the Battle of Midway, during the second world war. Chicago's O'Hare airport was named after Edward "Butch" O'Hare who was the first Medal of Honor recipient during the war.

The first thing I noticed about MDW. Short runways. One had to be very vigilant to set that aircraft down on the numbers. Especially in foul weather. Land too long and you may not stop in time before you run out of runway and end up on Central Avenue. As one air carrier did in a snowstorm many years later.

So began what was to be my final years of flying as a captain for another major airline before reaching age 60. At the time 60 was the max-age you could fly with a national air carrier under Part 121.

Still, in the back of my mind, I wanted to write. This time an idea came to me about Charles Lindberg's lone flight across the Atlantic Ocean on May 20/21, 1927. Except he was not the first to fly the Atlantic Ocean.

Two British Aviators, Capt. John Alcock, a 27-year pilot, and Lt. Arthur Whitten Brown, a 33-year navigator, accomplished that feat on June 14, 1916.

Although I was technically no longer an ALPA member I had submitted an article to their magazine called The Airline Pilot It was about the two aviators' famous flight. I had titled it, First Flight Across the Atlantic. They printed my article in their July 1993 issue. Along with a $250 check.

Once the line flying started and knowing the pilots, the flight attendants, crew schedulers, mechanics, operation agents, gate agents, and others who were ex-Eastern employees, made it seem like the old Eastern.

Of course, once the glitter began to wear off came some grumbling within the cockpit crew. Kiwi had something similar to what seat-swapping was like at Eastern when the first and second officers changed seats.

At Kiwi, there was also seat-swapping, except it was between the captain and the first officer who was also captain-qualified.

At first, it seemed like a good idea. If you flew a flight, say from EWR-PBI-EWR, the senior captain would sign all the required flight papers, and make all the decisions.

On the way back to EWR, the first officer, who was captain qualified would then be the captain and would sign all the flight papers and make all the decisions.

Of course, the flight attendants would scratch their heads wondering who the captain really was. Personally, I didn't like that idea. I felt that there should only be one captain, and one captain only.

On one occasion, the captain had been senior to me and flew the southbound leg. We then swapped seats for the northbound flight. I, as captain, had signed all the paperwork.

When the flight attendant came into the cockpit she had asked the captain who flew the flight southbound questions about the flight going northbound. It had left me no choice but to remind her who the captain was. I had heard that type of complaint from other captains before.

Afterward, I decided that if the captain of the flight was senior to me. He would be the captain throughout the day. That was probably the only grumble I had during those years with Kiwi. Except for one other that came years later.

Weather, mechanical breakdowns, and unruly passengers were all part of my flying career. For that matter, anyone's flying career.

Several incidents with Kiwi still stick in my mind.

BEING A CAPTAIN, HAD ITS BAD MOMENTS

I n mid-August of 1993, while signing our outbound flight papers from MDW-EWR, all flight paperwork was done at the gate, the agent in charge approached me and said one of my passengers wanted to talk to me in private.

When we stepped away from the passenger loading area the agent had pointed to a young woman sitting in a wheelchair. She appeared to be in her mid-twenties and looked rather frail, but had a smile on her face as she waited to be boarded. My first thought, she didn't have much time left.

The woman went on to explain that the woman in the wheelchair was her sister, and had been diagnosed with a brain tumor. She also confided to me, that according to the doctor whose patient her sister was, had told her. That there was the possibility of her having an aneurysm during the flight and dying.

The woman then went on to say, if that did occur during the flight, she would not get upset knowing the possibility of it happening. She then asked if Kiwi could set up a police escort from Newark to Hartford, Connecticut to where the woman lived.

Several thoughts popped into my head. Would my flight attendants accept the fact knowing that a passenger may die en route? How would the passengers react?

If I did allow her on the flight and she did require immediate attention. An emergency landing would have to be made before we got to Newark. If

I didn't land, most likely, there would be lawsuits against Kiwi and myself for not landing and seeking medical help.

I also didn't think the New Jersey State Police would be willing to do a police escort to another state, even under the circumstances.

When I presented those possibilities to my flight attendants. None had wanted her aboard.

Sadly, I had to refuse her sister's boarding. I implored her to hire an air ambulance service that had all the necessary equipment on board, and they could fly directly to Hartford.

When I told the boarding agent why I had to refuse the woman, she stared daggers at me. After that, she seldom talked to me when filling out flight papers.

I still think about that young woman sitting in that wheelchair waiting to be boarded with a smile on her face. Some things never go away.

ANOTHER CREW BASE BRINGS APPREHENSION

When Kiwi first began flexing its wings, our only flight crew base was Newark. Which meant anyone who wanted to be part of the program had to make his or her way to Newark. Enter out-basing. Something similar to what I had experienced when with Ryan International.

Many of Kiwi's pilots and flight attendants had lived in other states when they flew for Eastern where there had been crew bases. Atlanta, Boston, Washington D.C., and Miami.

Although the majority of those Kiwi pilots came from Atlanta. All of them flew to Newark using company pass privileges or requested the use of the cockpit jump seat. There were two of them on the aircraft that we used.

On several occasions when our flights were fully booked, five pilots would show up and request the jump seat. Two jump seats, a full aircraft. Well, let's just say, at times the cockpit could get quite crowded, as in, standing-room-only.

Eventually, Kiwi opened another crew base in Atlanta. That solved their commuting problems. Then it opened another can of worms.

As the saying goes, and because we were all part owners. "Too many chiefs and not enough Indians."

Incredible as it may seem there were those, within our group of pilots who thought they knew how to better run an airline than our founder.

Captain Bob Iverson.

For me, I invested to fly, not running an airline. I must say it again. You have to read his book to fully understand it all.

Wherever those few remaining years I had left to fly as an airline pilot was flying by quicker than I had wanted. Though it was not without several more incidents that were critical at the time.

IS MY AIRCRAFT ON FIRE?

I n the middle of May 1994, I had been going through my usual pre-flight cockpit check for our flight from Newark to Atlanta when I began to smell smoke coming from the cabin. At the time my second officer was outside pre-flighting the aircraft, and my first officer was inside the terminal at the boarding gate.

In the cabin were my three flight attendants. Just as I stepped out of the cockpit, I glanced at the rear of the cabin and saw thick black smoke coming out from underneath the left lavatory door.

At that same time, the first of our passengers began boarding the plane. I stopped them and told them and my cabin crew to get off the airplane immediately and go to the gate area.

At the same moment, a maintenance foreman had just come on board to sign the aircraft maintenance logbook and he too, saw the cabin was beginning to fill with smoke. He immediately reached into the cockpit and shut down the APU killing all electrical power to the aircraft.

Of course, the flight was canceled. Once the cabin was clear of the smoke, maintenance determined that one of the flight attendants had been in the lavatory and had flushed the toilet. Then had left closing the door behind her.

Unfortunately, the flush motor kept running. It had overheated, shorted out electrical wiring, and caught fire. In turn, it had melted the plastic casing that surrounded it causing the acrid and toxic black smoke.

According to the maintenance team, the electrical short should have tripped its circuit breaker. The circuit breaker that was located in the cockpit got fried and no matter what wasn't going to trip.

My thought at the time. If that had happened in flight while on our way to Atlanta. It would have been catastrophic. An airplane full of acrid toxic smoke would have undoubtedly overcome most passengers. Even if they were wearing oxygen masks. Case in point.

June 2, 1983. Air Canada flight 797, a DC-9-32, left Dallas, Texas on its way to Toronto, Ontario. Captain Donald Cameron was in command and had been assisted by First Officer Claude Ouimet. Onboard were 3 flight attendants and 41 passengers.

Midway through the flight, the pilots heard three snaps in succession. Behind them, they had spotted three circuit breakers that had popped out. When they tried to reset them, they popped again. One was the left toilet flushing motor. They had tried to reset them again but it only made them pop again. Then tried another time.

By that time smoke could be seen coming from under the door of the left lavatory. A flight attendant attempted to enter the toilet with a fire extinguisher but was driven back by the thick smoke.

The captain then sent the first officer back, but he had returned to get a pair of goggles to guard his eyes against the thickening smoke, and another attempt to control the smoke had failed.

In the cockpit, as AC and DC power systems were failing, the fire continued to burn in the space between the toilet wall and the aircraft's outer skin, allowing the fire to move forward above the ceiling panels and enter through the ceiling and sidewall panels. The first officer had returned to the cockpit and told the captain they should descend and land.

Smoke began to fill the cabin, and because the cockpit door had been left open began to fill the cockpit. Both pilots had donned their oxygen masks and declared a Mayday!

An emergency landing was made at Cincinnati/Northern Kentucky Airport in Boone County, Kentucky, near Cincinnati, Ohio. At night.

Because of the loss of electrical components, they had no anti-skid, blowing four tires as they tried to stop the aircraft. The fire swiftly enveloped the cabin. In the aftermath. Of the 46 total people, 23 three were fatalities. All five crew members survived.

In regards to the cockpit crew, under the dire circumstances of having a fire on board, and losing a major portion of their flight instruments, did a marvelous display of airmanship in bringing down their aircraft safely. Then came the report from the NTSB.

According to the NTSB report AAR-84/09 dated August 8, 1984.

"At 16:25h CDT flight, 797 took off from Dallas for a flight to Montreal via Toronto. At 18:15 EDT, while cruising at FL330, the three aft lavatory flush motor circuit breakers tripped. The captain thought the flush motor had probably seized and waited for about eight minutes before (unsuccessfully) trying to reset them. At about the same time, a strange odor was smelled in the aft cabin of the plane. After finding out that the lavatory was full of smoke, a cabin attendant used the CO2 bottle to put out the fire (though only black smoke was seen coming out of the seams of the lavatory's walls). The first officer went over to take a look, but had to return to the cockpit to get his goggles. When returning to the cockpit at 19:07, the 1st officer told the captain he thought it best to descend. Around the same time, the aircraft started developing electrical problems, and a Mayday call was issued. Flight 797 started to descend and contacted Cincinnati at 19:01h for an emergency. During the descent, smoke began to fill the passenger cabin. The emergency landing was carried out on runway 27L at 19:20h. The Cincinnati fire services were not able to put out the fire, which gutted the fuselage. The probable Cause: "A fire of undetermined origin, an underestimate of the fire severity, and conflicting fire progress information provided to the captain." Contributing to the severity of the accident was the flight crew's delayed decision to institute an emergency descent."

As to my aircraft's flush motor not shutting off. It was a fortuitous stroke of luck on that day for my passengers and myself that it had happened on the ground and not in flight. If it did happen in flight, who knows what might have been? Luck or guardian angels?

A FLYING FAMILY FOR KIWI

N ear the end of the year came great news! Both of my sons Scott and Keith, each experienced air force pilots, and who had received air medals for their combat service, had become part of Kiwi International Air Lines. Albeit as B-727 flight engineers.

On December 22, 1994, Scott and I finally get a chance to fly together. He was my second officer. A somewhat bittersweet flight.

On that day, our sequence of flights had called for us to fly from EWR-ATL-TPA-MDW. The first two legs had gone rather well. Flying from Tampa to Midway was another story.

The aircraft we were flying had a history of having pressurization problems. That maintenance supposedly had repaired. Pressurization of an aircraft is controlled by the operation of what are called outflow valves. The two valves are located on the bottom of the aft belly section of the fuselage. These two valves control the amount of pressurizing to the cabin and operated automatically. Or they could be operated manually if the auto-controller failed.

Forty minutes into our flight. Pressurization problems. The auto-controller had failed. Scott then tried to control pressurization manually. The manual operation controller had also failed.

When that happened the aircraft began to depressurize. I informed ATC of our problem and asked them for immediate descent to 10,0000 feet. 10,000 feet is considered a safe altitude without the need of having to wear an oxygen mask.

Followed by a landing at Atlanta. The aircraft was taken out of service and our passengers were rebooked on another flight to Chicago.

My crew and I then had to spend the night in Atlanta. The following morning we were assigned to ferry the same aircraft back to Newark.

With us was the maintenance crew who repaired the aircraft during the night. They assured me that the problem had been fixed. Though in the back of my mind, I thought we were going to have the same pressurization problem again and told them so.

I had given them the usual instructions a flight attendant would tell our passengers. "In the unlikely event—."

The head of the team asked me if he could ride the jump seat so he could monitor the auto-controller in flight. I told him okay but showed him how to use the sweep-on oxygen mask that hung over the jump seat. I know he wasn't happy about the way I went explaining it.

Sure enough, we had climbed to our cruising altitude of 33,000 feet and leveled off. Thirty minutes later the auto-controller failed again. As did the manual controller. Followed by another rapid descent to 10,000 feet.

When I turned and told the maintenance man to put on his oxygen mask. His eyes were as big as saucers. Talk about sucking on oxygen.

Once we were on the ground at Newark, we found that both outflow valves were wide open. There was no way we could have maintained pressurization under those circumstances. Eventually, maintenance would find the reason why. The outflow valve wiring had been inadvertently wired wrong.

Scott and I were able to fly together one more time on January 4, 1995. Shortly after that flight he left Kiwi and went with United Airlines where he is now a senior captain.

Five days later on January 9, 1995, Keith and I had become a flight crew. We would be able to fly together five more times before I would have to retire. Keith is now a senior captain with Southwest Airlines.

As a parent, the joy one has when you are fortunate enough to have both sons as part of your flight crew is enormous.

ROUGH WEATHER WITH ROGUE PILOTS

On February 2, 1995, rough weather for Kiwi. This time the turbulence came from rogue pilots who thought they knew how to run the airline better than Bob Iverson.

Leading up to that day, all had not been peaches and cream within the Kiwi family. Promises had been made, regarding having an Employee Stock Ownership Plan, or an Initial Public Offering (ESOP or an IPO) in place. Whereas all of us who had put up the $50,000, $10,000, and $3,000 to get Kiwi airborne were hoping we were going to capitalize on our investment.

Granted, unforeseen circumstances did arise concerning cash flow.

Then came dissension within the ranks when outside investors who had made promises, didn't.

Kiwi had a group called the Board of Directors, and The Voting Trust, which was made up of mostly rogue pilots, and who oversaw the company's operation. Their bad judgment, and bad decisions, began the death knell for Kiwi.

On that day, February 2, 1995, the group voted Bob Iverson off the board. Then he was unceremoniously escorted out the door. An in-house takeover had all the ear markings of what we Eastern pilots went through with Frank Lorenzo.

Now that Iverson was out, the Voting Trust made another bad decision, by improperly creating a new salary structure, not only for themselves but those who were allies within the rogue group of pilots.

346

Initially, base salary pay for pilots per year was anywhere between $25,000 to $48,000. Those who were now part of the chosen few were taking home somewhere between $85,000 to $140,000. Then came, their next thought. Let's screw with another, Holy Grail. The pilot's seniority list.

There were some family members whose parent was now part of management and went from being a junior second officer to captains. That alone ruffled a lot of feathers of those who were senior. Since we were not unionized, complaints fell on deaf ears. Although it didn't affect my seniority, then.

After Bob's ousting, there was less smiling, and more resentment toward those that were behind the coup. Over the next few years, CEOs had come and gone. All through that gloom-and-doom I think all of us knew there was never going to be either an ESOP or an IPO.

Setting all of that aside the good news had been that Keith and I were able to fly together quite often through 1995.

During all the turmoil I had been fast approaching the mandatory retirement age of 60 and had been looking forward to that special last flight as a captain.

When, after you had landed, an airport fire-truck would follow your aircraft to your gate. At the same time, they would be spraying your aircraft with their water cannons in a farewell salute to a career that had come to an end.

To me, the age 60 law was a bunch of malarkey. It meant you were being forced to retire which was strictly based on your birth date. It had nothing to do with your ability to fly an aircraft. The law at that time came under FAR Part 121 for the United States Air Carriers and were the rules and regulations at that time.

The quirkiness of that rule was a laugh. If you flew under another FAR, such as Part 91, or Part 135, you could be well over the age of 60, fly the same aircraft, and fly to the same cities, both domestic and foreign. Providing you met all the required physicals and flight checks. One has to wonder why you could fly after age 60 under one FAR and not the other.

Enter 1996 and, beware of the Ides of March.

THE FLIGHT FROM HELL

O n March 6, 1996, our flight plan called for us to fly from Newark
to Atlanta. From Atlanta to Tampa and then northbound to
Chicago's Midway Airport and layover.

With me, that day was First Officer Alan Cotrell and Second Officer Bill
Machauer. Bill who had been one of our premier captains had reached the
age of 60 and had retired as a captain. He then elected to become a second
officer to keep flying.

It was another quirk of the age 60 law. You could still fly, but not as a pilot.
As long as you passed all your physical exams, and flight checks. At the
time, there was no age limit to when you had to retire as a flight engineer.

The flight to Atlanta had been a little choppy due to the outreaches of a
large system of squall lines that had been making its way from the warm
waters of the Gulf of Mexico toward Atlanta. With it, came low ceilings,
visibility, and rain squalls.

By the use of our weather radar, we were able to navigate around most
of it. Then came our instrument approach to land on runway 27R.

As we descended below 500 feet, a departing Kiwi flight that had just taken
off from runway 27R reported encountering wind shear. Seconds later a
Delta flight who had been directly behind us reported having encountered
a severe micro-burst with wind shear and were aborting their landing.

At the same time, we also received a wind-shear alert through the use of
our Doppler weather radar. The system measures the presents of a micro-
burst and wind shear through the frequency of microwave pulses and issues
a warning to the flight crew.

Then came that sinking feeling knowing that the downward motion of the micro-burst was pushing your aircraft downward toward the ground and a long way from the end of the runway.

As trained, it was, ram the throttles full forward to max power, yank back on the control column far enough to stop the descent, and yet, not stall the aircraft. Leave the flaps, and landing gear as is. Abort the landing and climb out of the wind shear and the micro-burst.

Our missed approach procedure would have had us turning to the right and back toward the wind shear and micro-burst. That was when I told ATC we were not going to do that. That I intended to stay on the western side of the squall line and wanted to divert and land at Chattanooga.

As I was abandoning our approach to runway 27R Southern Airways Flight 242 had come to mind. Why? I don't know. The only thing that I could relate to it was later after we diverted to Chattanooga, Tennessee.

While with Eastern, we always had to do a yearly recurrent training program. That covered aircraft systems, FARs, and accident reports. Their cause, and how to prevent them. One of which was Southern Airways Flight 242.

On April 4, 1977, Southern Airways Flight 242, a DC-9 on its way from Northwest Alabama Regional Airport to Atlanta attempted to pick out a path through embedded thunderstorm cells, a squall line, using their onboard weather radar display.

They were misled by the radar's attenuation effect and proceeded toward what they believed was a low-intensity area, when in fact it was the peak convective activity point, attenuated by rain.

As the aircraft descended from its cruising altitude of 17,000 feet it entered a thunderstorm cell and encountered a massive amount of water and hail. The hail was intense enough to break the aircraft's windshield and because of the ingestion of both water and hail, both Pratt & Whitney JT8D-7A engines were damaged and flamed out.

Although the crew attempted to restart the engines, glided down unpowered looking for an emergency landing field within their range.

Unfortunately, none were to be found. The crew did break out into the clear and spotted a straight section of a rural highway below them.

Upon landing, collided with a gas station/convenience store and other buildings. Sadly, both pilots and 61 passengers were killed. Nine people on the ground were also killed. Of the total passengers on board, twenty survived as did the two flight attendants.

NTSB report: AAR78-03, dated January 26, 1978, stated: "The probable cause of this accident was the total and unique loss of thrust from both engines while the aircraft was penetrating an area of severe thunderstorms. The loss of thrust was caused by the ingestion of massive amounts of water and hail which in combination with thrust lever movement induced severe stalling and major damage to the engine compressors. Moreover, the crew had no training for a situation that involved total loss of engine thrust nor did Southern Airways require such training. FAA regulations had no such requirement either because the possibility of complete failure of all engines on a jet-powered carrier aircraft was deemed so remote as to not require training of special procedures."

After we refueled in Chattanooga, our flight back to Atlanta had been in clear skies, as was the landing on runway 27R. The front had moved through Atlanta so swiftly that there wasn't even a hint of foul weather.

The flight from Atlanta to Tampa had been uneventful. From Tampa to Midway, it seemed as though Mother Nature had been waiting for us in Chicago. From thunderstorms to blizzard conditions.

While we were en route to MDW, a heavy snowstorm struck the Chicago area, closing Midway Airport. After an hour and a half of doing race-tract circles in a holding pattern, it had become necessary, for the second time in the same day, to divert to an alternate airport.

Hello Rockford, Illinois. Its airport lies 77 miles west of Midway Airport. We landed in Rockford, amidst snow flurries.

Then came the calamity. There were no gates available to park the aircraft at the terminal. It also meant we had to park out on the ramp some two hundred yards away.

In the meantime, Kiwi had made alternate plans for our passengers to get to Midway by the use of chartered buses.

I announced to my passengers, that they had two choices. Take the buses, or remain with us until Midway re-opens. I also told them, there was no way I could guarantee when that would happen. Nor would I remove their luggage from the cargo compartments. They would have to stay on board until we arrived at Midway.

All of our passengers had decided to take the bus. Except for seven. All seven required the use of wheelchairs and had elected to remain on board. My crew dubbed them as. The Chicago Seven.

As to those passengers who left the aircraft. I can still visualize them walking across the ramp carrying what articles they had stowed in the overhead compartments. Heads down trying to duck under the snow flurries as they trudge to the terminal.

Two hours later Midway had reopened and we were on our way, landing just as more heavy snow began to fall.

As the Chicago Seven began to deplane using wheelchair after wheelchair, lo and behold, the three buses Kiwi chartered began to arrive from Rockford. Talk about timing.

The following day while back at Kiwi's headquarters, our chief pilot at the time, Don McCoy, said he wanted to talk to me about those two diversions the day before.

At first, I thought this was going to be one of those, second-guesses, of what I should have done.

It wasn't. He had radar weather map printouts of the area surrounding Atlanta the day before. When he showed them to me. He said.

"It's a good thing you made that missed approach to 27R when you did." His words, not mine. "According to them. You were encountering a 60-mph downburst when you went around."

I thanked him for the information and relayed it to the rest of my crew who were with me that day. I certainly hope that I never have to encounter another situation like that ever again.

AH, THE PHYSICAL SIDE OF MAN

The next six months had seemed to go very well, as far as the flying portion went. Keith and I did get to fly together one last time and that was on September 13, 1996.

On the physical side of man, mother nature has a bad habit of sneaking up on you when you least expect it.

Remember that landing in Richmond I had to make due to a male passenger being unable to urinate?

My wife and I had planned to spend a night in Atlantic City. While we were there mother nature invited me to the bathroom at 3 a.m. Nothing.

Thinking I was dehydrated, I drank two glasses of water. Nothing. Except for a nagging pain that was beginning to come from my Blatter. That was when I realized that I had a urination problem.

Long story short. Instead of going to the emergency room at the nearest hospital, I decided to drive the two hours back home. Dumb.

By the time I arrived at Dover General Hospital's emergency room, the pain had become excruciating. I then knew why that guy had tears in his eyes.

The on-duty female nurse had inserted a catheter in my lower anatomy and had strapped a urinary drain bag to my leg. Pain subsided. A smile was back on my face.

Only, the doctor who would become my urologist told me that he couldn't do a procedure called a TURP. A Transurethral Section of the Prostate, for at least two weeks.

For the next two weeks, I flew with a catheter and a bag strapped to my leg. The only good thing. I never had to get up in the middle of the night, nor did I ever have to leave the cockpit for the same reason.

Once the TURP operation was over, it took me another two weeks to get back to flying. By then Kiwi had filed for bankruptcy on September 30, 1996.

In the interim, with screwing with the seniority list, and the ineptness of management, some senior pilots were given little choice. Become a flight engineer or get terminated. I wasn't about to go backward.

My airline career unceremoniously ends some two months shy of my 60th birthday when I put in for early retirement.

No water cannon salutes from the airport's fire equipment as you would normally receive when you completed your last landing.

No escort to the gate. No hand-shakes.

No sharing of great flying memories with dear pilot friends I had known for over thirty years. Just the emptiness of that final act of flight. Knowing you haven't completed that mission you had in your mind when you first soloed

Kiwi stayed aloft for another three years, then took a final nose-dive and shut down all flight operations on March 24, 1999.

As Yogi Berra once said. "It's never over until it's over!"

THE FLYING FRISTERS

T hroughout those decades of flight, other members of my family had taken to the skies. Twelve pilots in all. Hopefully, more will follow.

Although I still manage to keep my hands and heart in aviation, I had always thought that there had to be more I could do to let others know about our flying family.

A brilliant thought struck me one early morning. Would the magazine Aircraft Owners and Pilots Association, (AOPA) be interested in writing a story about our family of pilots?

I contacted AOPA's Senior Features Editor, Julie Summers Walker in the spring of 2017 to see if she would be interested.

To my delightful surprise, she was. With Julie's guidance, we went about the process of trying to get all twelve of us pilots together at the same time. For most of our family are scattered throughout the United States.

It required five months in doing so. Largely because of the flight schedules of those who were still actively flying.

Finally, came the day when we all managed to get together at the Creve Coeur Airport located 24 miles west of downtown St. Louis in late September of 2017.

Julie was terrific in setting up the photo shoot. She photographed each family separately and ran her story about each family and our flying backgrounds separately.

But the best photo of all, had the twelve of us standing in front of Glenn's airplane standing side-by-side from wingtip to wingtip.

Engraved on the front upper portion of our black polo shirts was a design of a propeller-driven airplane and the words. "Frister Aviation." Which was quite impressive.

Background-wise, of the twelve, five of us were, or, are still captains for a major airline. Several of our family members hold certificates as commercial pilots, private pilots, and student pilots.

As you must know by now, I was a captain for Eastern Air Lines and captain for four other airlines. Those being. Air Aruba, Ryan International, Baltia, and Kiwi International Air Lines.

Our son Scott is now a senior captain for United Airlines. Scott's daughter, my granddaughter is a third-generation pilot and is an air force pilot flying KC-135s.

Our son Keith is a senior captain for Southwest Airlines.

My brother Glenn is a retired captain for Transworld Airlines. His wife Dee holds a commercial pilot's certificate. His son Justin holds a private pilot certificate. His daughter Jacqueline (Jackie) who had soloed, holds a student pilot certificate.

My brother Gregory had been a first officer with Eastern Air Lines but is now a Captain for Executive Jet Management. His son Gregory is also a private pilot working towards his commercial certificate.

My brother Ron holds a private pilot certificate, as does his son Ron. Twelve in all.

There are not enough accolades to commend Julie for presenting our family with photos pictured in the magazine. Or, for that magnificent featured story, she wrote about our family of flyers. The article appeared in AOPA's February 2018 issue.

Soon after the article was published other families contacted AOPA requesting to be recognized. But none came anywhere near having as many pilots in their families as we have.

GUINNESS BOOK OF WORLD RECORDS

While all of this was in the making for the AOPA magazine, I had in 2018, applied to "The Guinness Book Of World Records" as having our family of pilots set the record for having the most pilots in one family.

Needless to say, they required positive, evidence, as to us twelve being related. They said that they needed proof positive of us all having pilot certificates. I had agreed with that.

Then they required us to send them copies of our birth certificates that showed our parents' names on the certificates.

In some instances, they weren't. Fortunately, I had contacted the local town administration of the cities where we were born and they had sent them to me.

Then they said that they needed letters from our airline employer to verify that we flew for them. For Scott and Keith, it was not a problem as the airlines they flew for were still in business.

Glenn (TWA), Greg (EAL), and I (EAL, RYAN INTERNATIONAL, AIR ARUBA, BALTIA, AND KIWI) whose airlines we had flown for were all out of business.

Fortunately, we had kept pay records from those airlines and had sent copies of them to Guinness.

After many frustrating months of sending emails back and forth, and having to jump threw their hoops if you will. We sent them all of the evidence, and proof, they required.

This was their answer from their representative (Christine@GWR) who I had been corresponding with for nearly two years. It is dated July 2018 18:22.

"Hi, Bob,

Our team of expert Records of Managers receives thousands of new record proposals every year from all over the world which are carefully assessed to establish they meet our stringent criteria. Every record verified by Guinness World Records must be measurable by a single superlative, verifiable, standardizable, breakable, and also present an element of skill. (Remember all through their record book, are people who may have raised the biggest and heaviest tomato, potato, and pumpkin. Or, have set a record by having 300 people holding hands, of which none were related, and I'm sure weren't required to show them a birth certificate) We are unable to standardize the "most pilots in one family" because pilot licenses and certifications vary greatly. (European logic) A recreational pilot and a commercial pilot require two very different sets of qualifications. Additionally, on a global scale, a private pilot in the United States and a private pilot in a different country undergo different requirements to obtain their qualifications. Because of these differences, we are unable to define a pilot by qualifications. Rather we define a pilot by career. That is why the pilots who attempt this record have been paid commercial pilots as this is something that can be standardized across the globe.

Based on the documentation you have provided so far, there are five individuals in your family (including yourself) that have been paid, as commercial pilots. YOUR APPLICATION, THEREFORE, QUALIFIES FOR THE RECORD."

To this date, even though we qualified for the record, we have not been included in The Guinness Book of World Records. I have sent many requests to Christine@GWR asking why, and have yet to receive a response. Of course, we still hope they realize no one has or ever, or will ever come close to surpassing our family's record.

WRIGHT BROTHERS MASTER PILOT AWARD

S till, there was more history to be made.

Shortly after the February 2018 AOPA article was issued, Glenn, Greg, and I became recipients of one of the most prestigious awards that can be obtained as pilots. Notably the Wright Brother's Master Pilot Award.

The award had been presented through the offices of the (FAA) Federal Aviation Administration. In turn, it recognizes the efforts of pilots who have followed and continue to follow the precaution and awareness of safe flight operations. Most of all, the FAA recognizes pilots who have contributed and maintained safe flight operations for "50 or more consecutive years of piloting aircraft."

What brought this attention to us was my brother Greg. Greg lives in Geneva, Illinois, and flies for Executive Jet Management which is based at Du Page International Airport, St Charles, Illinois.

As a corporate pilot, he works closely with the local FAA and had mentioned to them that Glenn and I had flown for over 50 years without any violations or accidents, as did my brother Greg. Whereas, the FAA inspector suggested that we make an application for the award.

The application required proof positive, of our flying history, along with three letters of recommendation, per brother, from people who knew of our flying background.

We submitted our applications in April 2018 to the FAA's Greater Chicago

WRIGHT BROTHERS MASTER PILOT AWARD

Flight Standards District Office, Des Plains. Illinois.

What we did not know was that once they received our applications, they began an in-depth background check of our flying history.

How do they do that? All copies of our pilot certificates are kept at the FAA headquarters in Oklahoma City, Oklahoma. Any violations, or accident reports containing to us or any other pilot, would be on file. If so, we would have been eliminated from being recognized for the award.

Months had passed. No response from the FAA. Eight months later we were informed that we did qualify. The presentation was to be held at the Du Page International Airport. But the question then was when?

Glenn and I were now retired, which wasn't a problem. Greg, on the other hand, being a corporate pilot, was always on the go. Most of the time when he was away from home, to fly corporate management to some foreign country for weeks at a time.

When a date was chosen, something else would come up and create another postponement. Finally, sixteen months after submitting our applications the date was set for August 24, 2019.

Coincidently, the award came 65 years and almost to the date that I first soloed. Which was on August 22, 1954.

For my two brothers, Glenn and Greg their first solo dates were March 29, 1960, 59 years later, and August 31, 1968, 51 years later respectively.

With many friends and family members present, FAA Inspector, Lee J. Stenson, FAA Safety Team Program Manager, and Chet Cybuiski, Aviation Safety Operations Frontline Manager, made the presentation.

Astoundingly, my brothers and I received copies of all of our written exams, and our pilot certificates dating back to the day we had first soloed.

It all led to quite a stack of paperwork from each of our careers. Then came the presentation. We each received a beautiful plaque with both Orville and Wilbur Wright's photos engraved on them. It read.

The Wright Brothers "Master Pilot" Award.

"Fifty years of dedicated Service in Aviation Safety" and "In recognition of your contributions to building and maintaining the safest aviation system in the world, through practicing and promoting safe aircraft flight operations for 50 years."

In addition to the award, we also received a WBMPA pin. To honor our wives, each received a WBMPA stick pin, for supporting us through those many, many years.

As I look back and reflect on those five decades of flight. How fortunate that I, a star-eyed kid, had been able to do the thing I always wanted to do in my life. Above all, to have flown for such a great airline and the only one that I ever wanted to fly for. Eastern Air Lines.

As I reflect on my past fifty years of flight, I sometimes think about the numerous types of aircraft I had the opportunity to have flown, or taught students to fly.

Starting from a put-together balsa wood airplane to setting a world speed record. The aircraft that I have had the good fortune to fly are as follows:

The Piper Apache, Tri-Pacer, Colt, Vagabond, and that yellow Piper J-3 Cub. The ERCO Ercoupe. The V-Tail Beech Bonanza, The Beech Debonair. The Mooney Mark 20. The Luscombe E-8. The Cessna 120, 140, 150, 170, 172, 182, Skyhawk, 310. The twin-engine Lockheed Lodestar. For Eastern Air Lines, the Douglas DC-7, The Lockheed Super Constellation 1049 series, The Lockheed Electra (L-188), and The Lockheed L-1011. The Aero-Commander 500 (as part of North American Aviation), and my favorite, Boeing's B-727-100, 200 series.

Each aircraft I had flown had its characteristics, its personality if you will, but all were subject to the same aerodynamics. All in all, an airplane is an airplane, be it a single-engine piston-driven Piper J-3 Cub, a piston-driven four-engine DC-7, a four-engine turboprop-driven Lockheed Electra, or a jet-powered three-engine B-727, or the three engine Lockheed L-1011 Tri-Star.

I had logged well over 35,000 flight hours as a pilot and captain. Thousands more as a flight engineer. All of which equates to having lived five or more years of my life in the sky. Some of those moments were, "ho-hum." Others, "Holy s—-!" Years that were filled with fun, fear, emergencies, tragedies, lasting friendships, and great memories.

How could you not love every minute of it?

Then there's always that wonder. What makes a man or a woman, want to dream about wanting to leave the safety of the ground and challenging mother nature to fly?

The following poem was written by poet John Gillespie Magee Jr. A WWII Anglo-American, Royal Canadian Air Force fighter pilot who, shortly after writing it, was killed in an accidental mid-air collision over England in 1941. I believe, —answers it.

"High Flight"

Oh I have slipped the surly bonds of earth
And danced the skies on laughter-silvered wings;
Sunward I've climbed, and joined the tumbling mirth
Of sun-split clouds – and done a hundred things

You have not dreamed of – wheeled and soared and swung
High in the sunlit silence. Hov'ring there
I've chased the shouting wind along, and flung
My eager craft through footless halls of air.

Up, up the long delirious, burning blue,
I've topped the windswept heights with easy grace
Where never lark, or even eagle flew –
And, while with silent lifting mind I've trod
The high unsurpassed sanctity of space,
Put out my hand and touched the face of God.

Pilot Officer John Gillespie Magee

About the Author

This is the continuation of a young boy who heard the drone of an aircraft engine and looked skyward to see a small yellow aircraft circling overhead and flying away. He knew then he wanted to fly. His dream would become a reality that would lead him to fly for the only airline he wanted to fly for and that was. Eastern Air Lines. Fly with him in setting a World Speed Record. And, after fifty years of flight, receive the highest honor bestowed upon a pilot by the Federal Aviation Administration. The Wright Brothers Master Pilot Award. Learn what it is really like to be an airline pilot and captain. The good side and the bad side. Be with him when Mother Nature is at her worst, with lightning strikes, wind shears, and microbursts. This too, is about those pilots whom he had the privilege to fly with and who shared their stories of flying combat missions during World War Two with him. Read their stories of true heroism as told to him. This is the journey of his remarkable life in the heavens. Written as he lived it. One that you won't forget. "When you stand on the ground and look skyward, all you see is the sky. When you fly and look down, you see the world.

- Captain, Robert A. Frister Eastern Air Lines

Printed in the USA
CPSIA information can be obtained
at www.ICGtesting.com
LVHW011133220424
778080LV00019B/256